Śrī Devī Gīta

*

Dr. Ramamurthy N.

M.Sc., B.G.L., CAIIB, CCP, DSADP, CISA, PMP, CGBL, Ph.D.

*

*

Title:	*Śrī Devī Gīta*
First Edition:	2020
Author:	**Dr. Ramamurthy N,** http://ramamurthy.jāgruti.co.in/
Copyright ©:	With the author (No part of this book may be reproduced in any manner whatsoever without the written permission from the author).
Number of pages:	184
ISBN (13):	978-93-82237-72-3
Price:	₹ 400

*****

Table of Contents

Dedication 4

Blessings – 1 5

Blessings – 2 7

Introduction 9

Sri Devi Gita 12

Shrimad Bhagavad Gita and *Sri Devi Gita* 14

Sri Devi Gita Meditation Verses 20

Devi Appeared as Torch 21

Devi Gita 42

Devi Viśwarūpa Darśanam 56

The Specialty of *Gnanam* 72

Yoga-Mantra Siddhi 88

Dhyana Yogaḥ 106

Bhakti Yogaḥ 120

Virata Festivals of *Sri Devi* 134

Devi Pooja Vidhi 148

Devi Bāhya Pūja 162

Kṣamā Prārthaṇā 175

Dēvyaparāta Kṣamāpaṇa Stōtra 177

Other Books of the Author 181

Bibliography 184

*****

Dedication

मातृ देवो भव

या देवी सर्वभूतेषु मातृरूपेण संस्थिता ।
नमस्तस्यै नमस्तस्यै नमस्तस्यै नमो नमः ॥

Mātru Devo Bhava

Yā Devī Sarvabhūteṣu Mātru Rūpena Samstitā |

Namastasyai Namastasyai Namastasyai Namo Namaḥ ||

This book is dedicated with devotion to all the *upāsakas* of *Śrī Devī*. There cannot be even an iota of doubt that all will be blessed by *Śrī Ambikai*.

Dr. Ramamurthy N

*****

Blessings – 1

Śrī Gurubhyo Namaḥ

Dattatreya Hare Kriṣṇa Unmattānanda Dāyakaḥ
Digambara Mune Bāla Piṣaca Jnāna Sāgarā ||

Śāntam Dāntam Tapo Niṣṭam Śāntānanda Yatīśvaram |
Bajāmi Yaminām Śreṣṭam Avadhūtam Aharniśam ||

The author of this book <u>Dr. Ramamurthy</u> has written many spiritual books and his charity for Sanatana Dharma is well known to all.

As such, we are thrilled to learn that Dr. Ramamurthy is publishing this book, "The Devi Gita", which is an important subject for all those who are engaged in Shakta worship.

It is very special that the verses have been provided in Nagara script suitable for recitation and with English translation suitable for understanding and worship.

The Bhagavad Gita, which was preached to Arjuna by Lord Sri Krishna during the Mahabharata war, is well known in the spiritual world. But it is very important for everyone involved in Shakta worship to be aware of this Sri Devi Gita. Therefore, it is a commendable act to publish this book and make Sri Devi Gita known to all.

I pray to the Almighty Mother that all the devotees understand the supremacy of the author and buy and use this book and become recipients of Ambal's grace and that this spiritual work of the author should grow further.

We are very happy to see that Dr. Ramamurthy has compiled and published this book in Tamil also for all devotees. We pray to Goddess Srividya Maha Saubhagya Parashodashi daily, for him and his family and for all the loved ones who read this book to get Ambika's blessings and achieve the quadrupedal purusharthas.

Let everyone enjoy and live happily.

Happiness   Truth   Auspiciousness

Always in the service of *Sri Devi.*

Jaya Jaya Jagamba – Sri Gurudevadatta

With love

Ayyarmalai   श्रीप्रणवानन्द स्वामिन:
2020   *Srividya Parambika Trust*

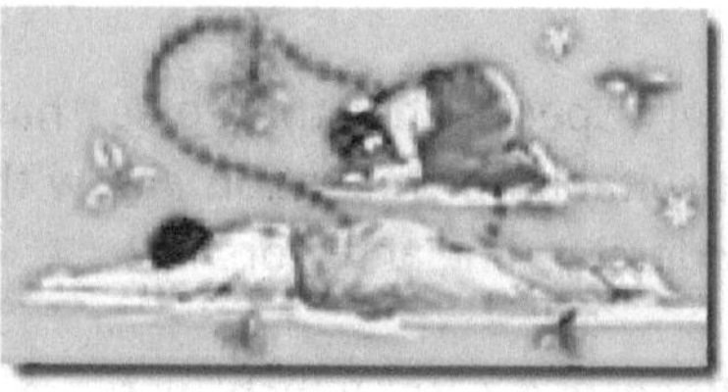

*****

Reg No : 87/2014 BKIV

ARSHA VIDYA VILASAM FOUNDATION

TRICHY · TUTICORIN · THANE

Tasmat Sastram Pramanam Te...

Blessings – 2

श्री गुरुभ्यो नमो नम:

परीक्ष्य लोकान् कर्म..............   मुण्डकोपनिषद्

If we look at this world through the body given to us as human beings, in the above *Upanishad mantra*, it becomes very clear to us that the world we are experiencing is an countenance of our previous karma-s.

The fruits of the deeds done or being done are also experienced as happiness (virtues) and miseries (sin). It is these two experiences that make us more addicted and give birth again and again.

Thus we realise the connection (ignorance) to ourselves and our experience of this world and carefully consider (hear-learn, memorise, spread to others) the *'Vedas'*, treasures praised by our Rishis and sages in order to free them from the grip of these (pleasures and sufferings), with the help of the Vedic Gurus by mastering, we can definitely achieve the moksha in this birth itself.

It is our privilege to have the wisdom of such Vedas available to us in the form of the *"Sri Devi Gita"* with

No.30, Linga Receidency, Yours Colony, 1st Main Road, Ramalinga Nagar, Woralyur, Trichy - 620 003. Mobile No : 94428 56102   e-mail : avvf.office@gmail.com   web : www.avvf.co.in

the compassion, grace and wisdom of the Mother of the Universe.

This book is a testament to the fact that the Vedic wisdom is the formal form of enlightened life in the form of worship called 'Srividya'.

With the blessings of Sri Devi and innumerable Gurus, the author, Dr. Ramamurthy N., in a very elegant way have effectively explained the wisdom of Vedanta and the greatness of Srividya and its nuances together, in this book.

In many places in the book in particular, his devotion to Ambika entirely surrendering to her and the Vedanta doctrines such as परिणामि उपादान कारणत्व and विवर्त उपादान कारण are very beautifully intertwined with the way of life (*Srividya*). It is definite that such an understanding is apparently the catalyst for a clearing all the confusions in the minds of all the people.

We offer our complete blessings with the prayers that this rare book will reach out to people of all walks of life and be read and understood by them and that the entire human society will attain the highest heavenly Siddhi and that the Sanatana Dharma will last forever.

Om Namo Narayanaya

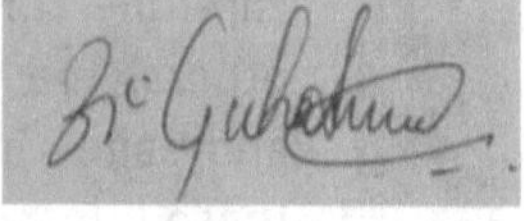

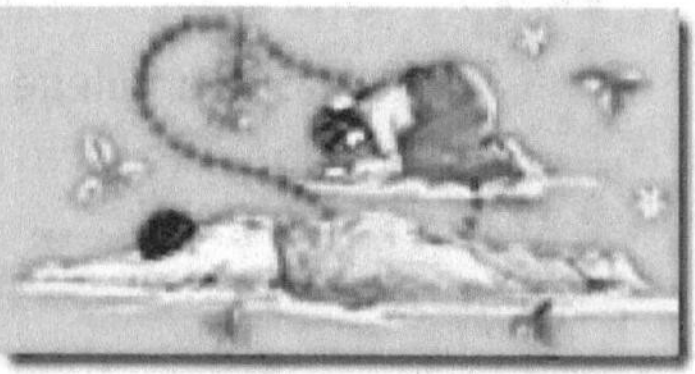

*****

Introduction

ॐ श्री गुरुभ्यो नम: । *Oṃ Śrī Gurubhyo Namaḥ* ।

Our humble *pranams* to all our *Gurus*.

सकल भुक्नमेतत् सृष्टुकामा यदात्वम्

सृजति जननि देवान् विष्णुरुद्राजमुख्यान् ।

स्थिति लय जननं तै: कारयस्येकरूपा

नखलु तवकथंचित् देवि संसार लेश ॥

Sakalu Bhuvaṉamētat Sruṣṭukāmā Yatātvam

Srujati Jaṉaṉi Dēvāṉ Viṣṇurudrājamukyāṉ ।

Stiti Laya Jaṉaṉam Taiḥ Kārayasyēkarūpā

Nakalu Tavakatamcit Dēvi Samsāra Lēśaḥ ॥

When the Goddess *Sri Devi* wanted to create the world, **She** created the trinity of *Brahma*, *Vishnu* and *Rudran*. Through those Gods **She** effectively runs the three professions of Srishti, Stiti and Samharam. All the three are running their respective businesses under *Sridevi's* direction. From time to time they make offerings to *Sri Devi* and become recipients of the blessings of the Goddess. *Paradevata*, on the pedestal of '*Bindu*', sits on the lap of *Sri Kameshwar*, the *Nirvisesha Brahmam* and guides all *devas*.

The title of this book as "*Śrī Devī Gīta*" might be surprising. Generally, when we hear the name '*Gīta*', immediately anyone, almost everyone, will remember *Shrimad Bhagavad Gita*, advised by *Bhagawan Krishna* to *Arjuna* – read in *Mahabharata*.

Similarly, when one hears of *Bhagavatam*, immediately *Sri Vishnu Bhagavatam* will only be remembered by everyone. The one sage *Shukha Brahmam* advised to king *Parikshit*.

All of us are aware that sage Vyasa has written 18 *Maha-Puranas* and 18 *Upa-Puranas*. He himself have listed them also. He has mentioned one *purana 'Bhagavatam'* both in the lists of 18 *Maha-Puranas* and 18 *Upa-Puranas*. One is a *Maha-Purana* and the other one is *Upa-Purana* – one is *Sri Vishnu Bhagavatam* and the other one is *Sri Devi Bhagavatam*. Which is *Maha-purana* and which is *Upa-purana* is a debatable question till date? This is beyond the scope of this book and we do not enter into it.

The *Purana*, called *Sri Devi Bhagavatam* contains 12 *Skandams*. In this text – in the 7th *Skanda* 10 chapters from 31 to 40 are called *"Sri Devi Gita"* – a very low profile – not so popular sacred text. The aim of this book is to bring this text to limelight. The verses are provided both in Samskrutam and English with lucid meaning in English. Normally any text relating to Devi is supposed to be secretive. That could be one more reason for this text being not so popular. *Devi Mahatmyam* (*Durga Saptashatee*) is a kind of summary of this *Devi Bhagavatam*. Both *Devi Mahatmyam* and *Devi Bhagavatam* are to be chant only by those who got initiated into by appropriate gurus.

The word *Gita* means 'song'. Accordingly, the title can be interpreted as "the Song of *Sri Devi*" or "the Divine Song" or "Celestial Song". *Sri Devi*, in this text, stresses – My sacred syllable (ह्रीम्) *'Hreem'*[1] transcends, the distinction of name and named, beyond all dualities. It is whole, infinite being, consciousness and bliss. One should meditate on that reality, within the flaming light of consciousness. Fixing the mind upon me, as the Goddess transcending all space and time, one quickly merges with me by realizing, the oneness of the soul and *Brahmam*[2].

Generally, it is very difficult to read Samskruta words in English with proper pronunciation. It is apt to read them in Samskruta script itself. But to benefit those who cannot read Samskruta

---

[1] *Om* is called general *Pranava Mantra*. *Hreem* is called *Shaakta Pranavam – Pranava mantra* related to *Sri Devi*.
[2] *Brahma* is different from *Brahmam*. *Brahma* is a lord head of *Devas*. *Brahmam* is the ultimate *Paramatma*.

script the *mantras* have been given in English also. The Samskruta words, when transliterated in English are denoted in *italics*. Normally diacritical marks will be used for transliteration of Samskruta words into English. But general readers are not fully conversant with diacritical marks and hence they find it difficult to read. Hence, it not been used in this book in normal texts. But for proper pronunciation it has been used in *mantras* and in some words.

Humble *pranams* are due to *Pujyasri Pranavananda Swamiji* of Ayyarmalai, who has given his blessings and some pleasantries about the author and the book.

Hearty thanks to all the good-hearted souls who enabled this book to be presented in this fashion. Attempts have been made to give this book as much error free as possible. Still if there are any errors, apologies are sought. If the errors are given as feedback, it will the next edition to be fault free.

There is no doubt that *Sri Devi* will shower her full compassion and blessings to all those who read this book.

This book has also been published in Tamil language simultaneously by the same author.

Chennai
2020   **Dr. Ramamurthy N.**

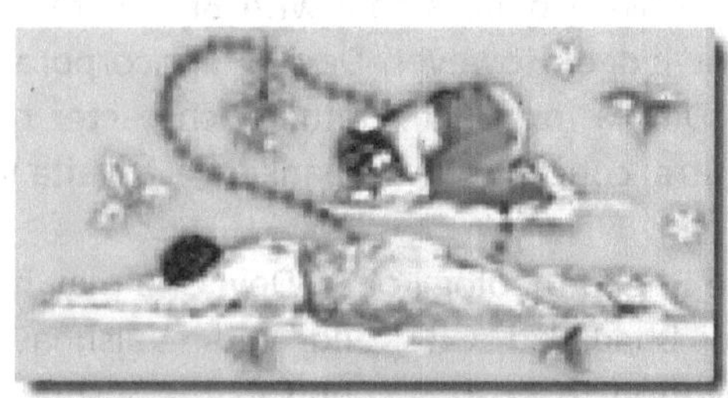

*****

Sri Devi Gita

त्वमेव माता च पिता त्वमेव त्वमेव बन्धुश्च सखा त्वमेव ।

त्वमेव विद्या द्रविणं त्वमेव त्वमेव सर्वं मम देवदेव ॥

Tvamēva Mātā Ca Pitā Tvamēva
Tvamēva Banduśca Sakā Tvamēva |
Tvamēva Vidyā Draviṇam Tvamēva
Tvamēva Sarvam Mama Dēvadēva ‖

Thou art my mother, my father, my relations, my friends, my wealth and my knowledge. You are everything Oh my *Devi*!

Sri Devi *Gita*, like the *Bhagavad Gita*, is a condensed philosophical treatise. It presents the divine female as a powerful and compassionate creator, pervader and protector of the universe. **She** is presented in the opening chapter of Sri Devi *Gita* as the benign and beautiful mother of the world, called *Bhuvaneshvari* (literally, ruler of the universe and the word is feminine). Thereafter, theological and philosophical teachings become the focus of the text, covering chapters 1 to 10 of Sri Devi *Gita* (or, chapters 31 to 40 of this *Purana's* Book 7). Some of the verses of *Devi Gita* are almost identical to Sri Devi *Upanishat*.

Sri Devi *Gita* frequently explains Shakta ideas by quoting from the Bhagavad Gita. Sri Devi is described by the text as "universal, cosmic energy" resident within each individual, weaving in the terminology of Samkhya school of Hindu philosophy. It is infused with Advaita Vedanta ideas, wherein nonduality is emphasized, all dualities are declared as incorrect and interconnected oneness of all living being's soul with Brahmam is held as the liberating knowledge. However, Devi Gita incorporates Tantric ideas giving Sri Devi a form and motherly character rather than the gender-neutral concept of Adi Shankara's Advaita Vedanta.

The Bhakti theology of Sri Devi Gita may have been influenced by the Bhagavad Gita and with Vaishnava concepts of loving devotion to Krishna found in the Vishnu Bhagavata Purana. All these texts highlight different types of devotion in a Samkhya philosophy framework. Tamasic Bhakti is one, asserts the text, where the devotee prays because he is full of anger, seeks to harm others, induce pain or jealousy to others. Rajasic Bhakti is one where the devotee prays not to harm others, but to gain personal advantage, fame or wealth. Sattvic Bhakti is the type where the devotee seeks neither advantage nor harm to others but prays to purify himself, renounce any sins and surrender to the ideas embodied as Goddess to liberate himself.

Sri Devi Bhagavata adds Para-Bhakti as the highest level of devotion, where the devotee seeks neither boon nor liberation, but weeps when he remembers her because he loves the Goddess, when he feels her presence everywhere and sees the Goddess in all living beings, he is intoxicated by her ideas and presence.

Number of verses in each chapter of *Sri Devi Gita*;

#	Chapter	No of verses
1.	*Devi Appeared as Torch*	74
2.	*Devi Gita*	50
3.	*Devi Vishwaroopa Darshanam*	56
4.	*The Specialty of Gnanam*	50
5.	*Yoga-Mantra Siddhi*	62
6.	*Dyana Yogaḥ*	30
7.	*Bhakti Yogaḥ*	45
8.	*Virata Festivals of Sri Devi*	49
9.	*Devi Pooja Vidhi*	47
10.	*Devi Baahya Pooja*	44
	Total	507

We will try to understand these ten chapters individually below – The verses are given both in Samskrutam and English. The meaning is given in English. Possibly a small comparison of relevant chapters with that of Shrimad Bhagawad Gita is also attempted.

*****

Shrimad Bhagavad Gita and Sri Devi Gita

Lord Shiva has many a form. One such form is *Shankara-Narayanar*. In that form left half of the *Shiva's* body is *Narayanar* and of course the right half is *Shiva*. One another form is *Arddhanaareeshwarar*. In this form left half of the *Shiva's* body is *Sri Devi* and again the right half is *Shiva*.

What does this imply – Lord Shiva has only one left half and hence both Lord Narayanar and Sri Devi are one and the same. Further they are part of Lord Shiva. Hence all the three Gods are one only. These three Gods(ess) are special in a way – there are 'n' number of Gods. Every *purana* or other stories reveal the birth of all the Gods and sometimes the end also. But no purana or story exposes the origin of these three Gods and naturally the end. Hence these three Gods are unique and one & the same. There cannot be any difference between the three. These three together is the *Brahmam*.

As already mentioned, there are *Bhagavatams* both in the names of *Vishnu* and *Sri Devi*. Similarly, there are Gita-s on both the names of *Vishnu* and *Sri Devi* – *Shrimad Bhagawad Gita* or *Sri Devi Gita*.

Be it *Bhagawad Gita* or *Devi Gita* – both advises the path of devotion. Both explains the *Brahmam* – one in the form of <u>*Vishnu*</u> and the other as <u>*Devi*</u>. Both lead to *Moksha* (liberation).

A chart comparing *Shrimad Bhagavad Gita* and *Sri Devi Gita*;

	Shrimad Bhagavad Gita	**Sri Devi Gita**
Author	*Veda Vyasa*	*Veda Vyasa*
Contained in	*Mahabharatam*	*Sri Devi Bhagavatam*
Number of chapters	18	10
Number of verses	700	507
As told by – to	Lord *Krishna* to *Arjuna*	*Śrī Devī* to *Devas* and King *Himavān*
Advised	*Shukar* (Vyasa's son) to king *Parikshit*	Vyasa (*Shukar's* father) to king Janamejayan (*Parikshit's* son)
Chapters	1. *Arjuna Vishada Yogaḥ* 2. *Sankhya Yogaḥ* 3. *Karma Yogaḥ* 4. *Jnana Yogaḥ* 5. *Karma-Sanyasa Yogaḥ* 6. *Atma Samyama - Yogaḥ* also called as *Dyana Yogaḥ* 7. *Vijnana Yogaḥ* 8. *Aksara-Para Brahma Yogaḥ* 9. *Raja-Vidya-Raja-Guhya Yogaḥ* 10. *Vibhuti-Vistara Yogaḥ* 11. *Viswarupa-Darsana Yogaḥ* 12. *Bhakti Yogaḥ* 13. *Ksetra-Ksetrajna Vibhaga Yogaḥ* 14. *Gunatraya-Vibhaga Yogaḥ*	1. *Devi appeared as Torch* 2. *Devi Gita* 3. *Devi Vishwaroopa Darshanam* 4. *The specialty of Gnanam* 5. *Yoga-Mantra Siddhi* 6. *Dyana Yogaḥ* 7. *Bhakti Yogaḥ* 8. *Virata Festivals of Sri Devi* 9. *Devi Pooja Vidhi* 10. *Devi Baahya Pooja*

	Shrimad Bhagavad Gita	*Sri Devi Gita*
	15. *Purushottama-Prapti Yogaḥ*	
	16. *Daivasura-Sampad-Vibhaga Yogaḥ*	
	17. *Shraddhatraya-Vibhaga Yogaḥ*	
	18. *Moksha-Sanyasa Yogaḥ*	

Chronologically, *Shrimad Bhagawad Gita* is earlier to *Sri Devi Gita*.

It is not a surprise that the following are defined and described uniformly in both the texts. Aptly both are called as Gita-s (songs).

Karma (Action) is not the cause of sufferings but attachments are;

- Leave the doer-ship of actions
- Love what you do, do it from heart
- Leave the attachment of every actions

Change your perceptions;

- Perceive everyone & everything as yourself
- Perceive equanimity in happiness & sorrows, profit & loss

Mind your mind;

- When your mind is controlled, you are your best friend or else you are alone your enemy
- Think from soul, not from mind
- Sensory organs are powerful than body, mind is powerful than senses, intellect is powerful than mind, Soul is powerful than intellect.
- One can be Monk & Yogi being without renouncing the world & actions;

- One who renounces the attachments of every action, who sees oneself on every living being, who does his duties is considered as Yogi or Sanyasi (Monk)
- Knowledge is better than practice without discernment, meditation on God is superior to knowledge and renunciation of the fruit of actions is even superior to meditation; for, peace immediately follows from renunciation.
- One who is renounced the world, forces the senses to shut down and thinking about sensory pleasure in mind is considered as A fake human (Or fake Monk & Yogi).

Nature has three qualities;

- Sattva – selflessness, active – Who is active on doing action for upliftment of society without any personal benefit, holds this quality.
- Rajas – selfishness, active – Who is active on pursuit of happiness of oneself, holds this quality.
- Tamas – laziness, sleepiness – Who is lazy and inactive, just living for pleasure of eating and sleeping holds this quality.

One can change their nature (basic quality);

- By reducing Rajas & Tamas, Sattva is uplifted
- By reducing Sattva & Tamas, Rajas is uplifted
- By reducing Sattva & Rajas, Tamas is uplifted
- Nature of mind is restlessness but by regular practice one can have complete control over the mind.

God;

- God is both spirit (his higher nature) and matter (his inferior nature)
- God is formless, but all forms belongs to him
- God is non-doer, but he is the one who create, sustains and destroy the universes & lives
- God is wisdom as well as real self of every being
- Krishna is personality of God, who born in the world to save Dharma

- Sole God is being worshiped through varies ways

Wisdom is the only purifier of sins;

- Wisdom is the goal of life
- Wisdom about the self has wisdom of everything

Surrender to The God;

- He who deals equally with friend and foe and is the same in honor and ignominy, who is alike in heat and cold, pleasure and pain and other contrary experiences and is free from attachment, he who takes praise and reproach alike and is given to contemplation and is contented with any means of subsistence available, entertaining no sense of ownership and attachment in respect of his dwelling-place and is full of devotion to Me, that person is dear to Me.
- He who, offering the highest love to Me, preaches the most profound gospel of the Gita among My devotees, shall come to Me alone; there is no doubt about it.
- Resigning all your duties to Me, the all-powerful and all supporting Lord, take refuge in Me alone; I shall absolve you of all sins, worry not.
- Give your mind to Me, be devoted to Me, worship Me and bow to Me. Doing so, you will come to Me alone, I truly promise you; for, you are exceptionally dear to Me.

If we can give a gist of the juice of *Gita*-s;

- Whatever happened, it happened well.
- Whatever is happening, it is happening well.
- Whatever will happen, it will also happen well.
- What of yours did you lose? Why or what for are you crying?
- What did you bring with you, for you to lose it?
- What did you create, for it to be wasted or destroyed?
- Whatever you took, it was taken from here.
- Whatever you gave, it was given from here.
- Whatever is yours today, will belong to someone else tomorrow, on another day, it will belong to yet another.

This change is the only thing that is permanent and is the law of the universe.

The chapters of Sri Devi Gita are discussed individually below. It can be observed both the Gita-s insist on Bhakti and Dhyanam to reach the Brahmam. It is obvious that both the Gita-s teach us the dharma to live, path to devotion and liberation.

Be it Devi Bhagavatam or Vishnu Bhagavatam, be it Bhagawad Gita or Devi Gita it is all written by same Veda Vyasa. Be it Krishna or Devi – as Veda says, in whichever language "एकं ब्रह्मम् - ब्रह्मं एक: - Brahmam *Eka – Brahmam Okate – Brahmam Onre* – only one *Brahmam*" – that Vishnu or Devi, whoever it is – it is the Brahmam.

It is He or She, the Brahmam – have belief and worship on that God without any other thought process – *"Ananya Chinta"*. Already we have discussed He and She are one and the same. Hence let us worship and pray to any God, take the right path of Dharma and attain liberation.

***Sri Devi Gita* Meditation Verses**

ॐ शुक्लाम्बरधरं विष्णुं शशिवर्णं चतुर्भुजम् ।
प्रसन्नवदनं ध्यायेत् सर्वविघ्नोपशान्तये ॥

Śukla-Ambara-Dharam Viṣṇum Śaśi-Varṇam Catur-Bhujam |
Prasanna-Vadanam Dhyāyet Sarva-Vighnopashāntaye ॥

गुरुर्ब्रह्मा गुरुर्विष्णु गुरुर्देवो महेश्वर: । गुरु साक्षात् परंब्रह्म तस्मै श्रीगुरवे नम॥

Gururbrahma Gururviṣṇuḥ Gururdevo Maheśvaraḥ |
Guru Sākśāt Parabrahma Tasmai Śrīgurave Namaḥ ॥

गुरुवे सर्वलोकानां भिषजेभवरोगिनां ।
निधये सर्वविद्यानां श्री दक्षिणामूर्तये नम:॥

Guruve Sarvloksansam Bhiṣaje Bhavaroginām |
Nidhaye Sarva Vidhyānām Dakśiṇa Mūrtaye Namaḥ ॥

कात्यायनाय विद्महे, कन्याकुमारी च धीमहि, तन्नो दुर्गा प्रचोदयात् ॥

Kātyāyaṉāya Vidmahē, Kaṉyākumarī Ca Dhīmahi,
Taṉṉō Durgā Piraccōdayāt ॥

महादेव्यै च विद्महे, विष्णुपत्न्यै च धीमहि, तन्नो लक्ष्मी प्रचोदयात् ॥

Mahādēvyai Ca Vidmahē, Viṣṇupatṉyai Ca Dhīmahi,
Taṉṉō Lakṣmī Piraccōdayāt ॥

वाग्देव्यै च विद्महे, विरिञ्चिपत्नी च धीमहि, तन्नो वाणी प्रचोदयात् ॥

Vāgdēvyai Ca Vidmahē, Viriñcipatṉyai Ca Dhīmahi,
Taṉṉō Vāṇī Piraccōdayāt ॥

व्यासं वसिष्ठ नप्तारं शक्तेः पौत्रमकल्मषं ।
पराशरात्मजं वन्दे शुकतातं तपोनिधिं ॥

Vyāsaṃ Vasiṣṭa Naptāraṃ Śakteḥ
Poutraṃakalmaṣam |
Parāśara Ātmajaṃ Vande Śukatātaṃ Tapo
Nidhim ॥

****

Devi Appeared as Torch
(*Devi Bhagavatam 7-31*)

This is the first chapter of *Sri Devi Gita*. Some schools view that *Sri Devi Gita* starts only from next chapter – Probably based on the name of the that chapter. However, we will follow the majority. This describes the conversation between the Devas and the Goddess Sri Devi on the birth of Parvati in the Himalayas.

ओं नम: चण्डिकायै । *Ōm Namaḥ Caṇḍikāyai* ।

जनमेजय उवाच

धराधराधीशमौलावाविरासीत्परं   मह: ।
यदुक्तं भवता पूर्व विस्तरात्तद्वदस्व मे ॥ १

Darādarādīśamoulāvāvirāsītparam Mahaḥ ।

Yaduktam Bhavatā Pūrvam Vistarāttadvadasva Mē ॥ 1

को विरज्येत मतिमान् पिबञ्छक्तिकथामृतम् ।
सुधां तु पिबतां मृत्यु: स नैतच्छृण्वतो भवेत् ॥ २

Kō Virajyēta Matimāṉ Pibañcaktikatāmrutam ।

Sudhām Tu Pibatām Mrutyuḥ Sa Naitaccruṇvatō Bhavēt ॥ 2

King Janamejaya asked Veda *Vyasa* - "Oh *Muni*! You earlier mentioned that "the Highest Light took Her birth on the top of the Himalayas". Now describe to me in detail about this Highest light. Which intelligent man can desist from hearing these nectar-like words about the *Shakti*? The danger of death may come even to the *Devas* who drink nectars but no such danger can possibly come to those that drink the nectar of Sri Devi's glorious deeds.

व्यास उवाच

धन्योऽसि कृतकृत्योऽसि शिक्षितोऽसि महात्मभि: ।
भाग्यवानसि यद्देव्यां निर्व्याजा भक्तिरस्ति ते ॥ ३

Vyāsa Uvāca

Dhaṉyōśi Krutakrutyōśi Śikṣitōśi Mahātmabhiḥ ।

Bhāgyavānasi Yadhdēvyām Nirvyājā Bhaktirasti Tē ‖ 3

शृणु राजन् पुरा वृत्तं सतीदेहेऽग्निभर्जिते।
भ्रान्तः शिवस्तु बभ्राम क्वचिद्देशे स्थिरोऽभवत्॥ ४

Śruṇu Rājaṇ Purā Vruttam Satīdēhēsgṇibharjitē |

Bhrāntaḥ Śivastu Babhrāma Kvacidhdēśē Stirōsbhavat ‖ 4

Vyasa said – "Oh King! You are blessed; you have attained what you are to attain in this life; you are taught by the high-souled men; you are fortunate since you are so sincerely devoted to Sri Devi. Oh King! Hear the ancient history.

प्रपञ्चभानरहितः   समाधिगतमानसः।
ध्यायन्देवीस्वरूपं तु कालं निन्ये स आत्मवान्॥ ५

Prapañcabhāṇarahitaḥ Samādhigatamāṇasaḥ |

Dhyāyandēvīsvarūpam Tu Kālam Niṇyē Sa Ātmavāṇ ‖ 5

सौभाग्यरहितं जातं त्रैलोक्यं सचराचरम्।
शक्तिहीनं जगत्सर्वं साब्धिद्वीपं सपर्वतम्॥ ६

Soubhāgyarahitam Jātam Trailōkyam Sacarācaram |

Śaktihīṇam Jagatsarvam Sābdhidvīpam Saparvatam ‖ 6

आनन्दः शुष्कतां यातः सर्वेषां हृदयान्तरे।
उदासीनाः   सर्वलोकाश्चिन्ताजर्जरचेतसः॥ ७

Āṇandaḥ Śuṣkatām Yātaḥ Sarvēṣām Hrudayāntarē |

Udāsīṇāḥ Sarvalōkāś Cintā Jarjaracētasaḥ ‖ 7

सदा दुःखोदधौ मग्ना रोगग्रस्तास्तदाभवन्।
ग्रहाणां देवतानां च वैपरीत्येन वर्तनम्॥ ८

Yatā Duḥkhōdadhou Magṇā Rōga Grastās Tadābhavan |

Grahāṇām Dēvatāṇām Ca Vaiparītyēṇa Vartaṇam ‖ 8

Earlier, when *Sateedevi* entered into the holy fire – the *Deva* of the *Devas*, the *Maheshvara* rested while – He was wandering all over the world in a distracted state, carrying the *Sati*'s body that as burnt by fire. He spent his time there with his senses controlled, in *Samadhi*, forgetting all his knowledge of *Samsara* in deep meditation of the form of Sri Devi. At this time, the three worlds, with their objects, moving and inmoving, with their oceans, mountains and islands became void of prosperity and power. The hearts of all the embodied beings became dried up, without any trace of joy; they were all burdened with anxious thoughts and remained indifferent. All were merged in the ocean of sorrows and became diseased. Planets retrograded and the *Devas* had their states reversed. The Kings were attacked with a series of ills and misfortunes - from material causes and from divine interference.

अधिभूताधिदैवानां सत्यभावान्नृपाभवन्।

अथास्मिन्नेव काले तु तारकाख्यो महासुरः ॥ ९

Adhibhūtādhidaivānām Satyabhāvānnrupābhavan |

Athāsminnēva Kālē Tu Tārakākhyō Mahāsurah ǁ 9

At this time a great Asura, named *Taaraka*, became unconquerable owing to his receiving a boon from *Brahma*.

ब्रह्मदत्तवरो दैत्योऽभवत्त्रैलोक्यनायकः।

शिवौरसस्तु यः पुत्रः स ते हन्ता भविष्यति ॥ १०

Brahma Dattavarō Daityō sBhavat Trailōkya Nāyakah |

Śivourasastu Yah Putrah Sa Tē Hantā Bhaviṣyati ǁ 10

Being intoxicated by his power and heroism, he conquered the three worlds and became the sovereign ruler. The Brahma Prajapati, gave him boon to this effect that the legitimate son of Lord Shiva would only be able to kill him.

इति कल्पितमृत्युः स देवदेवैर्महासुरः।

शिवौरससुताभावाज्जगर्ज च ननन्द च ॥ ११

Iti Kalpitamrutyuh Ca Dēva Dēvairmahāsurah |

Śivourasa Sutā bhāvājjagarja Ca Naṇanda Ca || 11

And as at that time Shiva had no son, the great Asura, elated with joy, became infatuated and carried off all victories.

तेन चोपद्रुता: सर्वे स्वस्थानात्प्रच्युता: सुरा: ।

शिवौंरससुताभावाच्चिन्तामापुर्दुरत्ययाम्   ॥१२

Tēṇa Cōpadrutāḥ Sarvē Svasthāṇāt Pracyutāḥ Surāḥ |

Śivourasa Sutābhāvāc Cintāmāpur Duratyayām || 12

All the Devas were banished from their places by his oppression; they remained always anxious owing to the want felt by them of a son of Shiva.

नाङ्गना शङ्करस्यास्ति कथं तत्सुतसम्भव: ।

अस्माकं भाग्यहीनानां कथं कार्यं भविष्यति॥ १३

Nāṅgaṇā Śaṅkarasyāsti Katham Tatsuta Sambhavaḥ |

Asmākam Bhāgyahīṇāṇām Katam Kāryam Bhaviṣyati || 13

Lord Shankara has no wife now (with him); how can He then have a son! We are very unfortunate; how can our work be accomplished?

इति चिन्तातुरा: सर्वे जग्मुर्वैकुण्ठमण्डले।

शशंसुर्हरिमेकान्ते स चोपायं जगाद ह॥१४

Iti Cintāturāḥ Sarvē Jagmur Vaikuṇṭha Maṇḍalē |

Śaśamsurharimēkāntē Sa Cōpāyam Jagāda Ha || 14

Thus, oppressed with thoughts, all the Devas went to Vaikunda and informed the Bhagavan Vishnu of all that had happened, in privacy.

कुतश्चिन्तातुरा: सर्वे कामकल्पद्रुमा शिवा।

जागर्ति भुवनेशानी मणिद्वीपाधिवासिनी॥ १५

Kutaścintāturāḥ Sarvē Kāmakalpadrumā Śivā |

Jāgarti Bhuvaṇēśāṇi Maṇidvīpādhivāsiṇī || 15

The Bhagavan Vishnu began to tell them the means, thus - "Oh Devas! Why are you all so anxious when the Auspicious Goddess of the Universe, the Dweller in the Mani Dveepa, the Yielder of all desires like a Kalpa Vruksha is always wakeful for you.

अस्माकमनया देव तदुपेक्षास्ति नान्यथा।

शिक्षैवेयं जगन्मात्रा कृतास्मच्छिक्षणाय च॥ १६

Asmākamanayā Dēva Tadupēkṣāsti Nānyatā |

Śikṣaivēyam Jaganmātrā Krutāsmacchikṣaṇāya Ca ‖16

It is due to your faults that She is showing Her indifference; it is meant to teach us (not for our destruction but to show Her infinite mercy).

लालने ताडने मातुर्नाकारुण्यं यथार्भके।

तद्वदेव जगन्मातुर्नियन्त्र्या गुणदोषयो: ॥ १७

Lālanē Tāḍanē Māturnākāruṇyam Yathārbhakē |

Tadvadēva Jaganmātur Niyantrayā Guṇadōṣayōḥ ‖ 17

When a mother nourishes and frightens and reprimands a son, it is not that she has become merciless; so also, the Mother of the world, the Controller of the Universe, will never be merciless to you as regards your qualifications and defects.

अपराधो भवत्येव तनयस्य पदे पदे।

कोऽपर: सहते लोके केवलं मातरं विना॥ १८

Aparādhō Bhavatyēva Taṇayasya Padē Padē |

Kōsparaḥ Sahatē Lōkē Kēvalam Mātaram Viṇā ‖ 18

A son commits offence at every step who can bear that in these three worlds except the mother!

तस्माद्यूयं पराम्बां तां शरणं यात मा चिरम्।

निर्व्याजया चित्तवृत्त्या सा व: कार्यं विधास्यति॥ १९

Tasmādyūyam Parāmbām Tām Śaraṇam Yāta Mā Ciram |

Nirvyājayā Cittavruttyā Sā Vaḥ Kāryam Vidhāsyati ‖ 19

Hence, soon take refuge to the Highest Mother, the Goddess of the universe, with the sincerest devotion. She will certainly take action and help your cause.

इत्यादिश्य सुरान्सर्वान्महाविष्णुः स्वजायया ।

संयुतो निर्जगामाशु देवैः सह सुराधिपः ॥ २०

Ityādiśya Surānsarvān Mahāviṣṇuḥ Svajāyayā |

Samyutō Nirjagāmāśu Tēvaiḥ Saha Surādhipaḥ ॥ 20

Thus, ordering the Devas, Vishnu with His consort Lakshmi and the other Devas quickly went out to worship Sri Devi.

आजगाम महाशैलं हिमवन्तं नगाधिपम् ।

अभवंश्च सुराः सर्वे पुरश्चरणकर्मिणः ॥ २१

Ājagāma Mahāśailam Himavantam Nagādhipam |

Abhavamśca Surā: Sarvē Purścaraṇakarmiṇaḥ ॥ 21

Going to the Himalayas, they soon engaged themselves in doing the Purashcharana Karma (act of repeating the names of the Deity, attended with burnt oblations and offerings, etc.).

अम्बायज्ञविधानज्ञा अम्बायज्ञं च चक्रिरे ।

तृतीयादिव्रतान्याशु चक्रुः सर्वे सुरा नृप ॥ २२

Ambāyakña Vidhānakñā Ambāyakñam Ca Cakrirē |

Trutīyādi Vratānyāśu Cakruḥ Sarvē Surā Nrupa ॥ 22

Oh King! Those who were well versed with the performance of sacrifice to the Mother, began their sacrificial ceremonies and all began to hold vows, viz., Triteeyaadi Vrataani.

केचित्समाधिनिष्णाताः केचिन्नामपरायणाः ।

केचित्सूक्तपराः केचिन्नामपारायणोत्सुकाः ॥ २३

Kēcitsamādhiniṣṇātāḥ Kēcinnāmaparāyaṇāḥ |

Kēcitsūktaparāḥ Kēcinnāmapārāyaṇōtsukāḥ ॥ 23

Some engaged themselves in incessantly meditating on Sri Devi; some began to repeat Her names constantly; some began to repeat Sri Devi Sukta.

मन्त्रपारायणपराः केचित्कृच्छ्रादिकारिणः ।

अन्तर्यागपराः केचित्केचिन्न्यासपरायणाः ॥ २४

Mantrapārāyaṇaparāḥ Kēcitkrucchrādikāriṇaḥ |

Antaryāgaparāḥ Kēcit Kēcin Nyāsa Parāyaṇāḥ ‖ 24

Thus, some devoted themselves to repeating names; others to repeating mantras. Again, some wore engaged in performing severe (painful) *Chandrayana* and other *Vratas*. Some wore doing *Antarayagas* (inner sacrifices); some wore doing *Pranagni-hotra* Yagas; whereas others engaged themselves in Nyaasaadhi, etc.

हल्लेखया पराशक्तेः पूजां चक्रुरतन्द्रिता ।

इत्येवं बहुवर्षाणि कालोऽगाज्जनमेजय ॥ २५

Hrullēkayā Parāśaktēḥ Pūjām Cakruratandritā |

Ityēvam Bahuvarṣāṇi Kālōskājjaṇamējaya ‖ 25

Again, some began to worship the Highest Shakti, the Goddess of the Universe, without any sleep or rest, by the seed *mantra* of Maya. Oh King! Thus, many years of the Devas passed.

अकस्माच्चैत्रमासीयनवम्यां च भृगोर्दिने ।

प्रादुर्बभूव पुरतस्तन्महः श्रुतिबोधितम् ॥ २६

Akasmāccaitramāsīya Navamyām Ca Brugōrdiṇē |

Prādurbabhūva Puratastaṇmahaḥ Śrutibōdhitam ‖ 26

On the ninth (tithi) day in the month of Chaitra on Friday, the Highest Light of the Supreme Force suddenly appeared in front of them.

चतुर्दिक्षु चतुर्वेदैर्मूर्तिमद्भिरभिष्टुतम् ।

कोटिसूर्यप्रतीकाशं चन्द्रकोटिसुशीतलम् ॥ २७

Caturdikṣu Caturvēdair Mūrtimad Bhirabhiṣṭutam |

Kōṭisūrya Pratīkāśam Candrakōṭi Suśītalam ||27

That Light was equal to crores of lightnings, of red in colour and cool like the crores of Moons. Again, the luster was like crores of Suns. The four Vedas personified, were chanting hymns all round Her.

विद्युत्कोटिसमानाभमरुणं तत्परं महः।

नैव चोर्ध्वं न तिर्यक्च न मध्ये परिजग्रभत्॥ २८

Vidyutkōṭi Samānābhamaruṇam Tatparam Mahaḥ |

Naiva Cōrdhvam Na Tiryakca Na Madhyē Parijagrabhat || 28

That mass of fire was above, below, on all sides, in the middle; nowhere it was obstructed.

आद्यन्तरहितं तत्तु न हस्ताद्यङ्गसंयुतम्।

न च स्त्रीरूपमथवा न पुंरूपमथोभयम्॥ २९

Ādyantarahitam Tattu Na Hastādyaṅga Samyutam |

Na Ca Strīrūpamathavā Na Pumrūpamathōpayam || 29

It had no beginning, nor end. It was of a form with hands and feet and all the limbs. The appearance was not that of a male nor that of a hermaphrodite.

दीप्त्या पिधानं नेत्राणां तेषामासीन्महीपते।

पुनश्च धैर्यमालम्ब्य यावत्ते ददृशुः सुराः॥ ३०

Dīptyā Pidāṉam Nētrāṇām Tēṣāmāsīṉ Mahīpatē |

Puṉaśca Dhairyamālambya Yāvattē Dadruśuḥ Surāḥ || 30

तावत्तदेव स्त्रीरूपेणाभादिव्यं मनोहरम्।

अतीव रमणीयाङ्गीं कुमारीं नवयौवनाम्॥ ३१

Tāvattadēva Strīrūpēṇābhādhdivyam Maṇōharam |

Atīva Ramaṇīyaṅgīm Kumārīm Navayauvaṇām || 31

The Devas, dazzled by the brilliant luster, first closed their eyes; but at the next moment, holding patience when they opened again their eyes, they found the Highest Light manifesting in the form of an exceedingly beautiful divine young woman.

उद्यत्पीनकुचद्वन्द्वनिन्दिताम्भोजकुड्मलाम् ।

रणत्किङ्किणिकाजालसिञ्जन्मञ्जीरमेखलाम् ॥ ३२

Udyat Pīṇa Kuca Dvandva Ninditām Bhōjakuṅmalām |

Raṇatkiṅkiṇi Kājā Lasiñjaṇmañjīra Mēkhalām || 32

कनकाङ्गदकेयूरग्रैवेयकविभूषिताम् ।

अनर्घ्यमणिसम्भिन्नगलबन्धविराजिताम् ॥ ३३

Kaṇakāṅgada Kēyūra Graivēya Kavi Bhūṣitām |

Aṇarghyamaṇi Sambhiṇṇagala Bandhavirājitām || 33

तनुकेतकसंराजन्नीलभ्रमरकुन्तलाम् ।

नितम्बबिम्बसुभगां रोमराजिविराजिताम् ॥ ३४

Taṇukētaka Samrājaṇṇīla Bhramarakuntalām |

Nitambabimbasubhagām Rōmarājivirājitām || 34

कर्पूरशकलोन्मिश्रताम्बूलपूरिताननाम् ।

कनत्कनकताटङ्कविटङ्कवदनाम्बुजाम् ॥ ३५

Karpūra Śakalōṇmiśra Tāmbūla Pūritāṇaṇām |

Kaṇatkakaka Tāṭaṅka Viṭaṅka Vadaṇāmbujām || 35

अष्टमीचन्द्रविम्बाभभललाटामायतभ्रुवम् ।

रक्तारविन्दनयनामुन्नसां मधुराधराम् ॥ ३६

Aṣṭamī Candra Vimbā Bhalalāṭāmāyatabhruvam |

Raktāravinda Nayaṇāmuṇṇasām Madhurātarām || 36

कुन्दकुड्मलदन्ताग्रां मुक्ताहारविराजिताम्।
रत्नसम्भिन्नमुकुटां चन्द्ररेखावतंसिनीम्॥ ३७

Kunta Kuṅmaladantāgrām Muktā Hāra Virājitām |
Ratnasambhinna Mukuṭām Candrarēkhāvatamsinīm ‖ 37

मल्लिकामालतीमालाकेशपाशविराजिताम्।
काश्मीरबिन्दुनिटिलां नेत्रत्रयविलासिनीम्॥ ३८

Mallikā Mālatī Mālā Kēśapāśa Virājitām |
Kāśmīra Bindu Niṭilām Nētratrayavilāsinīm ‖ 38

पाशाङ्कुशवराभीतिचतुर्बाहुं त्रिलोचनाम्।
रक्तवस्त्रपरीधानां दाडिमीकुसुमप्रभाम्॥ ३९

Pāśāṅkuśa Varābhīti Caturbāhum Trilōcanām |
Raktavastraparīdhānām Dāḍimī Kusumaprabhām ‖ 39

सर्वशृङ्गारवेषाढ्यां सर्वदेवनमस्कृताम्।
सर्वाशापूरिकां सर्वमातरं सर्वमोहिनीम्॥ ४०

Sarva Śruṅgāra Vēṣāḍyām Sarva Dēva Namaskrutām |
Sarvāśāpūrikām Sarvamātaram Sarva Mōhinīm ‖ 40

प्रसादसुमुखीमम्बां मन्दस्मितमुखाम्बुजाम्।
अव्याजकरुणामूर्ति ददृशुः पुरतः सुराः॥ ४१

Prasāda Sumukhīmambām Mantasmita Mukhāmbujām |
Avyāja Karuṇāmūrtim Dadruśuḥ Purataḥ Surāḥ ‖ 41

दृष्ट्वा तां करुणामूर्ति प्रणेमुः सादरं सुराः।
वक्तुं नाशक्नुवन् किञ्चिद्बाष्पसंरुद्धनिःस्वनाः॥ ४२

Druṣṭvā Tām Karuṇāmūrtim Praṇēmuḥ Sādaram Surāḥ |
Vaktum Nāśaknuvan Kiñcidbāṣpa Samruddhaniḥ Svanāḥ ‖ 42

कथञ्चित्स्थैर्यमालम्ब्य भक्त्या चानतकन्धरा: ।

प्रेमाश्रुपूर्णनयनास्तुष्टुवुर्जगदम्बिकाम्   ॥ ४३

Kathañcit Sthairyamālambya Bhaktyā Cānatakandharāḥ |

Prēmāśru Pūrṇa Nayaṇāstuṣṭuvur Jagadambikām ॥ 43

Her youth was just blooming and Her rising breasts, plump and prominent, vying as it were and with a lotus bud, added to the beauty all around. Bracelets were on Her hands; armlets on Her four arms; necklace on Her neck; and the garland made of invaluable gems and jewels spread very bright luster all around. Lovely ornaments on Her waist making tinkling sounds and beautiful anklets were on Her feet.

The hairs of Her head, flowing between Her ears and cheek sparkled bright like the large black bees shining on the flower leaves of the blooming Ketaki flower. Her loins were nicely shaped and exquisitely lovely and the hairs on Her navel gave additional beauty. Her exquisitely lively lotus mouth rendered more lustrous and beautiful by the shining golden ear-ornaments, was filled with betel leaves mixed with camphor, etc.; on Her forehead there was the half crescent moon; Her eye-brows were extended and Her eyes looked bright and beautifully splendid like the red lotus; Her nose was elevated and Her lips very sweet. Her teeth were very beautiful like the opening buds of Kunda flowers; from Her neck was suspended a necklace of pearls;

On Her head was the brilliant crown decked with diamonds and jewels; on Her ears, earrings were suspended like the lines on the Moon; Her hairs were ornamented with Jasmine and Malati flowers; Her forehead was pasted with Kashmiri Kumkum drops; and Her three eyes gave unparalleled luster to Her face. On Her one hand there was the noose and on Her other hand there was the goad; her two other hands made signs granting boons and dispelling fears; Her body shed luster like the flowers of a Daruma tree. Her wearing is a red coloured cloth. All these added great beauty to her.

Thus, the Devas saw before them the Mother Goddess, the Incarnate of unpreceded mercy, with a face ready to offer Her Grace, the Mother of the Whole Universe, the Enchantress of all, sweet-smiling, saluted by all the Devas, yielding all desires and wearing a dress, indicative of all lovely feelings. The Devas bowed at once they saw Her; but they could not speak with their voice as it was choked with tears. Then holding their patience, with much difficulty, they began to praise and chant hymns to the World Mother with their eyes filled with tears of love and devotion and with their heads bent low.

देवा ऊचु:

नमो देव्यै महादेव्यै शिवायै सततं नमः।

नमः प्रकृत्यै भद्रायै नियताः प्रणताः स्म ताम्॥ ४४

Dēvā Ūcu:

Namō Dēvyai MahāDēvyai Śivāyai Satatam Nama: |

Nama: Prakrutyai Bhadrāyai Niyatāḥ Praṇatāḥ Sma Tām || 44

तामग्निवर्णां तपसा ज्वलन्तीं

वैरोचनीं कर्मफलेषु जुष्टाम्।

दुर्गां देवीं शरणमहं प्रपद्ये

सुतरसि तरसे नमः॥ ४५

Tāmagṇivarṇām Tapasā Jvalantīm Vairōcaṇīm Karmapalēṣu Juṣṭām |

Durgām Dēvīm Śaraṇamaham Prapadyē Sutarasi Tarasē Namaḥ || 45

देवीं वाचमजनयन्त देवा-

स्तां विश्वरूपाः पशवो वदन्ति।

सा नो मन्द्रेषमूर्जं दुहाना

धेनुर्वागस्मानुपसुष्टुतैतु ॥ ४६

Dēvīm Vācamajaṇayanta Dēvāstām Viśvarūpāḥ Paśavō Vadanti |

Sā Nō Mandrēṣa Mūrjam Duhāṇā Dhēṇuvārgasmāṇupasuṣṭutaitu || 46

कालरात्रिं ब्रह्मस्तुतां वैष्णवीं स्कन्दमातरम्।

सरस्वतीमदितिं दक्षदुहितरं नमामः पावनां शिवाम्॥ ४७

Kālarātrim Brahmastutām Vaiṣṇavīm Skandamātaram |

Sarasvatīmaditim Dakṣaduhitaram Nāmāmaḥ Pāvanām Śivām ॥ 47

महालक्ष्म्यै च विद्महे सर्वशक्त्यै च धीमहि।

तन्नो देवी प्रचोदयात्॥ ४८

Mahālakṣmyai Ca Vidmahē Sarvaśaktyai Ca Dhīmahi |

Taṉṉō Dēvī Pracōtayāt ॥ 48

नमो विराट्स्वरूपिण्यै नमः सूत्रात्ममूर्तये।

नमोऽव्याकृतरूपिण्यै नमः श्रीब्रह्ममूर्तये॥ ४९

Namō Virāṭ Svarūpiṉyai Namaḥ Sūtrātmamūrtayē |

Namōᵛyākrutarūpiṉyai Namaḥ Śrībrahmamūrtayē ॥ 49

यदज्ञानाज्जगद्भाति रज्जुसर्पस्त्रगादिवत्।

यज्ज्ञानाल्लयमाप्नोति नुमस्तां भुवनेश्वरीम्॥ ५०

Yadagñāṉājjagadbhāti Rajjusrapasragādivat |

Yajkñāṉāllayamāpṉōti Numastām Bhuvaṉēśvarīm ॥ 50

नुमस्तत्पदलक्ष्यार्थां चिदेकरसरूपिणीम्।

अखण्डानन्दरूपां तां वेदतात्पर्यभूमिकाम्॥ ५१

Numastatpadalakṣyārthām Cidēkarasarūpiṇīm |

Akhaṇḍāṉandarūpām Tām Vēdatātparya Bhūmikām ॥ 51

पञ्चकोशातिरिक्तां तामवस्थात्रयसाक्षिणीम्।

नुमस्त्वंपदलक्ष्यार्थां प्रत्यगात्मस्वरूपिणीम्॥ ५२

Pañcakōśātiriktām Tāmavasthātrayasākṣiṇīm |

Numastvam Padalakṣayārthām Pratyagātma Svarūpiṇīm ॥ 52

नमः प्रणवरूपायै नमो ह्रींकारमूर्तये।

नानामन्त्रात्मिकायै ते करुणायै नमो नमः ॥ ५३

Namaḥ Praṇavarūpāyai Namō Hrīṅkāramūrtayē |

Nāṉāmantrātmikāyai Tē Karuṇāyai Namō Namaḥ ॥ 53

इति स्तुता तदा देवैर्मणिद्वीपाधिवासिनी।

प्राह वाचा मधुरया मत्तकोकिलनिःस्वना॥ ५४

Iti Stutā Tadā Dēvarmaṇidvīpādhivāsiṉī |

Prāha Vācā Madhurayā Mattakōkilaniḥsvaṉā ॥ 54

The *Devas* said – We bow down to Thee, Sri Devi and the Maha Devi, always obeisance to Thee! Thou art the *Prakruti* and the Auspicious One; we always salute to Thee. Oh Mother! Thou art of a fiery colour (residing as a Red Flame in the heart of a *Yogi*) and burning with Asceticism and Wisdom (shedding luster all around). Thou art specially shining everywhere as the Pure Chaitanya; worshipped by the Devas and all the Jeevas) for the rewards of their actions;

We take refuge to Thee, the Durga, Sri Devi, we bow down to Thee, that can well make others cross the ocean of Samsara; so that Thou help us in crossing this terrible ocean of world. Mother! The Devas have created the words (i.e., the words conveying ideas are uttered by the five *Vayus*, *Prana*, etc., which are called the Devas) which are of the nature of Vishvaroopa, pervading everywhere, like the Kamadhenu (the Heavenly Cow yielding all desires, riches, honor, food, etc.,) and by which the brutes (the gods) become egotistical.

Oh Mother! Thou art that language to us; hence Thou fulfill our desires when we praise with hymns to Thee. Oh *Devi*! Thou art the Night of Destruction at the end of the world; Thou art worshipped by Brahma; Thou art the Lakshmi, the Shakti of Vishnu; Thou art the Mother of Skanda the Shakti of Shiva; Thou art the Shakti Sarasvati of Brahma. Thou art Aditi, the Mother of the gods and Thou art Sati, the daughter of Daksha. Thus, thou art purifying the worlds in various forms and giving peace to all.

We bow down to Thee. We know Thee to be the great Maha Lakshmi; we meditate on Thee as of the nature of all the Shaktis as Bhaghavati.

Oh Mother! Illuminate us so that we can meditate and know Thee. Oh *Devi*! Obeisance to Thee, the Virat! Obeisance to Thee, the Sutratman, the Hiranyagarbha; obeisance to Thee, the transformed into sixteen Vikrutis (or transformations). Obeisance to Thee, of the nature of Brahma. We bow down with great devotion to Thee, the Goddess of the Universe, the Creatrix of Mayic Avidya (the Nescience) under whose influence this world is mistaken as the rope as a garland is mistaken for a rope and again that mistake is corrected by whose Vidya. We bow down to Thee who art indicated by both the letters *Tat* and *Tvam* in the sentence *Tat Tvamasi* (Thou art That), *Tat* indicating the *Chit* (Intelligence) of the nature of oneness and *Tvam* indicating the nature of *Akhanda Brahmam* (beyond the *Annamaya, Pranamaya, Manomaya, Vijnanamaya* and *Anandamaya* – the five Koshas, the Witness of the three states of wakefulness, dream and deep sleep states) and indicating Thee.

Oh Mother! Thou art of the nature of *Pranava Om*; Thou art *Hreem*; Thou art of the nature of various Mantras and Thou art merciful; we bow down again and again to Thy lotus Feet. When the Devas thus praised Sri Devi, the In-dweller of the Mani Dveepa, the Bhagavati spoke to them in a sweet cuckoo voice.

देव्युवाच

वदन्तु विबुधाः कार्यं यदर्थमिह सङ्गताः ।

वरदाहं सदा भक्तकामकल्पद्रुमास्मि च ॥ ५५

Dēvyuvāca

Vadantu Vibudhā: Kāryam Yadarthamiha Saṅgatāḥ |

Varadāham Sadā Bhaktakāma Kalpadrumāsmi Ca ॥ 55

Sri Devi Said - Oh *Devas*! What for have you come here? What do you want? I am always the Tree, yielding all desires to my *Bhaktas*; and I am ready to grant boons to them.

तिष्ठन्त्यां मयि का चिन्ता युष्माकं भक्तिशालिनाम् ।
समुद्धरामि   मद्भक्तान्दुःखसंसारसागरात् ॥ ५६

Tiṣṭhaṇtyām Mayi Kā Cintā Yuṣmākam Bhaktiśāliṇām |
Samuddharāmi MadbhaktāṇduḥKa Samsāra Sākarāt ॥ 56

इति प्रतिज्ञां मे सत्यां जानीथ विबुधोत्तमाः ।
इति प्रेमाकुलां वाणीं श्रुत्वा सन्तुष्टमानसाः ॥ ५७

Iti Pratigñām Mē Satyām Jāṇītha Vibudhōttamāḥ |
Iti Prēmākulām Vāṇīm Śrutvā Santuṣṭa Māṇasāḥ ॥ 57

निर्भया निर्जरा राजन्नूचुर्दुःखं स्वकीयकम् ।

Nirbhayā Nirjarā Rājaṇṇūcurduḥkham Svakīyakam |

You are my devotees; why do you worry, when I am on your side?
I will rescue you from the ocean of troubles, Oh Devas! Know this
as My true resolve.

Oh King! Hearing these words of deep love, the Devas became
very glad and gave out all their causes of troubles.

देवा ऊचुः

नाज्ञातं किञ्चिदप्यत्र भवत्यास्ति जगत्त्रये ॥ ५८

Dēvā Ūcu:

Nāgñātam Kiñcidapyatra Bhavatyāsti Jagattrayē ॥ 58

सर्वज्ञया   सर्वसाक्षिरूपिण्या   परमेश्वरि ।
तारकेणासुरेन्द्रेण पीडिताः स्मो दिवानिशम् ॥ ५९

Sarvagñayā Sarva Sākṣurūpiṇyā Paramēśvari |
Tārakēṇāsurēndrēṇa Pīḍitāḥ Smō Divāṇiśam ॥ 59

शिवाङ्गजाद्वधस्तस्य निर्मितो ब्रह्मणा शिवे ।
शिवाङ्गना तु नैवास्ति जानासि त्वं महेश्वरि ॥ ६०

Śivāṅgajādvadhastasya Nirmitō brahmaṇā Śivē |
Śivāṅgaṇā Tu Naivāsti Jāṇāsi Tvam Mahēśvari ॥ 60

सर्वज्ञपुरतः किं वा वक्तव्यं पामरैर्जनैः ।
एतदुद्देशतः प्रोक्तमपरं तर्कयाम्बिके ॥ ६१

Sarvagñapurataḥ Kim Vā Vaktavyam Pāmarairjanaiḥ |
Ētaduddēśataḥ Prōktamaparam Tarkayāmbikē || 61

सर्वदा चरणाम्भोजे भक्तिः स्यात्तव निश्चला ।
प्रार्थनीयमिदं मुख्यमपरं देहहेतवे ॥ ६२

Sarvadā Caraṇāmbhōjē Bhaktiḥ Syāttava Niścalā |
Prārthaṉīyamidam Mukhyamaparam Dēhahētavē || 62

इति तेषां वचः श्रुत्वा प्रोवाच परमेश्वरी ।
मम शक्तिस्तु या गौरी भविष्यति हिमालये ॥ ६३

Iti Tēṣām Vacaḥ Śrutvā Prōvāca Paramēśvarī |
Mama Śaktistu Yā Gourī bhaviṣyati Himālayē || 63

शिवाय सा प्रदेया स्यात्सा वः कार्यं विधास्यति ।
भक्तिर्मच्चरणाम्भोजे भूयाद्युष्माकमादरात् ॥ ६४

Śivāya Sā Pradēyā Syātsā Vaḥ Kāryam Vidhāsyati |
Bhaktirmaccaraṇāmbhōjē Bhūyādyuṣmākamādarāt || 64

हिमालयो हि मनसा मामुपास्तेऽतिभक्तितः ।
ततस्तस्य गृहे जन्म मम प्रियकरं मतम् ॥ ६५

Himālayō Hi Maṉasā Māmupāstēstibhaktitaḥ |
Tatastasya Gruhē Jaṉma Mama Priyakaram Matam || 65

Oh *Parameshvari!* Thou art omniscient and witness of all these worlds. What is there in the three worlds that is not known to Thee! Oh, Auspicious Mother! The Demon Taraka is giving us troubles day and night. Brahma has given him boon that he will be killed by the Shiva's son. Oh Maheshwari! Sati, the wife of Shiva has cast aside Her body. It is known to Thee. What will the ignorant low people inform the one, who is Omniscient? Oh Mother! We have described in brief all what we had to say. What more shall we say? Thou know all our other troubles and causes of sorrows. Bless us so that our devotion remains undiverted at Thy lotus feet; this is our earnest prayer. That Thou take the body to have a son of Shiva is our fervent Prayer to Thee.

Hearing the words of Devas, Parameshvari, with a graceful countenance, spoke to them, thus - "My Shakti will incarnate as Gauri in the house of Himalayas; She will be the wife of Shiva and will beget a son that will destroy Taraka Damon and will serve your purpose. And your devotion will remain steadfast at My Lotus feet. Himalayas, too, is worshipping Me with his wholehearted devotion; so, to take birth in his house is to my greatest liking; know this.

व्यास उवाच

हिमालयोऽपि तच्छुत्वात्यनुग्रहकरं वचः।
बाष्पैः संरुद्धकण्ठाक्षो महाराज्ञीं वचोऽब्रवीत्॥ ६६

Vyāsa Uvāca

Himālayōspi Tacchrutvātyaṉugrahakaram Vacaḥ |

Bāṣpaiḥ Samruddhakaṇṭhākṣō Mahārāgñīm Vacōsbravīt || 66

महत्तरं तं कुरुषे यस्यानुग्रहमिच्छसि।
नोचेत्क्वाहं जडः स्थाणुः क्व त्वं सच्चित्स्वरूपिणी॥ ६७

Mahattaram Tam Kuruṣē Yasyāṉugrahamicchasi |

Nōcētkvāham Jaḍaḥ Sthāṉuḥ Kva Tvam Saccit Svarūpiṇī || 67

असम्भाव्यं जन्मशतैस्त्वत्पितृत्वं ममानघे।
अश्वमेधादिपुण्यैर्वा पुण्यैर्वा तत्समाधिजैः॥ ६८

Asambhāvyam Jaṉmaśataistvatpitrutvam Mamāṉaghē |

Aśvamēdhādipuṇyairvā Puṇyairvā Tat Samādhijaiḥ || 68

अद्य प्रपञ्चे कीर्तिः स्याजगन्माता सुताभवत्।
अहो हिमालयस्यास्य धन्योऽसौ भाग्यवानिति॥ ६९

Adya Prapañcē Kīrtiḥ Syājjagaṉmātā Sutābhavat |

Ahō Himālayasyāsya Dhaṉyōsou Bhākyavāṉiti || 69

यस्यास्तु जठरे सन्ति ब्रह्माण्डानां च कोटयः।
सैव यस्य सुता जाता को वा स्यात्तत्समो भुवि॥ ७०

Yasyāstu Jaṭharē Santi Brahāṇḍāṇām Ca Kōṭayaḥ |

Saiva Yasya Sutā Jātā Kō Vā Syāt Tatsamō Bhuvi ‖ 70

न जानेऽस्मत्पितृणां किं स्थानं स्यान्निर्मितं परम्।
एतादृशानां वासाय येषां वंशेऽस्ति मादृशः॥ ७१

Na Jāṇēśmatpitruṇām Kim Stāṇam Syāṇṇirmitam Param |

Ētādruśāṇām Vāsāya Yēṣām Vamśēśti Mātruśaḥ ‖ 71

इदं यथा च दत्तं मे कृपया प्रेमपूर्णया।
सर्ववेदान्तसिद्धं च त्वद्रूपं ब्रूहि मे तथा॥ ७२

Idam Yathā Ca Dattam Mē Krupayā Prēmapūrṇayā |

Sarvavēdāntasiddham Ca Tvadrūpam Brūhi Mē Tathā ‖ 72

योगं च भक्तिसहितं ज्ञानं च श्रुतिसम्मतम्।
वदस्व परमेशानि त्वमेवाहं यतो भवेः॥ ७३

Yōgam Ca Bhaktisahitam Ñāṇam Ca Śrutisam'matam |

Vadasva Paramēśāṇi Tvamēvāham Yatō Bhavēḥ ‖ 73

Vyasa said – "Oh King! Hearing the kind words of Sri Devi, the King of mountains was filled with love; and, with voice choked with feelings and with tears in his eyes spoke to the Goddess of the world, the Queen. of the three worlds. Thou hast raised me much higher, that Thou dost me so great a favour; otherwise where am I inert and unmoving and where art Thou, of the nature of Existence, Intelligence and Bliss! It manifests the Greatness of Thy Glory. Oh, Sinless One! My becoming the father of Thee indicates nothing less than the merits earned by me for doing, countless Ashvamedha sacrifices or for my endless *Samadhi*. Oh! What a favour hast Thou shewn towards me! Henceforth my unparalleled fame will be spread throughout the whole Universe of five original elements that "The Upholder of the Universe, the World Mother has become the daughter of this

Himalayas! This man is blessed and fortunate!" Who can be so fortunate, virtuous and merited as he whose daughter She has become, whose belly contains millions of Brahmandas! I cannot describe what pre-eminent heavens are intended for my Pitrus, my, family predecessors, wherein virtuous persons like myself are born. Oh Mother! Oh *Parameshvari*! Now describe to me Thy Real Self as exemplified in all the Vedantas; and also, Jnana with Bhakti approved by the *Vedas* in the same way that Thou hast shown already this favour to me, so that by That Know ledge I will be able to realise Thy Self.

व्यास उवाच

इति तस्य वच: श्रुत्वा प्रसन्नमुखपङ्कजा।

वक्तुमारभताम्बा सा रहस्यं श्रुतिगूहितम्॥ ७४

Vyāsa Uvāca

Iti Tasya Vacaḥ Śrutvā Prasaṇṇamukhapaṅkajā |

Vaktumārabhatāmbā Sā Rahasyam Śrutigūhitam || 74

Vyasa said – Oh King! Thus, hearing the praise of Himalayas, the Goddess of the Universe, with a graceful look, began to speak the very secret essences of the *Shrutis*.

ओं श्री जगदंबार्पणमस्तु । श्री चण्डिकापरमेश्वरी प्रीयताम् ।

Ōm Śrī Jagadambārpaṇamastu |

Śrī Caṇḍikā Paramēśvarī Prīyatām |

इति श्रीमद् देवी भागवते महापुराणेऽष्टादश साहस्रयां संहितायां श्री देवीगीतायां हिमालय गृहे पार्वतीजन्मविषये देवान् प्रति देवीकथनवर्णनं नाम प्रथमोऽध्याय: ॥

Iti Śrīmad Dēvī Bhāgavatē Mahāpurāṇēɔṣṭātaśa Sāhasrayām Samhitāyām Śrī Dēvī Gītāyām Himālaya Gruhē Pārvatī Jaṇma Viṣayē Dēvāṇ Prati Dēvī Kathaṇa Varṇaṇam Nāma Pratamōdyāyaḥ ||

Here ends the first Chapter of Sri Devi Gita named as the birth of Parvati in the House of Himalayas in the Mahapuranam *Shrimad Devi Bhagavatam* having 18,000 verses, by Maharshi Veda Vyasa.

Devi Gita
(*Devi Bhagavatam 7-32*)

This is the second chapter of *Sri Devi Gita*. In Sri Devi Bhagavatam, sage Vyasa has named this chapter as *"Sri Devi Gitai"*. However, alongwith the previous chapter "Appearing of Sri Devi" and further chapters like Dhyana Yoga and all, the ten chapters, entirely are called *Sri Devi Gita*. This chapter explains the individual and combined form of *Sri Devi*.

ओं नमः चण्डिकायै । *Ōm Namaḥ Caṇḍikāyai* ।

देव्युवाच

श्रृण्वन्तु निर्जराः सर्वे व्याहरन्त्या वचो मम।

यस्य श्रवणमात्रेण मद्रूपत्वं प्रपद्यते॥ १

Dēvyuvāca

Śruṇvantu Nirjarāḥ Sarvē Vyāharantyā Vacō Mama |

Yasya Śravaṇamātrēṇa Madrūpatvam Prapadyatē ‖ 1

अहमेवास पूर्वं तु नान्यत्किञ्चिन्नगाधिप।

तदात्मरूपं चित्संवित्परब्रह्मैकनामकम्॥ २

Ahamēvāsa Pūrvam Tu Nānyatkiñciṇṇagādhipa |

Tadātmarūpam Citsamvit Parabrahmaika Nāmakam ‖ 2

Sri Devi said to Devas and the Parvata king – "Hear, you Immortals! My words with attention, that I am now going to speak to you, hearing which will enable the Jeevas to realise My Essence. Before the creation, I, only I, existed; nothing else was existent then. My Real Self is known by the names *Chit*, *Samvit* (Intelligence), Parabrahmam and others.

अप्रतर्क्यमनिर्देश्यमनौपम्यमनामयम्　　　 ।

तस्य काचित्स्वतः सिद्धा शक्तिर्मायेति विश्रुता॥ ३

Apratakryamaṇirtēśyamaṇaupamyamaṇāmayam |

Tasya Kācitsvataḥ Siddhā Śaktirmāyēti Viśurutā || 3

न सती सा नासती सा नोभयात्मा विरोधतः।

एतद्विलक्षणा काचिद्वस्तुभूतास्ति सर्वदा॥ ४

Na Satī Sā Nāsatī Sā Nōbhayātmā Virōdhataḥ |

Ētadvilakṣaṇā Kācidvastu Bhūtāsti Sarvadā || 4

पावकस्योष्णतेवेयमुष्णांशोरिव दीधितिः।

चन्द्रस्य चन्द्रिकेवेयं ममेयं सहजा धुवा॥ ५

Pāvakasyōṣṇatēvēyamuṣṇāṁśōriva Dīdhitiḥ |

Candrasya Candrikēvēyam Mamēyam Sahajā Dhruvā || 5

तस्यां कर्माणि जीवानां जीवाः कालाश्च सञ्चरे।

अभेदेन विलीनाः स्युः सुषुप्तौ व्यवहारवत्॥ ६

Tasyām Karmāṇi Jīvānām Jīvāḥ Kālāśca Sañcarē |

Abhēdēna Vilīnāḥ Syuḥ Suṣuptau Vyavahāravat || 6

My Atman is beyond mind, beyond thought, beyond any name or mark, without any parallel and beyond birth, death or any other change or transformation. My Self has one inherent power called Maya. This Maya is not existent, nor non-existent, nor can it be called both. This unspeakable substance Maya always exists (till the final emancipation or Moksha).

स्वशक्तेश्च समायोगादहं बीजात्मतां गता।

स्वाधारावरणात्तस्या दोषत्वं च समागतम्॥ ७

Svaśaktēśca Samāyōgādaham Bījātmatām Gatā |

Svādhārāvaraṇāttasyā Dōṣatvam Ca Samāgatam || 7

चैतन्यस्य समायोगान्निमित्तत्वं च कथ्यते।

प्रपञ्चपरिणामाच्च समवायित्वमुच्यते॥ ८

Caitanyasya Samāyōgān Nimittatvam Ca Kathyatē |

Prapañca Pariṇāmācca Samavāyitvamucyatē || 8

केचित्तां तप इत्याहुस्तमः केचिज्जडं परे।

ज्ञानं मायां प्रधानं च प्रकृतिं शक्तिमप्य्यजाम्॥ ९

Kēcittām Tapa Ityāhustamaḥ Kēcijjaḍam Parē |

Ñāṉam Māyām Pradhāṉam Ca Prakrutim Śaktimayyajām || 9

Maya can be destroyed by Brahma-Jnana; so, it cannot be called existent, again if Maya does not exist, the practical world cannot exist. So, it cannot be called non-existent. Of course, it cannot be called both, for it would involve contradictions. This Maya (without beginning but with end at the time of Moksha) naturally arises as heat comes out of fire, as the rays come out of the Sun and as the cooling rays come out of the Moon. Just as all the Karmas of the Jeevas dissolve in deep sleep (Sushupti), so at the time of Pralaya or the General Dissolution, the Karmas of the Jeevas, the Jeevas and Time all become merged, in one uniform mass in this great Maya. United with My Shakti, I am the Cause of this world; this Shakti has this defect that it has the power of hiding Me, its Originator.

विमर्श इति तां प्राहुः शैवशास्त्रविशारदाः।

अविद्यामितरे प्राहुर्वेदतत्त्वार्थचिन्तकाः॥ १०

Vimarśa Iti Tām Prāhuḥ Śavaśāstraviśāradāḥ |

Avidyāmitarē Prāhur Vēdatatvārtha Cintakāḥ || 10

I am Nirguna. And when I am united with my Shakti, Maya, I become Saguna, the Great Cause of this world. This Maya is divided into two, Vidya and Avidya. Avidya Maya hides Me; whereas Vidya Maya does not. Avidya creates whereas Vidya Maya liberates.

एवं नानाविधानि स्युर्नामानि निगमादिषु।

तस्या जडत्वं दृश्यत्वाज्ज्ञानिनशाक्तितोऽसती॥ ११

Ēvam Nāṉāvidhāṉi Syurnāmāṉi Nigamādiṣu |

Tasyā Jaḍatvam Druśyatvāñ Gñāṉa Nāśāt Tatōśatī || 11

चैतन्यस्य न दृश्यत्वं दृश्यत्वे जडमेव तत्।

स्वप्रकाशं च चैतन्यं न परेण प्रकाशितम्॥१२

Caitaṉyasya Na Druśyatvam Druśyatvē Jaḍamēva Tat |

Svaprakāśam Ca Caitaṉyam Na Parēṇa Prakāśitam || 12

Maya united with Chaitanya (Intelligence), i.e., Chidakhasha is the efficient cause of this Universe; whereas Maya reduced to and united with five original elements is the material Cause of the Universe. Some call this Maya tapas; some call Her inert, material; some call Her knowledge; some call Her Maya, Pradhana, Prakriti, Aja (unborn) and sonic others call Her Shakti. The Saiva authors call Her Vimarsha and the other Vedantists call Her Avidya; in short, this Maya is in the heads of all the Pundits. This Maya is called various in the Nigamas.

अनवस्थादोषसत्त्वान स्वेनापि प्रकाशितम्।

कर्मकर्त्रींविरोध: स्यात्तस्मात्तद्दीपवत्स्वयम्॥१३

Aṉavastā Dōṣasatvāṉṉa Svēṉāpi Prakāśitam |

Karmakartrī Virōdhaḥ Syāt Tasmāt Tat Dīpavat Svayam || 13

प्रकाशमानमन्येषां भासकं विद्धि पर्वत।

अतएव च नित्यत्वं सिद्धसंवित्तनोर्मम॥१४

Prakāśamāṉamaṉyēṣām Bhāsakam Viddhi Parvata |

Ataēva Ca Nityatvam Siddhasamvittaṉōrmama || 14

जाग्रत्स्वजसुषुप्त्यादौ दृश्यस्य व्यभिचारत:।

संविदो व्यभिचारश्च नानुभूतोऽस्ति कर्हिचित्॥१५

Jāgrat Svapṉa Suṣuptyādou Druśyasya Vyabhicārataḥ |

Samvidō Vyabhicāraśca Nāṉubhūtōśti Karʾhicit || 15

यदि तस्याप्यनुभवस्तर्ह्ययं येन साक्षिणा।
अनुभूतः स एवात्र शिष्टः संविद्वपुः पुरा॥ १६

Yati Tasyāpyanubhavas Tar'hyayam Ēna Sākṣiṇā |
Anubhūtaḥ Sa Ēvātra Śiṣṭaḥ Samvidvapuḥ Purā || 16

अतएव च नित्यत्वं प्रोक्तं सच्छास्त्रकोविदैः।
आनन्दरूपता चास्याः परप्रेमास्पदत्वतः॥ १७

Atayēva Ca Nityatvam Prōktam Sacchāstra Kōvidaiḥ |
Āṇanda Rūpatā Cāsyāḥ Paraprēmāspadatvataḥ || 17

मा न भूवं हि भूयासमिति प्रेमात्मनि स्थितम्।
सर्वस्यान्यस्य मिथ्यात्वादसङ्गत्वं स्फुटं मम॥ १८

Mā Na Bhūvam Hi Bhūyāsamiti Prēmātmaṇi Sthitam |
Sarvasyāṇyasya Mithyātvāda Saṅgatvam Sphuṭam Mama || 18

अपरिच्छिन्नताप्येवमत एव मता मम।
तच्च ज्ञानं नात्मधर्मो धर्मत्वे जडतात्मनः॥ १९

Aparicchiṇṇatāpyēvamata Ēva Matā Mama |
Tacca Ñāṇam Nātmadharmō Dharmatvē Jaḍatātmaṇaḥ || 19

ज्ञानस्य जडशेषत्वं न दृष्टं न च सम्भवि।
चिद्धर्मत्वं तथा नास्ति चितश्चिन्न हि भिद्यते॥ २०

Ñāṇasya Jaḍaśēṣatvam Na Druṣṭam Na Ca Sambhavi |
Ciddharmatvam Tathā Nāsti Citaściṇṇa Hi Bhidyatē || 20

तस्मादात्मा ज्ञानरूपः सुखरूपश्च सर्वदा।
सत्यः पूर्णोऽप्यसङ्गश्च द्वैतजालविवर्जितः॥ २१

Tasmādātmā Ñāṇarūpa: Sukharūpaśca Sarvadā |
Satyaḥ Pūrṇopyasaṅgaśca Dvaitajālavivarjitaḥ || 21

स पुनः कामकर्मादियुक्तया स्वीयमायया।
पूर्वानुभूतसंस्कारात् कालकर्मविपाकतः॥ २२

Ya Puṇaḥ Kāmakarmādiyuktayā Svīyamāyayā |
Pūrvāṇubhūta Samskārāt Kālakarmavipākataḥ || 22

अविवेकाच्च तत्त्वस्य सिसृक्षावान्प्रजायते।
अबुद्धिपूर्वः सर्गोऽयं कथितस्ते नगाधिप॥ २३

Avivēkācca Tatvasya Sisrukṣāvāṇ Prajāyatē |
Abuddhipūrvaḥ Sargōyam Kathitastē Nagādhipa || 23

एतद्धि यन्मया प्रोक्तं मम रूपमलौकिकम्।
अव्याकृतं तदव्यक्तं मायाशबलमित्यपि॥ २४

Ētaddhi Yaṇmayā Prōktam Mama Rūpamalaukikam |
Avyākrutam Tadavyaktam Māyāśabalamityapi || 24

प्रोच्यते सर्वशास्त्रेषु सर्वकारणकारणम्।
तत्त्वानामादिभूतं च सच्चिदानन्दविग्रहम्॥ २५

Prōcyatē Sarva Śāstrēṣu Sarva Kāraṇa Kāraṇam |
Tatvānāmādi Bhūtam Ca Saccidāṇanda Vigraham || 25

सर्वकर्मघनीभूतमिच्छाज्ञानक्रियाश्रयम्।
ह्रींकारमन्त्रवाच्यं तदादितत्त्वं तदुच्यते॥ २६

Sarva Karma Ghaṇībhūtamiccāñāṇa Kriyāśrayam |
Hrīṅkāra Mantravācyam Tadāditatvam Taducyatē || 26

तस्मादाकाश उत्पन्नः शब्दतन्मात्ररूपकः।
भवेत्स्पर्शात्मको वायुस्तेजोरूपात्मकं पुनः॥ २७

Tasmādākāśa Utpaṇṇaḥ Śabdataṇmātrarūpakaḥ |
Bhavētsparśātmakō Vāyustējōrūpātmakam Puṇaḥ || 27

जलं रसात्मकं पश्चात्ततो गन्धात्मिका धरा।

शब्दैकगुण आकाशो वायुः स्पर्शरवान्वितः ॥ २८

Jalam Rasātmakam Paścāttatō Gandhātmikā Dharā |

Śabdaikaguṇa Ākāśō Vāyuḥ Sparśaravāṇvitaḥ ‖ 28

शब्दस्पर्शरूपगुणं तेज इत्युच्यते बुधैः।

शब्दस्पर्शरूपरसैरापो वेदगुणाः स्मृताः ॥ २९

Śabta Sparśa Rūpaguṇam Tēja Ityucyatē Budhaiḥ |

Śapta Sparśa Rūparasairāpō Vēdaguṇāḥ Smrutāḥ ‖ 29

शब्दस्पर्शरूपरसगन्धैः पञ्चगुणा धरा।

तेभ्योऽभवन्महत्सूत्रं यल्लिङ्गं परिचक्षते ॥ ३०

Śabdasparśa Rūparasagantaiḥ Pañcaguṇā Dharā |

Tēbhyōbhavan Mahat Sūtram Yalliṅgam Paricakṣatē ‖ 30

सर्वात्मकं तत्सम्प्रोक्तं सूक्ष्मदेहोऽयमात्मनः।

अव्यक्तं कारणो देहः स चोक्तः पूर्वमेव हि ॥ ३१

Sarvātmakam Tatsamprōktam Sūkṣma Dēhō śYamātmaṇaḥ |

Avyaktam Kāraṇō Dēhaḥ Sa Cōktaḥ Pūrvamēva Hi ‖ 31

That which is seen is inert; for this reason, Maya is Jada (inert) and as the knowledge it conveys is destroyed, it is false. Chaitanya (Intelligence) is not seen; if It were seen, it would have been Jada. Chaitanya is self-luminous; not illumined by any other source. Were It so, Its Enlightener would have to be illumined by some other? thing and so the fallacy of Anavastha creeps in (an endless series of causes and effects). Again, one thing cannot be the actor and the thing, acted upon (being contrary to each other); so, Chaitanya cannot be illumined by itself. So, it is Self-luminous; and it illumines Sun, Moon, etc., as a lamp is self-luminous and illumines other objects. So, Oh Mountain! This My Intelligence is established as eternal and everlasting. The waking, dreaming and deep sleep states do not remain constant but the sense of "I" remains the same, whether in waking, dreaming or deep sleep state; its anomaly is never felt. (The Bouddhas say that) The sense of intelligence, Jnana, is also not, felt; there in the absence of it; so, what is existent is also temporarily existent. But (it can then be argued that) then the Witness by which that absence is sensed, that Intelligence, in the shape of the Witness, is eternal. So, the Pundits of all the reasonable Sastras declare that Samvit (Intelligence) is Eternal and it is Blissful the fountain of all love. Never the Jeevas or embodied souls feel "I am not"; but "I am" this feeling is deeply established in the soul as Love. Thus, it is clearly evident that I am quite Separate from anything else which are all false. Also, I am one continuous (no interval or separation existing within Me). Again, Jnana is not the Dharma (the natural quality) of Atman but it is of the very nature of Atman. If Jnana ware the Dharma of Atman, then Jnana would have been material; so, Jnana is immaterial. If (for argument's sake) Jnana be denominated as material, that cannot be. For Jnana is of the nature of Intelligence and Atman is of the so, nature of Intelligence. Intelligence has not the attribute of being Dharma. Here the thing Chit is not different from its quality (Chit). So, Atman is always of the nature of Jnana and happiness; Its nature is Truth; It is always Full, unattached and void of duality. This Atman again, united with Maya, composed of desires and Karmas, wants to create, due to the want of discrimination, the twenty-four tattvas, according to the previous Samskaras (tendencies), time and Karma. Oh Mountain! The re-awakening after Pralaya Sushupti is not done with Buddhi (for then Buddhi is not at all manifested). So, this creation is said to be affected without any Buddhi (proper intelligence). Oh, Chief of the Immovables! The Tattva (Reality) that I have spoken to you is most excellent and it is my Extraordinary Form merely. In the Vedas it is known as Avyakruta (unmodified), Avyakta (unmanifested).

यस्मिञ्जगद्बीजरूपं स्थितं लिङ्गोद्भवो यत: ।

तत: स्थूलानि भूतानि पञ्चीकरणमार्गत: ॥ ३२

Yasmiñjagadbījarūpam Stitam Liṅkōdbhavō Yataḥ ।

Tata: Sthūlāṉi Bhūtāṉi Pañcīkaraṇamārgataḥ ‖ 32

पञ्चसंख्यानि जायन्ते तत्प्रकारस्त्वथोच्यते।
पूर्वोक्तानि च भूतानि प्रत्येकं विभजेद् द्विधा॥ ३३

Pañcasaṅkhyāṉi Jāyantē Tatprakārastvathōcyatē |
Pūrvōktāṉi Ca Bhūtāṉi Pratyēkam Vibhajēt Dvidhā ‖ 33

एकैकं भागमेकस्य चतुर्धा विभजेद् गिरे।
स्वस्वेतरद्वितीयांशे योजनात्पञ्च पञ्च ते॥ ३४

Ēkaikam Bhāgamēkasya Caturdhā Vibhajēt Girē |
Svasvētaradvitīyāmśē Yōjaṉātpañca Pañca Tē ‖ 34

तत्कार्यं च विराड्देहः स्थूलदेहोऽयमात्मनः।
पञ्चभूतस्थसत्त्वांशैः श्रोत्रादीनां समुद्भवः॥ ३५

Tatkāryam Ca Virāḍḍēhaḥ Stūla Dēhō śYamātmaṉaḥ |
Pañcabhūtasta Satvāmśaiḥ Śrōtrādīṉām Samudbhavaḥ ‖ 35

ज्ञानेन्द्रियाणां राजेन्द्र प्रत्येकं मिलितैस्तु तैः।
अन्तःकरणमेकं स्याद् वृत्तिभेदाच्चतुर्विधम्॥ ३६

Ñāṉēntriyāṉām Rājēndra Pratyēkam Militaistu Taiḥ |
Antaḥ Karaṇamēkam Syād Vrutti Bhēdāccaturvidham ‖ 36

यदा   तु   संकल्पविकल्पकृत्यं
        तदा   भवेत्तन्मन   इत्यभिख्यम्।
स्याद्   बुद्धिसंज्ञं   च   यदा   प्रवेत्ति
        सुनिश्चितं   संशयहीनरूपम्॥ ३७

Yadā Tu Saṅkalpa Vikalpa Krutyam
        Tadā Bhavēttaṉmaṉa Ityabhikhyam |
Syād Buddhisaṇṇam Ca Yadā Pravētti

अनुसन्धानरूपं तच्चित्तं च परिकीर्तितम्।
अहङ्कृत्यात्मवृत्त्या तु तदहङ्कारतां गतम्॥ ३८

Anusandhānarūpam Taccittam Ca Parikīrtitam |
Ahaṅkrutyātma Vrutyā Tu Tadahaṅkāratām Gatam ‖ 38

तेषां रजोंशैर्जातानि क्रमात्कर्मेन्द्रियाणि च।
प्रत्येकं मिलितैस्तैस्तु प्राणो भवति पञ्चधा॥ ३९

Tēṣām Rajōmśairjātāni Kramāt Karmēndriyāṇi Ca |
Pratyēkam Militaistaistu Prāṇō Bhavati Pañcadhā ‖ 39

हृदि प्राणो गुदेऽपानो नाभिस्थस्तु समानकः।
कण्ठदेशेऽप्युदानः स्याद् व्यानः सर्वशरीरगः॥ ४०

Hruti Prāṇō Gudēpāṇō Nābhistastu Samāṇaka: |
Kaṇṭhadēśēpyudāṇaḥ Syād Vyāṇaḥ Sarvaśarīragaḥ ‖ 40

ज्ञानेन्द्रियाणि पञ्चैव पञ्चकर्मेन्द्रियाणि च।
प्राणादिपञ्चकं चैव धिया च सहितं मनः॥ ४१

Gñāṇēndriyāṇi Pañcaiva Pañcakarmēndriyāṇi Ca |
Prāṇādi Pañcakam Caiva Dhiyā Ca Sahitam Maṇaḥ ‖ 41

एतत्सूक्ष्मं शरीरं स्यान्मम लिङ्गं यदुच्यते।
तत्र या प्रकृतिः प्रोक्ता सा राजन्द्विविधा स्मृता॥ ४२

Ētatsūkṣmam Śarīram Syānmama Liṅgam Yaducyatē |
Tatra Yā Prakrutiḥ Prōktā Sā Rājandvividhā Smrutā ‖ 42

Maya Sabala (divided into various parts) and so forth. In all tantric
Shastras, it is stated to be the Cause of all causes, the Primeval
Tattva and Sachchidananda Vigraha. Where all the Karmas are
solidified and where Ichcha Shakti, (will), Jnana Shakti

(intelligence) and Kriya Shakti (action) all are melted in one, that is called the Mantra Hreem, that is the first Tattva. From this comes out Akasha, having the property of sound, thence Vayu (air) with 'touch' property; then fire with form, then water having 'Rasa' property; and lastly the earth having the quality 'smell'. The Pundits say that the 'sound' is the only quality of Akasha; air has two qualities viz., sound and touch, fire has three qualities sound, touch, form; water has four qualities sound, touch, form, taste; and the earth has five qualities sound, touch, form, taste and smell, Out of these five original elements, the all-pervading, Sutra (string or thread) arose. This Sutratman (soul) is called the "Linga Deha," comprising within itself all the Pranas; this is the subtle body of the Paramatman. And what is said in the previous lines as Avyakta or Unmainfested and in which the Seed of the World is involved and whence the Linga Deha has sprung, that is called the Causal body (Karana body) of the Paramatman.

सत्त्वात्मिका तु माया स्यादविद्या गुणमिश्रिता ।

स्वाश्रयं या तु संरक्षेत्सा मायेति निगद्यते ॥ ४३

Satvātmikā Tu Māyā Syādavidyā Guṇamiśritā |

Svāśrayam Yā Tu Samrakṣētsā Māyēti Nigadyatē ॥ 43

तस्यां यत्प्रतिबिम्बं स्याद् बिम्बभूतस्य चेशितुः ।

स ईश्वरः समाख्यातः स्वाश्रयज्ञानवान्परः ॥ ४४

Tasyām Yatpratibimbam Syāt Bimbabhūtasya Cēśituḥ |

Sa Īśvaraḥ Samākhyātaḥ Svāśrayagñānavānparaḥ ॥ 44

सर्वज्ञः सर्वकर्ता च सर्वानुग्रहकारकः ।

अविद्यायां तु यत्किञ्चित्प्रतिबिम्बं नगाधिप ॥ ४५

Sarvagñaḥ Sarvakartā Ca Sarvānu Grahakārakaḥ |

Avidyāyām Tu Tatkiñcit Pratibimbam Nagādhipa ॥ 45

तदेव जीवसंज्ञं स्यात्सर्वदुःखाश्रयं पुनः ।

द्वयोरपीह सम्प्रोक्तं देहत्रयमविद्यया ॥ ४६

Tadēva Jīvasamñam SyātsarvaduḥKāśrayam Punaḥ |

Dvayōrapīha Samprōktam Dēhatrayama Vidyayā ‖ 46

देहत्रयाभिमानाच्चाप्यभून्नामत्रयं   पुनः ।

प्राज्ञस्तु कारणात्मा स्यात्सूक्ष्मदेही तु तैजसः ‖ ४७

Dēhatrayābhimānāccāpya Bhūṉṉāmatrayam Puṉaḥ |

Prākñastu Kāraṇātmā Syātsūkṣmadēhī Tu Taijasaḥ ‖ 47

स्थूलदेही तु विश्वाख्यस्त्रिविधः परिकीर्तितः ।

एवमीशोऽपि   सम्प्रोक्त   ईशसूत्रविराट्पदैः ‖ ४८

Stūladēhī Tu Viśvākhyastrividha: Parikīrtitaḥ |

Ēvamīśōpi Samprōkta Īśasūtravirāṭpadaih ‖ 48

प्रथमो व्यष्टिरूपस्तु समष्ट्यात्मा परः स्मृतः ।

स हि सर्वेश्वरः साक्षाज्जीवानुग्रहकाम्यया ‖ ४९

Pratamō Vyaṣṭirūpastu Samaṣṭyātmā Parah Smrutaḥ |

Sa Hi Sarvēśvaraḥ Sākṣājjīvāṉugraha Kāmyayā ‖ 49

करोति विविधं विश्वं नानाभोगाश्रयं   पुनः ।

मच्छक्तिप्रेरितो नित्यं मयि राजन् प्रकल्पितः ‖ ५०

Karōti Vividham Viśvam Nāṉābhōgāśrayam Puṉaḥ |

Macchakti Prēritō Nityam Mayai Rājaṉ Prakalpitaḥ ‖ 50

The five original elements (Apancheekruta called the five Tan Matras) being created, next by the Pancheekarana process, the gross elements are created. The process is now being stated – Oh Girija! Each of the five original elements is divided into two parts; one part of each of which is subdivided into four parts. This fourth part of each is united with the half of four other elements different from it and thus each gross element is formed. By these five gross elements, the Cosmic (Virat) body is formed and this is called the Gross Body of the God. Jnanendriyas (the organs of knowledge) arise from Sattva Gunas of each of these five elements. Again, the Sattva Gunas of each of the Jnanendriyas united become the Antah-Karana. This Antah-karana is of four kinds, according as its functions vary. When it is engaged in forming Sankalpas, resolves and Vikalpas (doubts) it is called 'mind'. When it is free from doubts and when it arrives at the decisive conclusion, it is called 'Chitta'; and when it rests simply on itself in the shape of the feeling 'I', it is called Ahamkara. From the Rajo Guna of each of the five elements arises Vak (speech), Pani (hands) Pada (feet), Payu (Anus) and Upastha (organs of generation). Again, their Rajo parts united give rise to the five Pranas (Prana, Apana, Samana, Udana and Vyana) the Prana Vayu resides in the heart; Apana Vayu in the Arms; Samana Vayu resides in the Navel; Udana Vayu resides in the Throat; and the Vyana Vayu resides, pervading all over the body. My subtle body (Linga Deha) arises from the union of the five Jnanendriyas, the five Karmendriyas (organs of action), the five Pranas and the mind and Buddhi, these seventeen elements. And the Prakriti that resides there is divided into two parts; one is pure (Shuddha Satbava) Maya and the other is the impure Maya or Avidya united with the Gunas. By Maya is meant She, who, without concealing Her refugees, protects them. When the Supreme Self is reflected on this Shuddha Sattva, Maya, He is called Ishvara. This Shuddha Maya does not conceal Brahmam, its receptacle; therefore, she knows the All-pervading Brahmam and She is omniscient, omnipotent, the Lady of all and confers favours and blessings on all. When the Supreme Self is reflected on the Impure Maya or Avidya, He is called Jeeva. This Avidya conceals Brahma, whose nature is Happiness; therefore, this Jeeva is the source of all miseries. Both Ishvara and Jeeva have, by the influence of Vidya and Avidya three bodies and three names. When the Jeeva lives in his causal body, he is named Prajna; when he lives in subtle body he is known as Taijasa; while he has the gross body, he is called Vishva. So, when Ishvara is in His causal body, he is denominated as Isha; when He is in His subtle body, he is known as Sutra; and when He is in His gross body, He is known as Virat.

The Jeeva glories in having three (as above-mentioned) kinds of differentiated bodies and Ishvara glories in having three (as above-mentioned) kinds of cosmic bodies. Thus, Ishvara is the

Lord of all and though He feels Himself always happy and satisfied, yet to favour the Jeevas and to give them liberation (Moksha) He has created various sorts of worldly things for their Bhogas (enjoyments). This Ishvara creates all the Universe, impelled by My Brahma-Shakti. I am of the nature of Brahmam; and Ishvara in conceived in Me as a snake is imagined in a rope. Therefore, Ishvara has to remain dependent on My Shakti.

ओं श्री जगदंबार्पणमस्तु । श्री चण्डिकापरमेश्वरी प्रीयताम् ।

Ōm Śrī Jagadambārpaṇamastu |

Śrī Caṇḍikā Paramēśvarī Prīyatām |

इति श्रीमद् देवी भागवते महापुराणेऽष्टादश साहस्रयां संहितायां श्री देवी गीतायां देव्या व्यष्टि समष्टि रूपवर्णनं नाम द्विदीयोऽध्याय: ॥

Iti Śrīmad Dēvī Bhāgavatē Mahāpurāṇēʂʂṭātaśa Sāhasrayām

Samhitāyām Śrī Dēvī Gītāyām Devyā Vyaʂṭi Samaʂṭi Rūpa

Varṇaṇam Nāma Dvideeyōḍyāyaḥ ‖

Here ends the second Chapter of *Sri Devi Gita* named as *Śrī Dēvī Gītā* in the Mahapuranam *Shrimad Devi Bhagavatam* having 18,000 verses, by Maharshi Veda Vyasa.

Devi Viśwarūpa Darśanam
(Devi Bhagavatam 7-33)

This is the third chapter of *Sri Devi Gita*. The name of the chapter "*Śrī Devī Viśvarūpa Darśanam*". This is comparable with the 11th chapter of *Shrimad Bhagawad Gīta*. This explains the *Virātrūpa/Viśvarūpa* form of *Śri Devī*. '*Vi*' = no and '*rāt*' = head, hence '*Virāt*' = nobody above her.

ओं नम: चण्डिकायै । *Ōm Namaḥ Caṇḍikāyai* ।

देव्युवाच

मन्मायाशक्तिसंक्लृप्तं जगत्सर्वं चराचरम्।
सापि मत्त: पृथङ्माया नास्त्येव परमार्थत: ॥ १

Dēvyuvāca

Maṇmāyāśakti Saṅkluptam Jagatsarvam Carācaram ।

Sāpi Mattaḥ Pruthaṅmāyā Nāstyēva Paramārthataḥ ॥ 1

व्यवहारदृशा सेयं विद्या मायेति विश्रुता।
तत्त्वदृष्ट्या तु नास्त्येव तत्त्वमेवास्ति केवलम्॥ २

Vyavahāradruśā Sēyam Vidyā Māyēti Viśrutā ।

Tatvadruṣṭyā Tu Nāstyēva Tatvamēvāsti Kēvalam ॥ 2

साहं सर्वं जगत्सृष्ट्वा तदन्त: प्रविशाम्यहम्।
मायाकर्मादिसहिता गिरे प्राणपुर:सरा ॥ ३

Sāham Sarvam Jagatsruṣṭvā Tadantaḥ Praviśāmyaham ।

Māyākarmādisahitā Girē PrāṇapuraḥSarā ॥ 3

लोकान्तरगतिर्नोचेत्कथं स्यादिति हेतुना।
यथा यथा भवन्त्येव मायाभेदास्तथा तथा॥ ४

Lōkāntara Gatirṇōcētkatham Syāditi Hētuṇā ।

Yathā Yathā Bhavantyēva Māyābhētāstathā Tathā || 4

उपाधिभेदाद्भिन्नाहं घटाकाशादयो यथा ।
उच्चनीचादिवस्तूनि भासयन्भास्करः सदा ॥ ५

Upādhi Bhēdādbhinnāham Ghaṭākāśādayō Yathā |
Uccanīcādi Vastūni Bhāsayan Bhāskaraḥ Sadā || 5

न दुष्यति तथैवाहं दोषैर्लिप्ता कदापि न ।
मयि बुद्ध्यादिकर्तृत्वमध्यस्यैवापरे जनाः ॥ ६

Na Duṣyati Tathaivāham Dōṣarliptā Kadāpi Na |
Mayi Buddhyādikartrutvamadhyasyaivāparē Janāḥ || 6

वदन्ति चात्मा कर्मेति विमूढा न सुबुद्धयः ।
अज्ञानभेदतस्तद्वन्मायाया भेदतस्तथा ॥ ७

Vadanti Cātmā Karmēti Vimūḍā Na Subuddhayaḥ |
Akñāna Bhēdatastadvanmāyāyā Bhēdatastathā || 7

जीवेश्वरविभागश्च कल्पितो माययैव तु ।
घटाकाशमहाकाशविभागः कल्पितो यथा ॥ ८

Jīvēśvaravibhāgaśca Kalpitō Māyayaiva Tu |
Ghaṭākāśa Mahākāśa Vibhāgaḥ Kalpitō Yathā || 8

तथैव कल्पितो भेदो जीवात्मपरमात्मनोः ।
यथा जीवबहुत्वं च माययैव न च स्वतः ॥ ९

Tathaiva Kalpitō Bhēdō Jīvātma Paramātmanōḥ |
Yathā Jīva Bahutvam Ca Māyayaiva Na Ca Svataḥ || 9

तथेश्वरबहुत्वं च मायया न स्वभावतः ।
देहेन्द्रियादिसङ्घातवासनाभेदभेदिता ॥ १०

Tathēśvara Bahutvam Ca Māyayā Na Svabhāvataḥ |

Dēhēndriyādi Saṅghāta Vāsanāpēta Bhēditā || 10

Sri Devi said – Oh Giriraja! This whole universe, moving and unmoving, is created by My Maya Shakti. This Maya is conceived in Me. It is not, in reality, different or separate from Me. Hence, I am the only Chit, Intelligence. There is no other intelligence than Me. Viewed practically, it is known variously as Maya, Vidya; but viewed really from the point of Brahmam, there is no such thing as Maya; only one Brahman exists, I am that Brahmam, of the nature of Intelligence I create this whole world on this Unchangeable Eternal (Mountain-like) Brahmam, (composed of Avidya, Karma and various Samskaras) and enter first as Prana (vital breath) within it in the form of Chidakhasha.

Oh Mountain! Unless I enter as Breath, how can this birth and death and leaving and retaking bodies after bodies be accounted for! As one great Akasha is denominated variously Ghatakasha (Akasha in the air), Patakasha (Akasha in cloth or picture), so I too appear variously by acknowledging this Prana in various places due to Avidya and various Anta-karanas. As the Sun's rays are never defiled when they illumine various objects on earth, so I, too, am not defiled in entering thus into various high and low Anta-karanas (hearts). The ignorant people attach Buddhi and other things of activity on Me and say that Atman is the Doer; the intelligent people do not say that. I remain as the Witness in the hearts of all men, not as the Doer.

Oh Achalendra! There are many Jeevas and many Ishvaras due to the varieties in Avidya and Vidya. Really it is Maya that differentiates into men, beasts and various other Jeevas; and it is Maya that differentiates into Brahma, Vishnu and other Ishvaras. As the one pervading sky (Akasha) is called Mahakasha Ghatakasha (being enclosed by jars), so the One All-pervading Paramatma is called Paramatma, Jeevatma (being enclosed within Jeevas). As the Jeevas are conceived many by Maya, not in reality; so Ishvaras also are conceived many by Maya; not in essence.

Oh Mountain! This Avidya and nothing else, is the cause of the difference in Jeevas, by creating differences in their bodies, indriyas (organs) and minds. Again, due to the varieties in the three Gunas and their wants (due to the differences between Saattvik, Raajasik and Taamasik desires), Maya also appears various. And their differences are the causes of different Ishvaras, Brahma, Vishnu and others.

Oh Mountain! This whole world is interwoven in Me; It is I that am the Ishvara that resides in causal bodies; I am the "Sutratman, Hiranyagarbha that resides in subtle bodies and it is I that am the Virat, residing in the gross bodies. I am Brahma, Vishnu and Maheshvara; I am the Brahma, Vaishnavi and Roudri Shaktis. I am the Sun, I am the Moon, I am the Stars; I am beast, birds, Chandalas and I am the Thief, I am the cruel hunter; I am the virtuous high-souled persons and I am the female, male and hermaphrodite. There is no doubt in this.

अविद्या जीवभेदस्य हेतुर्नान्यः प्रकीर्तितः ।

गुणानां वासनाभेदभेदिता या धराधर ॥ ११

Avidyā Jīvabhēdasya Hēturnānyaḥ Prakīrtitaḥ |

Guṇāṉām Vāsaṉābhēdabhēditā Yā Dharādhara ǁ 11

माया सा परभेदस्य हेतुर्नान्यः कदाचन ।

मयि सर्वमिदं प्रोतमोतं च धरणीधर ॥ १२

Māyā Sa Parabhēdasya Hēturnāṉyaḥ Kadācaṉa |

Mayi Sarvamidam Prōtamōtam Ca Dharaṇīdhara ǁ 12

ईश्वरोऽहं च सूत्रात्मा विराडात्माऽहमस्मि च ।

ब्रह्माहं विष्णुरुद्रौ च गौरी ब्राह्मी च वैष्णवी ॥ १३

Īśvarōham Ca Sūtrātmā Virāḍātmā 'Hamasmi Ca |

Brahmāham Viṣṇu Rudrou Ca Gourī Brāhmī Ca Vaiṣṇavī ǁ 13

सूर्योऽहं तारकाश्चाहं तारकेशस्तथास्म्यहम् ।

पशुपक्षिस्वरूपाहं चाण्डालोऽहं च तस्करः ॥ १४

Sūryōham Tārakāścāham Tārakēśas Tatāsmyaham |

Paśupakṣisvarūpāham Cāṇḍālōham Ca Taskaraḥ || 14

व्याधोऽहं क्रूरकर्माहं सत्कर्माहं महाजनः।

स्त्रीपुन्पुंसकाकारोऽप्यहमेव न संशयः॥ १५

Vyādhōham Krūra Karmāham Satkarmāham Mahājaṉaḥ |

Strīpuṉ Napumsakākārō Pyahamēva Na Samśayaḥ || 15

यच्च किञ्चित्क्वचिदुस्तु दृश्यते श्रूयतेऽपि वा।

अन्तर्बहिश्च नत्सर्वं व्याप्याहं सर्वदा स्थिता॥ १६

Yacca Kiñcitkvacidvastu Druśyatē Śrūyatēpi Vā |

Antarbahiśca Tatsarvam Vyāpyāham Sarvadā Sthitā || 16

न तदस्ति मया त्यक्तं वस्तु किञ्चिच्चराचरम्।

यद्यस्ति चेत्तच्छून्यं स्याद्वन्ध्यापुत्रोपमं हि तत्॥ १७

Na Tadasti Mayā Tyaktam Vastu Kiñciccarācaram |

Yadyasti Cēttacchūṉyam Syād Vandhyā Putrōpamam Hi Tat || 17

रज्जुर्यथा सर्पमालाभेदैरेका विभाति हि।

तथैवेशादिरूपेण भाम्यहं नात्र संशयः॥ १८

Rajjuryathā Sarpamālā Bhēdairēkā Vibhāti Hi |

Tathai Vēśādirūpēṇa Bhāmyaham Nātra Samśayaḥ || 18

अधिष्ठानातिरेकेण कल्पितं तन्न भासते।

तस्मान्मत्सत्तयैवैतत्सत्तावान्नान्यथा भवेत्॥ १९

Adhiṣṭhāṉātirēkēṇa Kalpitam Taṉṉa Bhāsatē |

Tasmāṉ Matsattayaivaitat Sattāvāṉṉāṉyathā Bhavēt || 19

Oh Mountain! Wherever there is anything, seen or heard, I always exist there, within and without, there is nothing moving or unmoving, that can exist without Me. If there be such, that is like the son of a barren woman. Just as one rope is mistaken for a snake or a garland, so I am the One Brahmam and appears as Ishvara, etc. There, is no doubt in this. This world cannot appear without a substratum. And That Substratum is My Existence. There can be nothing else.

हिमालय उवाच

यथा वदसि देवेशि समष्ट्यात्मवपुस्त्विदम्।

तथैव द्रष्टुमिच्छामि यदि देवि कृपा मयि॥ २०

Himālaya Uvāca

Yahtā Vadasi Dēvēśi Samaṣṭyātmavapustvidam |

Tathaiva Draṣṭumicchāmi Yadi Dēvi Krupā Mayi ǁ 20

King Himalayas said - "Oh Devi! If Thou art merciful on me, I desire, then, to see Thy Virat form in the Fourth Dimensional Space. This sight is developed when the mind resides in the heart center or in the center of the eye-brows. A proper teacher is necessary.

व्यास उवाच

इति तस्य वचः श्रुत्वा सर्वे देवाः सविष्णवः।

ननन्दुर्मुदितात्मानः   पूजयन्तश्च   तद्वचः॥ २१

Vyāsa Uvāca

Iti Tasya Vacaḥ Śrutvā Sarvē Dēvāḥ Saviṣṇavaḥ |

Naṇandurmuditātmāṇaḥ Pūjayantaśca Tadvacaḥ ǁ 21

अथ देवमतं ज्ञात्वा भक्तकामदुघा शिवा।

अदर्शयन्निजं   रूपं   भक्तकामप्रपूरणी॥ २२

Atha Dēvamatam Ñātvā Bhaktakāmadughā Śivā |

Adarśayaṇṇijam Rūpam bhaktakāma Prapūraṇī ǁ 22

Vyasa said – Oh King! Hearing the words of Giriraja, Vishnu and all the other Devas gladly seconded him. Then Sri Devi, the Goddess of the Universe, knowing the desires of the Devas, showed Her Own Form that fulfils the desires of the Bhaktas, that is auspicious and that is like the Kalpa Vruksha towards the Bhaktas. They saw Her Highest Virat Form.

अपश्यंस्ते महादेव्या विराड्रूपं परात्परम्।
द्यौर्मस्तकं भवेद्यस्य चन्द्रसूर्यौ च चक्षुषी॥ २३

Apaśyamstē Mahādēvyā Virāḍrūpam Parātparam |

Dhourmastakam Bhavēdyasya Candra Sūryou Ca Cakṣuṣī || 23

दिश: श्रोत्रे वचो वेदा: प्राणो वायु: प्रकीर्तित:।
विश्वं हृदयमित्याहु: पृथिवी जघनं स्मृतम्॥ २४

Diśa: Śrōtrē Vacō Vēdāḥ Prāṇō Vāyuḥ Prakīrtitāḥ |

Viśvam Hrudayamityāhuḥ Pruthivī Jaghaṇam Smrutam || 24

नभस्तलं नाभिसरो ज्योतिश्चक्रमुर:स्थलम्।
महलोंकस्तु ग्रीवा स्याज्जनोलोको मुखं स्मृतम्॥ २५

Nabhastalam Nābhisarō Jyōtiścakramura:Sthalam |

Maharlōkastu Grīvā Syājjaṇōlōkō Mukham Smrutam || 25

तपोलोको रराटिस्तु सत्यलोकादध: स्थित:।
इन्द्रादयो बाहव: स्यु: शब्द: श्रोत्रं महेशितु:॥ २६

Tapōlōkō Rarāṭistu Satyalōkādadhaḥ Stitaḥ |

Indrādayō Bāhavaḥ Syuḥ Śabtaḥ Śrōtram Mahēśituḥ || 26

नासत्यदस्त्रौ नासे स्तो गन्धो घ्राणं स्मृतो बुधै:।
मुखमग्नि: समाख्यातो दिवारात्री च पक्ष्मणी॥ २७

Nāsatyadastrou Nāsē Stō Gandhō Ghrāṇam Smrutō Budhaiḥ |

Mukamagṇiḥ Samākyātō Divārātrī Ca Pakṣmaṇī || 27

ब्रह्मस्थानं भ्रूविजृम्भोऽप्यापस्तालुः प्रकीर्तिताः ।

रसो जिह्वा समाख्याता यमो दंष्ट्राः प्रकीर्तिताः ॥ २८

Brahmasthānam Bhrūvitrumbhōpyāpastāluḥ Prakīrtitāḥ |

Rasō Jihvā Samākyātā Yamō Damṣṭrāḥ Prakīrtitāḥ || 28

दन्ताः स्नेहकला यस्य हासो माया प्रकीर्तिता ।

सर्गस्त्वपाङ्गमोक्षः स्याद् व्रीडोर्ध्वोष्ठो महेशितुः ॥ २९

Dantā: Snēhakalā Yasya Hāsō Māyā Prakīrtitā |

Sargastva Pāṅgamōkṣaḥ Syād Vrīḍōdhrvōṣṭhō Mahēśituḥ || 29

लोभः स्यादधरोष्ठोऽस्याधर्ममार्गस्तु पृष्ठभूः ।

प्रजापतिश्च मेढ्रं स्याद्यः स्रष्टा जगतीतले ॥ ३०

Lōbha: Syādadharōṣṭhōśyādharma Mārgastu Pruṣṭhabhūḥ |

Prajāpatiśca Mēḍhram Syādyaḥ Srasṭā Jagatītalē || 30

कुक्षिः समुद्रा गिरयोऽस्थीनि देव्या महेशितुः ।

नद्यो नाड्यः समाख्याता वृक्षाः केशाः प्रकीर्तिताः ॥ ३१

Kukṣiḥ Samudrā Girayōṣtīṇi Dēvyā Mahēśituḥ |

Nadyō Nāḍyaḥ Samākyātā Vrukṣāḥ Kēśāḥ Prakīrtitāḥ || 31

कौमारयौवनजरा वयोऽस्य गतिरुत्तमा ।

बलाहकास्तु केशाः स्युः सन्ध्ये ते वाससी विभोः ॥ ३२

Koumāra Yauvaṇa Jarā Vayōśya Gatiruttamā |

Balāhakāstu Kēśāḥ Syuh Sandhyē Tē Vāsasī Vibhōḥ || 32

राजञ्छ्रीजगदम्बायाश्चन्द्रमास्तु मनः स्मृतः ।

विज्ञानशक्तिस्तु हरी रुद्रोऽन्तःकरणं स्मृतम् ॥ ३३

Rājañcrī Jagadambāyāccandramāstu Maṇaḥ Smrutaḥ |

Viññaṇaśaktistu Harī RudrōhtaḥKaraṇam Smrutam || 33

अश्वादिजातयः सर्वाः श्रोणिदेशे स्थिता विभोः ।
अतलादिमहालोकाः कट्यधोभागतां गताः ॥ ३४

Aśvādi Jātayaḥ Sarvāḥ Śrōṇidēśē Stitā Vibhōḥ |
Atalādi Mahālōkāḥ Kaṭyadhō Bhāgatām Gatāḥ || 34

एतादृशं महारूपं ददृशुः सुरपुङ्गवाः ।
ज्वालामालासहस्राढ्यं लेलिहानं च जिह्वया ॥ ३५

Ētādruśam Mahārūpam Dadruśuḥ Surapuṅgavāḥ |
Jvālā Mālā Sahasrāḍyam Lēlihāṉam Ca Jihvyā || 35

दंष्ट्राकटकटारावं वमन्तं वह्निमक्षिभिः ।
नानायुधधरं वीरं ब्रह्मक्षत्रौदनं च यत् ॥ ३६

Damṣṭrākaṭakaṭārāvam Vamantam Vahṉimakṣibhiḥ |
Nāṉāyudhadharam Vīram Brahmakṣatroudaṉam Ca Yat || 36

सहस्रशीर्षनयनं सहस्रचरणं तथा ।
कोटिसूर्यप्रतीकाशं विद्युत्कोटिसमप्रभम् ॥ ३७

Sahasra Śīrṣa Nayaṉam Sahasra Caraṇam Tathā |
Kōṭisurya Pratīkāśam Vidyukōṭi Samaprabham || 37

भयङ्करं महाघोरं हृदक्ष्णोस्त्रासकारकम् ।
ददृशुस्ते सुराः सर्वे हाहाकारं च चक्रिरे ॥ ३८

Bhayaṅkaram Mahāghōram Hruda Kṣṇōstrā Sakārakam |
Dadruśustē Surāḥ Sarvē Hāhākāram Ca Cakrirē || 38

विकम्पमानहृदया मूर्च्छामापुर्दुरत्ययाम् ।
स्मरणं च गतं तेषां जगदम्बेयमित्यपि ॥ ३९

Vikampa Māṉahrudayā Mūrcchāmāpur Duratyayām |
Smaraṇam Ca Gatam Tēṣām Jagadambēyamityapi || 39

अथ ते ये स्थिता वेदाश्चतुर्दिक्षु महाविभो: ।
बोधयामासुरत्युग्रं मूर्च्छतो मूर्च्छितान्सुरान् ॥ ४०

Ata Tē Yē Sthitā Vēdāś Caturdikṣu Mahā Vibhōḥ |

Bōdhayāmāsuratyugram Mūrcchātō Mūrcchitān Surān ॥ 40

अथ ते धैर्यमालम्ब्य लब्ध्वा च श्रुतिमुत्तमाम् ।
प्रेमाश्रुपूर्णनयना रुद्धकण्ठास्तु निर्जरा: ॥ ४१

Ata Tē Dhairyamālambya Labdhvā Ca Śruti Muttamām |

Prēmāśrupūrṇa Nayaṇā Ruddhakaṇṭhāstu Nirjarāḥ ॥ 41

बाष्पगद्गदया वाचा स्तोतुं समुपचक्रिरे ।

Bāṣpagadgadayā Vācā Stōtum Samupacakrirē |

In that virat form of Sri Devi – The Satyaloka is situated on the topmost part and is Her head; the Sun and Moon are Her eyes; the directions Her ears; the Vedas are Her words; the Universe is Her heart; the earth is Her loins; the Bhuvarloka is Her navel; the asterisms are Her Thighs; the Maharloka is Her neck; the Janarloka is Her Face; the Tapoloka is Her head, situated below the Satyaloka Indra and the Devas; and the Svarloka is Her arms; the sound is the organ of Her ears; the Ashvin twins, Her nose; the smell is the organ of smell; the fire is within Her face; day and night are like Her two wings.

The four-faced Brahma is Her eyebrows; water is Her palate; the juice thereof is Her organ of taste; Yama, the God of Death, is Her large teeth; the affection is Her small teeth; Maya is Her smile; the creation of Universe is Her side-looks; modesty is Her upper lip; covetousness is Her lower lip; unrighteousness is Her back. The Prajapati is Her organ of generation; the oceans are Her bowels; the mountains are Her bones; the rivers are Her veins; and the trees are the hairs of Her body.

Oh King! Youth, virginity cand old age are Her best gaits, positions or ways (courses) paths, the clouds are Her handsome hairs; the two twilights are Her clothings; the Moon is the mind of the

Mother of the Universe; Hari is Her Vijnana Shakti (the knowledge power); and Rudra is Her all-destroying power. The horses and other animals are Her loins; the lower regions Atala, etc., are Her lower regions from Her hip to Her feet. The Devas began to behold Her this Cosmic (Virata) appearance with eyes, wide awake, with wonder. Thousands of fiery rays emitted from Her form; She began to lick the whole universe with Her lips; the two rows of teeth began to make horrible sounds; fires came out from Her eyes; various weapons were seen in Her hands; and the Brahmanas and Kshatriyas are become the food of that Awful Deity.

Thousands of heads, eyes and feet were seen in that form. Crores of Suns, crores of lightnings flashes, mingled there. Horrible, Awful, that appearance looked terrific to the eyes, heart and mind. The Devas thus beheld and began to utter cries of horror and consternation; their hearts trembled and they were caught with immoveable senselessness. "Here is Sri Devi, our Mother and Preserver. This idea vanished away at once from their minds. At this moment the Vedas that were on the four sides of Sri Devi, removed the swoon of the Devas and made them conscious.

The Devas got, then, heard excellent Vedas; and, having patience, began to praise and chant hymns in words choked with feelings and with tears flowing from their eyes.

देवा ऊचुः

अपराधं क्षमस्वाम्ब पाहि दीनांस्त्वदुद्भवान् ॥ ४२

Dēvā Ūcuḥ

Aparādham Kṣamasvāmba Pāhi Dīnāstvadudbhavān ॥ 42

कोपं संहर देवेशि सभया रूपदर्शनात् ।

का ते स्तुतिः प्रकर्तव्या पामरैर्निर्जरैरिह ॥ ४३

Kōpam Samhara Dēvēśi Sabhayā Rūpadarśanāt ।

Kā Tē Stutiḥ Prakartavyā Pāmarairnirjarairiha ॥ 43

स्वस्याप्यज्ञेय एवासौ यावान्यश्च स्वविक्रमः।
तदर्वाग्जायमानानां कथं स विषयो भवेत्॥ ४४

Svasyāpyakñēya Ēvāsou Yāvānyaśca Svavikramaḥ |

Tadarvāgjāyamānānām Katham Sa Viṣayō Bhavēt || 44

The Devas said – Oh Mother! Forgive our faults. Protect us, the miserable, that are born of Thee. Oh, Protectress of the Devas! Withhold Thy anger we are very much terrified at the sight of Thy this form.

नमस्ते भुवनेशानि नमस्ते प्रणवात्मिके।
सर्ववेदान्तसंसिद्धे नमो ह्रींकारमूर्तये॥ ४५

Namastē Bhuvaṇēśāṇi Namastē Praṇavātmikē |

Sarva Vēdānta Samsiddhē Namō Hrīṅkāra Mūrtayē || 45

यस्मादग्निः समुत्पन्नो यस्मात्सूर्यश्च चन्द्रमाः।
यस्मादोषधयः सर्वास्तस्मै सर्वात्मने नमः॥ ४६

Yasmādagṇiḥ Samutpaṇṇō Yasmāt Sūryaśca Candramāḥ |

Yasmādōṣadhayah Sarāstasmai Sarvātmaṇē Namaḥ || 46

यस्माच्च देवाः सम्भूताः साध्याः पक्षिण एव च।
पशवश्च मनुष्याश्च तस्मै सर्वात्मने नमः॥ ४७

Yasmācca Dēvāḥ Sambhūtāḥ Sādhyāḥ Pakṣiṇa Ēva Ca |

Paśavaśca Maṇuṣyāśca Tasmai Sarvātmaṇē Namaḥ || 47

प्राणापानौ व्रीहियवौ तपः श्रद्धा ऋतं तथा।
ब्रह्मचर्य विधिश्चैव यस्मात्तस्मै नमो नमः॥ ४८

Prāṇāpāṇou Vrīhiyavou Tapaḥ Śraddhā Rutam Tathā |

Brahmacaryam Vidhiścaiva Yasmāttasmai Namō Namaḥ || 48

सप्तप्राणार्चिषो यस्मात्समिध: सप्त एव च।

होमा: सप्त तथा लोकास्तस्मै सर्वात्मने नम: ॥ ४९

Sapta Prāṇārciṣō Yasmātsamita: Sapta Ēva Ca |

Hōmā: Sapta Tatā Lōkāstasmai Sarvātmaṉē Namah ॥ 49

यस्मात्समुद्रा गिरय: सिन्धव: प्रचरन्ति च।

यस्मादोषधय: सर्वा रसास्तस्मै नमो नम: ॥ ५०

Yasmāt Samudrā Girayah Sindhavah Pracaranti Ca |

Yasmādōṣadhayah Sarvā Rasāstasmai Namō Namah ॥ 50

यस्माद्यज्ञ: समुद्भूतो दीक्षा यूपश्च दक्षिणा:।

ऋचो यजूंषि सामानि तस्मै सर्वात्मने नम: ॥ ५१

Yasmādyañah Samudbhūtō Dīkṣā Yūpaśca Dakṣiṇāḥ |

Rucō Yajūmṣi Sāmāṉi Tasmai Sarvātmaṉē Namah ॥ 51

नम: पुरस्तात्पृष्ठे च नमस्ते पार्श्वयोर्द्वयो:।

अध ऊर्ध्वं चतुर्दिक्षु मातर्भूयो नमो नम: ॥ ५२

Nama: Purastātpruṣṭē Ca Namastē Pārśvayōr Dvayōḥ |

Adha Ūrdhvam Caturdikṣu Mātarbhūyō Namō Namah ॥ 52

उपसंहर देवेशि रूपमेतदलौकिकम्।

तदेव दर्शयास्माकं रूपं सुन्दरसुन्दरम् ॥ ५३

Upasamhara Dēvēśi Rūpamētadaloukikam |

Tadēva Darśayāsmākam Rūpam Sundara Sundaram ॥ 53

Oh Devi! We are inferior immortals; what prayers can we offer to Thee! Thou Thyself canst not measure Thy powers; how then can we, who are born later, know of Thy greatness! Obeisance to Thee, the Lady of the Universe! Obeisance to Thee of the nature of the Pranava Om; Thou art the One that is proved in all the Vedantas. Obeisance to Thee, of the form of Hreem! Obeisance to Thee, the Self of all, whence has originated the Fire, the Sun and the Moon and whence have sprung all the medicinal plants. Obeisance to Sri Devi, the Cosmic Deity, the Self in all whence have sprung all the Devas, Sadhyas, the beasts, birds and men!

We bow down again and again to the Great Form, Maha Maya, the Self of all, whence have-sprung the vital breath Prana, Apana, grains and wheats and Who is the source of asceticism, faith, truth, continence and the rules what to do and what not to do under the present circumstances. The seven Pranas, the seven Lokas, the seven Flames, the seven Samits, the seven Oblations to Fire, have sprung from Thee! Obeisance to Thee, the Great Self in all! Obeisance to the Universal form of the Deity of the Universe whence have sprung all the oceans, all the mountains, all the rivers, all the medicinal plants and all the Rasas (the tastes of all things). We bow down to that Virat Form, the Great Self, the Maha Maya, whence have originated the sacrifices, the sacrificial post (to which the victim about to be immolated is bound) and Dakshinas (the sacrificial fees) and the Rik, the Yajus and the Sama Vedas.

Oh Mother! Oh Maha Maya! We bow down to Thy front, to Thy back, to Thy both the sides, to Thy top, to Thy bottom and on all sides of Thee. Oh Devi! Be kind enough to withhold this Extraordinary Terrific Form of Thine and show us Thy Beautiful Lovely Form.

व्यास उवाच

इति भीतान्सुरान्दृष्ट्वा जगदम्बा कृपार्णवा।

संहृत्य रूपं घोरं तद्दर्शयामास सुन्दरम्॥५४

Vyāsa Uvāca

Iti Bhītānsurān Druṣṭvā Jagadambā Krupārṇavā |

Samhrutya Rūpam Ghōram Taddharśayāmāsa Sundaram || 54

पाशाङ्कुशवराभीतिधरं   सर्वाङ्गकोमलम्।

करुणापूर्णनयनं   मन्दस्मितमुखाम्बुजम्॥५५

Pāśāṅkuśa Varābhītidharam Sarvāṅga Kōmalam |

Karuṇā Pūrṇanayaṇam Maṇḍasmita Mukhāmbujam ‖ 55

दृष्ट्वा तत्सुन्दरं रूपं तदा भीतिविवर्जिता: ।

शान्तचित्ता: प्रणेमुस्ते हर्षगद्गदनि:स्वना: ॥ ५६

Druṣṭvā Tatsundaram Rūpam Tadā Bhītivivarjitāḥ |

Śāntacittāḥ Praṇēmustē HarṣagadgadaṇiḥSvaṇaḥ ‖ 56

Vyasa said – "Oh King! The World Mother, the Ocean of mercy, seeing the Devas terrified, withheld Her Fearful Cosmic Form and showed Her very beautiful appearance, pleasing to the whole world. Her body became soft and gentle.

In one hand She held the noose and in another She held the goad. The two other hands made signs to dispel all their fears and ready to grant the boons. Her eyes emitted rays of kindness; Her face was adorned with beautiful smiles.

The Devas became glad at this and bowed down to Her in a peaceful mind and then spoke with great joy.

ओं श्री जगदंबार्पणमस्तु । श्री चण्डिकापरमेश्वरी प्रीयताम् ।

Ōm Śrī Jagadambārpaṇamastu |

Śrī Caṇḍikā Paramēśvarī Prīyatām |

इति श्रीमद् देवी भागवते महापुराणेऽष्टादश साहस्त्रयां संहितायांश्री देवी विराड् रूप दर्शन सहितं देवकृत तत्स्तव वर्णनम् नाम तृतीयोऽध्याय: ॥

Iti Śrīmad Dēvī Bhāgavatē Mahāpurāṇēṣṣṭātaśa Sāhasrayām Samhitāyām Śrī Dēvī Gītāyām Devi Virat Roopa Darshana Sahita Devakrutā TatStava Varnanam Nāma Triteeyōtyāyaḥ ‖

Here ends the third Chapter of Sri Devi Gita named as *Śrī Dēvī Gītāyām Devi Virat Roopa Darshana Sahita Devakruta Tat-atava Varnanam* in the Mahapuranam *Shrimad Devi Bhagavatam* having 18,000 verses, by Maharshi Veda Vyasa.

Shrimad Bhagavad Gita chapter 11 – Lord Krishna grants Arjuna divine vision and reveals His spectacular unlimited form as the cosmic universe. Thus, He conclusively establishes His divinity. Krishna explains that His own all-beautiful humanlike form is the original form of Godhead. One can perceive this form only by pure devotional service.

One may not be prepared or qualified to see God, but by regarding the world as the manifestation of God as explained in Chapter 11, everybody can see the cosmic form of God anywhere anytime. God can be seen in four-armed form by devotional love only. One who dedicates all works to Me and to whom I am the supreme goal, who is my devotee, who has no attachment and is free from enmity towards any being – attains Me, Oh Arjuna.

One should always remember that we are merely His instrument.

Thus, the two cosmic forms – virat forms of Krishna and Devi are similar and one and the same.

The Specialty of *Gnanam*
(Devi Bhagavatam 7-34)

This is the fourth chapter of *Sri Devi Gita*. This explains the Knowledge and Final Emancipation.

ओं नमः चण्डिकायै । *Ōm Namaḥ Caṇḍikāyai* ।

देव्युवाच
क्व यूयं मन्दभाग्या वै क्वेदं रूपं महाद्भुतम्।
तथापि भक्तवात्सल्यादीदृशं दर्शितं मया॥ १

Dēvyuvāca

Kva Yūyam Mandabhāgyā Vai Kvēdam Rūpam Mahādbhutam |

Tathāpi Bhaktavātsalyādīdruśam Darśitam Mayā ‖ 1

न वेदाध्ययनैर्योगैर्न दानैस्तपसेज्यया।
रूपं द्रष्टुमिदं शक्यं केवलं मत्कृपां विना॥ २

Na Vēdādhyayaṉairyōgairṉa Dāṉais Tapa Sējyayā |

Rūpam Draṣṭumidam Śakyam Kēvalam Matkrupām Viṉā ‖ 2

प्रकृतं शृणु राजेन्द्र परमात्मात्र जीवताम्।
उपाधियोगात्सम्प्राप्तः कर्तृत्वादिकमप्युत॥ ३

Prakrutam Śruṇu Rājēndra Paramātmātra Jīvatām |

Upādhi Yōgāt Samprāptaḥ Kartrutvādikamapyuta ‖ 3

क्रियाः करोति विविधा धर्माधर्मैकहेतवः।
नानायोनीस्ततः प्राप्य सुखदुःखैश्च युज्यते॥ ४

Kriyāḥ Karōti Vividhā Dharmādharmaikahētavaḥ |

Nāṉāyōṉīstataḥ Prāpya SukhaduḥKhaiśca Yujyatē ‖ 4

पुनस्तत्संस्कृतिवशान्नानाकर्मरतः सदा।
नानादेहान्समाप्नोति सुखदुःखैश्च युज्यते॥ ५

Puṇastat Samskruti Vaśāṇṇāṇā Karmarataḥ Sadā |

Nāṇādēhāṇ Samāpṇōti SukhaduḥKhaiśca Yujyatē ‖ 5

घटीयन्त्रवदेतस्य न विरामः कदापि हि।

अज्ञानमेव मूलं स्यात्ततः कामः क्रियास्ततः॥ ६

Ghaṭīyantra Vadētasya Na Virāmaḥ Kadāpi Hi |

Agñāṇamēva Mūlam Syāttataḥ Kāmaḥ Kriyāstataḥ ‖ 6

तस्मादज्ञाननाशाय यतेत नियतं नरः।

एतद्धि जन्मसाफल्यं यदज्ञानस्य नाशनम्॥ ७

Tasmādakñāṇa Nāśāya Yatēṇa Niyatam Naraḥ |

Ētaddhi Jaṇmasāphalyam Yadakñāṇasya Nāśaṇam ‖ 7

Sri *Devi* said - Oh Devas! You are not at all worthy to see this My Wonderful Cosmic Form. Where are Yet and where is this My Form! But it is my affection towards the Bhaktas that I have shewn to You all this great form of mine. Nobody can see this form without My Grace; the study of the *Vedas*, the *Yoga*, the gift, the Sacrifice, the austerities or any other Sadhanas are quite incompetent to make this form visible to anybody.

Oh, King of mountains! Now hear the real instructions. The Great Self is the only Supreme Thing in this world of *Maya* (Illusions). He it is that under the various *Upadhis* of an actor and enjoyer performs various functions leading to the Dharma (righteousness) and the Adharma (unrighteousness). Then he goes into various wombs and enjoys pleasure or pain according to his *Karma*. Then again owing to the tendencies pertaining to these births he becomes engaged in various functions and gets again various bodies and enjoys varieties of pleasures and pains.

Oh, Best of Mountains! There is no cessation of these births and deaths; it in like a regular clockwork machine; it has no beginning and it goes on working to an endless period. Ignorance or Avidya is the Cause of this Samsara. Desire comes out of this and action flows thence. So, men ought to try their best to get rid of this Ignorance.

पुरुषार्थसमाप्तिश्च जीवन्मुक्तदशापि च।
अज्ञाननाशने शक्ता विद्यैव तु पटीयसी॥८

Puruṣārtha Samāptiśca Jīvanmukta Daśāpi Ca |
Agñāna Nāśanē Śaktā Vidyaiva Tu Paṭīyasī ǁ 8

न कर्म तज्जं नोपास्तिर्विरोधाभावतो गिरे।
प्रत्युताशाज्ञाननाशे कर्मणा नैव भाव्यताम्॥९

Na Karma Tajjam Nōpāstir Virōdhā Bhāvatō Girē |
Pratyutāśāgñāna Nāśē Karmaṇā Naiva Bhāvyatām ǁ 9

अनर्थदानि कर्माणि पुनः पुनरुशन्ति हि।
ततो रागस्ततो द्वेषस्ततोऽनर्थो महान्भवेत्॥१०

Anarthadāni Karmāṇi Punaḥ Punaruśanti Hi |
Tatō Rāgastatō Dvēṣastatōḫarthō Mahāṉ Bhavēt ǁ 10

तस्मात्सर्वप्रयत्नेन ज्ञानं सम्पादयेन्नरः।
कुर्वन्नेवेह कर्माणीत्यतः कर्माप्यवश्यकम्॥११

Tasmāt Sarva Prayatṉēṉa Ñāṉam Sampādayēṉṉaraḥ |
Kurvaṉṉēvēha Karmāṇītyataḥ Karmāpyavaśyakam ǁ 11

ज्ञानादेव हि कैवल्यमतः स्यात्तत्समुच्चयः।
सहायतां व्रजेत्कर्म ज्ञानस्य हितकारि च॥१२

Ñāṉādēva Hi Kaivalyamataḥ Syāttat Samuccayaḥ
Sahāyatām Vrajētkarma Ñāṉasya Hitakāri Ca ǁ 12

इति केचिद्वदन्त्यत्र तद्विरोधान्न सम्भवेत्।
ज्ञानाद्धृद्ग्रन्थिभेदः स्याद्धृद्ग्रन्थौ कर्मसम्भवः॥१३

Iti Kēcidvadantyatra Tadvirōdhāṉya Sambhavēt |
Ñāṉāddhrud Granthibhētaḥ Syāddhrudgranthou Karma

Sambhavaḥ ǁ13

यौगपद्यं न सम्भाव्यं विरोधात्तु ततस्तयो: ।
तम:प्रकाशयोर्यद्वद्यौगपद्यं न सम्भवि ॥ १४

Yougapadyam Na Sambhāvyam Virōdhāttu Tatastayōḥ |
Tamaḥ Prakāśayōryadvadyougapadyam Na Sampavi ॥ 14

Oh, King of Mountains! What more to say than this that the Goal of life is attained when this Ignorance is destroyed. The highest goal is attained by a *Jeeva*, when he becomes liberated, while living. And *Vidya* is the only thing that is able and skillful in destroying this ignorance. (As darkness cannot dispel darkness so) the *Karma* done out of ignorance is ignorance itself; and such a work cannot destroy ignorance. So, it is not proper to expect that this Avidya can be destroyed by doing works. The works are entirely futile. The Jeevas want again and again the sensual enjoyments out of this *Karma*. Attachment arises out of this desire; discrepancies creep in and out of this ignorant attachment great calamities befall when such faults or discrepancies are committed.

So, every sane man ought to make his best effort to get this *Jnanam* (knowledge). And as it is also enjoined in the Shrutis that one ought to do actions (and try to live one hundred years) so it is advisable to do works also. Again, the *Shrutis* declare that the "final liberation comes from Knowledge" so one ought to acquire Jnanam. If both these be collectively followed, then works become beneficial and helping to Jnanam. (Therefore, the Jeevas should take up both of these.) Others say that this is impossible owing to their contradictory natures. The knots of heart are let loose by Jnanam and the knots are knit more by Karma. So how can they be reconciled? They are so very diametrically opposite. Darkness and light cannot be brought together, so Jnanam and Karma cannot be brought together. Therefore, one ought to do all the Karmas as best as one can, as enjoined in the Vedas, until one gets *Chittashuddhi* (the purification of one's heart and mind).

तस्मात्सर्वाणि कर्माणि वैदिकानि महामते ।
चित्तशुद्ध्यन्तमेव स्युस्तानि कुर्यात्प्रयत्लत: ॥ १५

Tasmāt Sarvāṇi Karmāṇi Vaidikāṇi Mahāmatē |

Citta Śuddhyantamēva Syustāṇi Kuryāt Prayatnataḥ ‖ 15

शमो दमस्तितिक्षा च वैराग्यं सत्त्वसम्भव: ।
तावत्पर्यन्तमेव स्यु: कर्माणि न तत: परम्॥१६

Śamō Damastitikṣā Ca Vairāgyam Satva Sambhavaḥ |

Tāvatparyantamēva Syuḥ Karmāṇi Na Tataḥ Param ‖ 16

तदन्ते चैव संन्यस्य संश्रयेद् गुरुमात्मवान् ।
श्रोत्रियं ब्रह्मनिष्ठं च भक्त्या निर्व्याजया पुन: ॥१७

Tadantē Caiva Samnyasya Samśrayēd Gurumātmavāṇ |

Śrōtriyam Brahmaniṣṭham Ca Bhaktyā Nirvyājayā Puṇaḥ ‖ 17

वेदान्तश्रवणं   कुर्यान्नित्यमेवमतन्द्रित: ।
तत्त्वमस्यादिवाक्यस्य नित्यमर्थं विचारयेत्॥१८

Vēdānta Śravaṇam Kuryāṇnitya Mēvamatandritaḥ |

Tatvamasyādi Vākyasya Nityamartham Vicārayēt ‖ 18

तत्त्वमस्यादिवाक्यं तु जीवब्रह्मैक्यबोधकम् ।
ऐक्ये ज्ञाते निर्भयस्तु मद्रूपो हि प्रजायते॥१९

Tatvamasyādi Vākyam Tu Jīva Brahmaikya Bōdhakam |

Aikyē Ñātē Nirbhayastu Madrūpō Hi Prajāyatē ‖ 19

पदार्थावगति: पूर्वं वाक्यार्थावगतिस्तत: ।
तत्पदस्य च वाक्यार्थो गिरेऽहं परिकीर्तित: ॥ २०

Padārthāvagatiḥ Pūrvam Vākyārthāvagatistataḥ |

Tatpadasya Ca Vākyārthō Girēham Parikīrtitaḥ ‖ 20

त्वंपदस्य च वाच्यार्थो जीव एव न संशय: ।
उभयोरैक्यमसिना पदेन प्रोच्यते बुधै:॥२१

Tvampadasya Ca Vācyārthō Jīva Ēva Na Samśayaḥ |

Ubhayōraikyamasiṉā Padēṉa Prōcyatē Bhudhaiḥ ‖ 21

वाच्यार्थयोर्विरुद्धत्वादैक्यं नैव घटेत ह।

लक्षणातः प्रकर्तव्या तत्त्वमोः श्रुतिसंस्थयोः ॥ २२

Vācyārthayōrviruddhatvādaikyam Naiva Ghaṭēta Ha |

Lakṣaṇātaḥ Prakartavyā Tatvamōḥ Śrutisamsthayōḥ ‖ 22

चिन्मात्रं तु तयोर्लक्ष्यं तयोरैक्यस्य सम्भवः।

तयोरैक्यं तथा ज्ञात्वा स्वाभेदेनाद्वयो भवेत्॥ २३

Ciṉmātram Tu Tayōrlakṣyam Tayōraikyasya Sambhavaḥ |

Tayōraikyam Tathā Ñātvā Svābhēdēṉādvayō Bhavēt ‖ 23

Karmas are to be done until *Shama* (the control of the inner organs of senses), *Dama* (the control of the outer organs of senses), Titeeksha (the power to endure heat and cold and other dualities), *Vairagyam* (Dispassion), *Sattva Sambhava* (the birth of pure *Sattva Guna* in one's own heart) take place. After those, the *Karmas* cease for that man. Then one ought to take *Sannyasa* from a *Guru* (Spiritual Teacher) who has got his senses under control, who is versed in the Shrutis, attached to Brahmam (practicing the Yogic union with *Brahmam*). He should approach to him with an unfeigned Bhakti. He should day and night, without any laziness, do *Shravanam*, *Mananam* and *Nididhyasanam* (hearing, thinking and deeply realising) the Vedanta sayings.

He should constantly ponder over the meanings of the *Mahavakyam* "Tat Tvam Asi". "Tat Tvam Asi" means Thou art That; it asserts the identity of the Supreme Self (*Brahmam*) and Embodied Self (*Jeevatma*). When this identity is realised, fearlessness comes and he then gets My nature. First of all, he should try to realise (by reasoning) the idea conveyed by that sentence. By the word '*Tat*' is meant Myself, of the nature "of Brahmam"; and by the word '*Tvam*' is meant is 'Jeeva' embodied self and the word '*Asi*' indicates, no doubt, the identity of these two. The two words '*Tat*' and '*Tvam*' cannot be apparently identified, as they seem to convey contradictory meanings ('*Tat*' implying omniscience, omnipresence and other universal qualities and '*Tvam*' implying non-omniscience and other qualities of a limited nature). So, to establish the identity between the two, one ought to adopt *Bhagalakshana* and *Tyagalakshana*. (*Bhagalakshana* – kind of *Lakshana* or secondary use of a word by which it partly loses and partly retains its primary meaning also called *Jahadajahallakshana*. *Tyaga Lakshana* - a secondary use of a word by which it loses partly it as primary meaning.

देवदत्तः स एवायमितिवल्लक्षणा स्मृता।

स्थूलादिदेहरहितो   ब्रह्म सम्पद्यते नरः ॥ २४

Dēvadattaḥ Sa Ēvāyamiti Vallakṣaṇā Smrutā |

Sthūlādidēharahitō Brahma Sampadyatē Naraḥ ॥ 24

The Supreme Self is Brahmam – Consciousness, endowed with the omniscience, etc. and the Embodied Self is Limited *Jeeva* Consciousness, etc.). Leaving aside both the adjuncts, we take the Consciousness, when both of them are identical and we come to *Brahmam*, without a second. The example is now quoted to illustrate what is called *Bhagalakshana* and *Tyagalakshana*. "This is that *Devadatta*" means *Devadatta* seen before and Devadatta seen now means one and the same person, if we leave aside the time past and the time present take the body of *Devadatta* only.

पञ्चीकृतमहाभूतसम्भूतः   स्थूलदेहकः।

भोगालयो जराव्याधिसंयुतः सर्वकर्मणाम् ॥ २५

Pañcīkruta Mahābhūta Sambhūtaḥ Sthūladēhakaḥ |

Bhōgālayō Jāvyāti Samyutaḥ Sarva Karmaṇām ॥ 25

मिथ्याभूतोऽयमाभाति स्फुटं मायामयत्वतः।

सोऽयं स्थूल उपाधिः स्यादात्मनो मे नगेश्वर ॥ २६

Mithyābhūtōyamābhāti Sphuṭam Māyāmayatvataḥ |
Sōyam Sthūla Upādhiḥ Syātādmaṉō Mē Nagēśvara ‖ 26

ज्ञानकर्मेन्द्रिययुतं प्राणपञ्चकसंयुतम् ।
मनोबुद्धियुतं चैतत्सूक्ष्मं तत्कवयो विदुः ॥ २७

Ñāṉa Karmēndriyayutam Prāṇa Pañcaka Samyutam |
Maṉōbuddhiyutam Caitatsūkṣmam Tatkavayō Viduḥ ‖ 27

अपञ्चीकृतभूतोत्थं सूक्ष्मदेहोऽयमात्मनः ।
द्वितीयोऽयमुपाधिः स्यात्सुखादेरवबोधकः ॥ २८

Apañcīkruta Bhūtōttham Sūkṣma Dēhō Yamātmaṉaḥ |
Dvitīyōyamupādhiḥ Syātsukhādēravabōdhakaḥ ‖ 28

अनाद्यनिर्वाच्यमिदमज्ञानं तु तृतीयकः ।
देहोऽयमात्मनो भाति कारणात्मा नगेश्वर ॥ २९

Anādya Nirvācyamidamakñāṉam Tu Trutīyakaḥ |
Dēhōyamātmaṉō Bhāti Kāraṇātmā Nagēśvara ‖ 29

उपाधिविलये जाते केवलात्मावशिष्यते ।
देहत्रये पञ्चकोशा अन्तःस्थाः सन्ति सर्वदा ॥ ३०

Upādhivilayē Jātē Kēvalātmāvaśiṣyatē |
Dēhatrayē Pañcakōśā AntaḥSthāḥ Santi Sarvadā ‖ 30

पञ्चकोशपरित्यागे ब्रह्मपुच्छं हि लभ्यते ।
नेतिनेतीत्यादिवाक्यैर्मम रूपं यदुच्यते ॥ ३१

Pañcakōśa Parityāgē Brahma Puccam Hi Labhyatē |
Nētinētītyādi Vākyair Mama Rūpam Yaducyatē ‖ 31

This gross body arises from the Pancheekruta gross elements. It is the receptacle of enjoying the fruits of its Karma and liable to disease and old age. This body is all Maya; therefore, it has certainly no real existence.

Oh Lord. of Mountains! Know this to be the gross Upadhi (limitation) of My real Self. The five Jnanendriyas (organs of senses), five Karmendriyas (working organs), the Prana Vayus, mind and Buddhi (rational intellect), in all, these seventeen go to form the subtle body, Sookshma Deha. So, say the Pundits. This body of the Supreme Self is caused by the Apancheekruta five original elements. Through this body, pain and pleasure are felt in the heart. This is the second Upadhi of the Atman. The Ajnana or Primeval Ignorance, without beginning and indescribable, is the third body of the Atman. Know this also to be my third Upadhi. When all these Upadhis subside, only the Supreme Self, the Brahmam remains. Within these three gross and subtle bodies, the five sheaths, Annamaya, Pranamaya, Manomaya, Vijnanamaya and Anandamaya always exist. When these are renounced, Brahmapuccha is obtained. That is Brahmam and My Nature, too.

The Taitreeya Upanishat elaborates on these five sheaths (envelopes) - Annamaya, Pranamaya, Manomaya, Vijnanamaya and Anandamaya.

न जायते म्रियते तत्कदाचि-
न्नायं भूत्वा न बभूव कश्चित्।
अजो नित्यः शाश्वतोऽयं पुराणो
न हन्यते हन्यमाने शरीरे॥ ३२

Na Jāyatē Mriyatē Tatkadācinnāyam
Bhūtvā Na Babhūva Kaścit |
Ajō Nityaḥ Śaśvatōyam Purāṇō
Na Haṇyatē Haṇyamāṇē Śarīrē || 32

हतं चेन्मन्यते हन्तुं हतश्चेन्मन्यते हतम्।
उभौ तौ न विजानीतो नायं हन्ति न हन्यते॥ ३३

Hatam Cēnmanyatē Hantum Hataścēnmanyatē Hatam
Ubhou Tau Na Vijānītō Nāyam Hanti Na Hanyatē ||33

अणोरणीयान्महतो महीया-
नात्मास्य जन्तोर्निहितो गुहायाम्।
तमक्रतुः पश्यति वीतशोको
धातुः प्रसादान्महिमानमस्य॥ ३४

Anōraṇīyān Mahatō Mahīyānāt-
Māsya Jantōrnihitō Guhāyām |
Tamakratuḥ Paśyati Vītaśōkō
Dhātuḥ Prasādān Mahimānamasya || 34

आत्मानं रथिनं विद्धि शरीरं रथमेव तु।
बुद्धिं तु सारथिं विद्धि मनः प्रग्रहमेव च॥ ३५

Ātmānam Rathinam Viddhi Śarīram Rathamēva Tu |
Buddhim Tu Sārathim Viddhi Manaḥ Pragrahamēva Ca || 35

इन्द्रियाणि हयानाहुर्विषयांस्तेषु गोचरान्।
आत्मेन्द्रियमनोयुक्तं भोक्तेत्याहुर्मनीषिणः॥ ३६

Indriyāṇi Hayānahur Viṣayāmstēṣu Gōcarān |
Ātmēndraya Manōyuktam Bhōktētyākurmaṇīṣiṇaḥ || 36

This is the Goal of "Not this, Not this" the Vedanta words. This Self is not born nor It dies. It does not live also, being born. (But it remains constant, though It is not born). This Self is unborn, eternal, everlasting, ancient. It is not killed, when the body is killed. If one wants to kill it or thinks It as slain, both of them do not know; this does not kill nor is it killed. This Atman, subtler than the subtlest and greater than the greatest, resides within the cave (the Buddhi) of the Jeevas.

Yajur Veda Upanishats, mainly Taitreeya Upanishat (Naraaya-navalli), also vouches same concept that the soul is unmeasurable – it is Upanishats larger than the largest and smaller than the smallest.

In the Bhagavad Gita verse (2-18) Lord Krishna says that the soul is larger than the largest and smaller than the smallest (*Aṇōraṇīyāṇ Mahatō Mahīyān*).

He whose heart is purified and who is free from Sankalpa and Vikalpa (doubt and mental phenomena), knows It and Its glory and is free from sorrows and troubles. Know this Atman and Buddhi as the charioteer, this body as the chariot and the mind as the reins. The senses and their organs are the horses and the objects of enjoyments are their aims. The sages declare that the Atman united with mind and organs of senses enjoys the objects. He who is non-discriminating, unmindful and always impure, does not realise his Atman; rather he is bound in this world.

यस्त्वविद्वान्भवति चामनस्कश्च सदाशुचि: ।

न तत्पदमवाप्नोति संसारं चाधिगच्छति ॥ ३७

Yastva Vidvāṇ Bhavati Cāmaṇaskaśca Sadāśuciḥ |

Na Tatpadamavāpṇōti Samsāram Cādhigaccati ॥ 37

यस्तु विज्ञानवान्भवति समनस्क: सदा शुचि: ।

स तु तत्पदमाप्नोति यस्माद्भूयो न जायते ॥ ३८

Yastu Vikñāṇavāṇ Bhavati Samaṇaskaḥ Sadā Śuciḥ |

Sa Tu Tatpadamāpṇōti Yasmādbhūyō Na Jāyatē ॥ 38

विज्ञानसारथिर्यस्तु मन:प्रग्रहवान्नर: ।

सोऽध्वन: पारमाप्नोति मदीयं यत्परं पदम् ॥ ३९

Vikñāṇa Sārathiryastu Maṇaḥ Pragrahavāṇnaraḥ |

Sōdhvaṇaḥ Pāramāpṇōti Madīyam Yatparam Padam ॥ 39

इत्थं श्रुत्या च मत्या च निश्चित्यात्मानमात्मना ।
भावयेन्मामात्मरूपां निदिध्यासनतोऽपि च ॥ ४०

Ittham Śrutyā Ca Matyā Ca Niściṭyātmāṉamātmaṉā |
Bhāvayēṉmāmātmarūpām Nididhyāsaṉatōpi Ca || 40

He who is not discriminating, mindful and always pure reaches the Goal, realises the Highest Self; and he is not fallen again from That. That man becomes able to cross the Ocean of Samsara and gets My Highest Abode, of the nature of everlasting Existence, Intelligence and Bliss, whose charioteer is Discrimination and who keeps his senses under control by keeping tight the reins of his mind. Thus, one should always meditate intensely on Me to realise the nature of Self by *Shravanam* (hearing), *Mananam* thinking and realising one's own self by one's Self (pure heart).

योगवृत्तेः पुरा स्वस्मिन्भावयेदक्षरत्रयम् ।
देवीप्रणवसंज्ञस्य ध्यानार्थं मन्त्रवाच्ययोः ॥ ४१

Yōgavruttēḥ Purā Svasmiṉ Bhāvayēdakṣaratrayam |
Dēvīpraṇavasaññasya Dhyāṉārtham Mantravācyayōḥ || 41

हकारः स्थूलदेहः स्याद्रकारः सूक्ष्मदेहकः ।
ईकारः कारणात्मासौ ह्रींकारोऽहं तुरीयकम् ॥ ४२

Hakāraḥ Stūlatēhaḥ Syātrakāraḥ Sūkṣmatēhakaḥ |
Īkāraḥ Kāraṇātmāsau Hrīṅkārōham Turīyakam || 42

एवं समष्टिदेहेऽपि ज्ञात्वा बीजत्रयं क्रमात् ।
समष्टिव्यष्ट्योरेकत्वं भावयेन्मतिमान्नरः ॥ ४३

Ēvam Samaṣṭi Dēhēpi Ñātvā Bījatrayam Kramāt |
Samaṣṭi Vyaṣṭyōrēkatvam Bhāvayēṉmatimāṉṉaraḥ || 43

समाधिकालात्पूर्वं तु भावयित्वैवमादृतः ।
ततो ध्यायेन्निलीनाक्षो देवीं मां जगदीश्वरम् ॥ ४४

Samādhikālātpūrvam Tu Bhāvayitvaivamādrutaḥ |

Tatō Dhyāyēṉṉilīṉākṣō Dēvīm Mām Jagadīśvaram || 44

When by the constant practice, as mentioned above, one's heart is fit for *Samadhi* (being absorbed in the Spirit), just before that, he should understand the meanings of the separate letters in the seed Mantra of *Mahamaya*. The letter '*Ha*' means gross body and the letter '*Ra*' means subtle body and the letter '*I*' means the causal body; the fourth; (dot over the semicircle) is the fourth '*Tureeya*' state of Mine. Thus, meditating on the separate delineated states, the intelligent man should meditate on the aforesaid three letters in the Cosmic body also and he should then try to establish the identity between the two. Before entering into *Samadhi*, after very carefully thinking the above, one should close one's eyes and meditate on Me, the Supreme Deity of the Universe, the Luminous and Self-Eluent Brahmam.

प्राणापानौ समौ कृत्वा नासाभ्यन्तरचारिणौ।

निवृत्तविषयाकाङ्क्षो वीतदोषो विमत्सरः ॥ ४५

Prāṇāpāṉou Samou Krutvā Nāsābhyantaracāriṇau |

Nivrutta Viṣayākāṅkṣau Vītadōṣō Vimatsarah || 45

भक्त्या निर्व्याजया युक्तो गुहायां निःस्वने स्थले।

हकारं विश्वमात्मानं रकारे प्रविलापयेत्॥ ४६

Bhaktyā Nirvyājayā Yuktō Guhāyām NiḥSvaṉē Sthalē |

Hakāram Vicvamātmāṉam Rakārē Pravilāpayēt || 46

रकारं तेजसं देवमीकारे प्रविलापयेत्।

ईकारं प्राज्ञमात्मानं ह्रींकारे प्रविलापयेत्॥ ४७

Rakāram Taijasam Dēvamīkārē Pravilāpayēt |

Īkāram Prāgñamātmāṉam Hrīṅkārē Pravilāpayēt || 47

वाच्यवाचकताहीनं द्वैतभावविवर्जितम्।

अखण्डं सच्चिदानन्दं भावयेत्तच्छिखान्तरे ॥ ४८

Vācyavācakatāhīṉam Dvaita Bhāva Vivarjitam |

Akhaṇtam Saccidāṉandam Bhāvayēttacchikhāntarē || 48

इति ध्यानेन मां राजन् साक्षात्कृत्य नरोत्तमः ।
मद्रूप एव भवति द्वयोरप्येकता यतः ॥ ४९

Iti Dhyāṉēṉa Mām Rājaṉ Sākṣātkrutya Narōttamaḥ |

Madrūpa Ēva Bhavati Dvayōrayēkatā Yataḥ ‖ 49

योगयुक्त्यानया दृष्ट्वा मामात्मानं परात्परम् ।
अज्ञानस्य सकार्यस्य तत्क्षणे नाशको भवेत् ॥ ५०

Yōgayuktyāṉayā Druṣṭvā Māmātmāṉam Parātparam |

Agñāṉasya Sakāryasya Tatkṣaṉē Nāśakō Bhavēt ‖ 50

Oh, Chief of Mountains! Putting a stop to all worldly desires, free from jealousy and other evils, he should (by constant practice of Pranayama) make equal according to the rules of *Pranayama*, the *Prana* (the inhaled breath) and *Apana* (the exhaled breath) *Vayus* and with an unfeigned devotion get the gross body (*Vaishvanara*) indicated by the letter 'Ha' dissolved in the subtle body *Taijasa*. The Taijasa body, the letter 'Ra' is in a cave where there is no noise (in the *Sushumna* cave). After that He should dissolve the *Taijasa*, 'Ra' into the Causal body 'I'. He should then dissolve the Causal body, the *Prajna* 'I' into the *Tureeya* state *Hreem*. Then he should go into a region where there is no speech or the thing spoken, which is absolutely free from dualities, that *Akhanda Sachchidananda* and meditate on that Highest Self in the midst of the Fiery Flame of Consciousness.

Oh, King of Mountains! Thus, men by the meditation mentioned above, should realise the identity between the Jeeva and Brahmam and see Me and get My Nature.

Oh Lord of Mountains! Thus, the firmly resolved intelligent man, by the practice of this Yoga sees and realises the nature of My Highest Self and destroys immediately the Ignorance and all the actions thereof.

As discussed in the above verses 46 and 47 – *Sri Devi Atharvasheersha Upanishat* explains the structure of the letter

'*Hreem*' as below – yes repeat – it is not a word it is only a letter in Samskrutam. It is also called as *Shakta pranava mantra*. This is single letter mantra, that is explained here, of Sri *Bhuvaneshwari*.

Sri Devi shines with the combination of *ha* – the root letter of ether, *ra* – the root letter of *Agni* (the fire god), alongwith '*Ee*', the half-moon '*m*'. The combined root letter '*Hreem*' of *Sri Devi*, has the power of to do anything and everything.

ओं श्री जगदंबार्पणमस्तु । श्री चण्डिकापरमेश्वरी प्रीयताम् ।

Ōm Śrī Jagadambārpaṇamastu |

Śrī Caṇḍikā Paramēśvarī Prīyatām |

इति श्रीमद् देवी भागवते महापुराणेऽष्टादश साहस्रयां संहितायां श्री देवी गीतायां ज्ञानस्य मोक्षहेतुत्व वर्णनं नाम चतुर्थोऽध्याय: ॥

Iti Śrīmad Dēvī Bhāgavatē Mahāpurāṇēṣṣṭātaśa Sāhasrayām Samhitāyām Śrī Dēvī Gītāyām Gnānasya Mokśa Hetutva Varṇanam Nāma Caturthoṣdyāyaḥ ॥

Here ends the fourth Chapter of Sri Devi Gita named as *Gnānasya Mokśa Hetutva Varṇanam* in the Mahapuranam *Shrimad Devi Bhagavatam* having 18,000 verses, by Maharshi Veda Vyasa.

In the Bhagavad Gita, chapter 4, this jnana yoga is referred to as buddhi yoga and its goal is self-realization. The text considers jnana marga as the most difficult, slow, confusing for those who prefer it because it deals with "formless reality", the avyakta. It is the path that intellectually oriented people tend to prefer.

Krishna reveals that he is transmitting an ancient teaching to Arjuna. Though Krishna has taught this wisdom to gods and others before Arjuna, it has become diluted and lost with time. Arjuna inquires that this loss is possible because Krishna was "born countless eons/ later than the god of the sun". Krishna clarifies that he has been born countless times, is eternal and comes to earth in human form when "righteousness falters/ and chaos threatens to prevail". In his present incarnation, Krishna is here to help Arjuna understand the complex nature of action. Krishna explains that God is in action through worship and that in this context God is both the actor and the action. Worship, or sacrifice, has many paths, including the paths of meditation, self-denial and study of scriptures. However, these paths are subsets of the main path of right action. Wisdom is the outcome of right action. Thus, it is important to have a wise teacher as a guide.

Yoga-Mantra Siddhi
(*Devi Bhagavatam* 7-35)

This is the fifth chapter of *Sri Devi Gita*. The name of the chapter *Mantra Siddhi Sādhana Varṇanam*. This explains the steps to get the fruits of any mantra.

ओं नमः चण्डिकायै । *Ōm Namaḥ Caṇḍikāyai* ।

हिमालय उवाच

योगं वद महेशानि साङ्गं संवित्प्रदायकम्।
कृतेन येन योग्योऽहं भवेयं तत्त्वदर्शने॥ १

Himālaya Uvāca

Yōgam Vada Mahēśāṉi Sāṅgam Samvit Pradāyakam |

Krutēṉa Yēṉa Yōgyōham Bhavēyam Tatvadarśaṉē || 1

Himalaya said – Oh Mahesvari! Now tell me the Yoga with all its Angas (limbs) giving the knowledge of the Supreme Consciousness so that, I may realise my Self, when I practice according to those instructions.

देव्युवाच

न योगो नभसः पृष्ठे न भूमौ न रसातले।
ऐक्यं जीवात्मनोराहुर्योगं योगविशारदाः॥ २

Dēvyuvāca

Na Yōgō Nabhasaḥ Pruṣṭē Na Bhūmau Na Rasātalē |

Aikyam Jīvātmaṉōrākuryōgam Yōgaviśāradāḥ || 2

Sri Devi said – The Yoga does not exist in the Heavens; nor does it exist on earth or in the nether regions (*Pataala*). Those who are skilled in the Yogas say that the realisation of the identity between the Jeevaatma and the Paramaatma is 'Yoga'.

तत्प्रत्यूहाः षडाख्याता योगविघ्नकरानघ।
कामक्रोधौ लोभमोहौ मदमात्सर्यसंज्ञकौ॥ ३

Tatpratyūhāḥ Ṣaḍākhyātā Yōgavighnakarāṇagha |

Kāmakrōdhou Lōbhamōhau Madamātsarya Sannakou ‖ 3

योगाङ्गैरेव भित्त्वा तान्योगिनो योगमाप्नुयुः ।

यमं नियममासनप्राणायामौ ततः परम् ‖ ४

Yōgāṅgairēva Bhitvā Tāṇyōgiṇō Yōgamāpṇuyuḥ |

Yamam Niyamamāsaṇaprāṇāyāmou Tataḥ Param ‖ 4

प्रत्याहारं धारणाख्यं ध्यानं सार्धं समाधिना ।

अष्टाङ्गान्याहुरेतानि योगिनां योगसाधने ‖ ५

Pratyāhāram Dhāraṇākhyam Dhyāṇam Sārdham Samādhiṇā |

Aṣṭāṅgāṇyāhurētāṇi Yōgiṇām Yōga Sādhaṇē ‖ 5

Oh, Sinless One! The enemies to this Yoga are six; and they are lust, krodha (anger), lobha (greed), mada (pride), moha (attachment) and matsarya (jealousy). The Yogis attain the Yoga when they become able to destroy these six enemies by practising the accompaniments to Yoga – Yama, Niyama, Asana, Pranayama, Pratyahara, Dharana, Dhyana and Samadhi, these are the eight limbs of Yoga.

अहिंसा सत्यमस्तेयं ब्रह्मचर्यं दयार्जवम् ।

क्षमा धृतिर्मिताहारः शौचं चेति यमा दश ‖ ६

Ahimsā Satyamastēyam Brahmacaryam Dayārjavam |

Kṣamā Dhrutirmitāhāraḥ Śaucam Cēti Yamā Daśa ‖ 6

तपः सन्तोष आस्तिक्यं दानं देवस्य पूजनम् ।

सिद्धान्तश्रवणं चैव ह्रीर्मतिश्च जपो हुतम् ‖ ७

Tapaḥ Santōṣa Āstikyam Dāṇam Dēvasya Pūjaṇam |

Siddhānta Śravaṇam Caiva Hrīrmatiśca Japō Hutam ‖ 7

दशैते नियमाः प्रोक्ता मया पर्वतनायक ।

पद्मासनं स्वस्तिकं च भद्रं वज्रासनं तथा ‖ ८

Daśaitē Niyamāḥ Prōktā Mayā Parvataṇāyaka |

Padmāsaṇam Svastikam Ca Bhadram Vajrāsaṇam Tathā ‖ 8

वीरासनमिति प्रोक्तं क्रमादासनपञ्चकम् ।

ऊर्वोरुपरि विन्यस्य सम्यक्पादतले शुभे ॥ ९

Vīrāsaṇamiti Prōktam Kramādāsaṇa Pañcakam |

Ūrvorupari Viṇyasya Samyakpādatalē Śubhē ‖ 9

अङ्गुष्ठौ च निबध्नीयाद्धस्ताभ्यां व्युत्क्रमात्ततः ।

पद्मासनमिति प्रोक्तं योगिनां हृदयङ्गमम् ॥ १०

Aṅguṣṭou Ca Nibadhṇīyāddhastābhyām Vyutkramāttataḥ |

Padmāsaṇamiti Prōktam Yōgiṇām Hrudayaṅgamam ‖ 10

These eight limbs of Yoga;

- Yama includes Ahimsa (non-injuring; non- killing); truthfulness; Asteyam (non-stealing by mind or deed) Brahmacharya (continence); Daya (mercy to all beings); Uprightness; forgiveness, steadiness; eating frugally, restrictedly and cleanliness (external and internal). These are ten in number.
- Niyama also includes ten qualities;
  (1) Tapasya (austerities and penances);
  (2) Contentment;
  (3) Astikya (faith in the God and the Vedas, Devas, Dharma and Adharma)
  (4) Charity (in good causes);
  (5) Worship of God;
  (6) Hearing the Siddhantas (established sayings) of the Vedas;
  (7) Hreem or modesty (not to do any irreligious or blamable acts);
  (8) Sraddha (faith to go do good works that are sanctioned);
  (9) Japam (uttering silently the mantrams, Gayatris or sayings of Puranas) and
  (10) Homam (offering oblations daily to the Sacred Fire). There are five kinds of Asanas (Postures) that are commendable: Padmasan, Svastikasan, Bhadrasan, Vajrasan and Virasan. Padmasan consists in crossing the legs and placing the fact on the opposite thighs (the right foot on the left thigh and the left foot on the right thigh)

and catching by the right hand brought round the back, the toes of the right foot and catching by the left hand brought round the back the toes of the left foot; sitting then straight and with ease. This is recommended by the Yogis (and by this one can raise oneself in the air).

N.B.; The hands, according to some, need not be carried round the back; both the hands can be crossed and placed similarly on the thighs.

जानूर्वोरन्तरे सम्यक्कृत्वा पादतले शुभे।

ऋजुकायो विशेद्योगी स्वस्तिकं तत्प्रचक्षते॥ ११

Jānūrvōrantarē Samyakkrutvā Pādatalē Śubhē |

Rujukāyō Viśēdyōgī Svastikam Tat Pracakṣatē || 11

सीवन्या: पार्श्वयोर्न्यस्य गुल्फयुग्मं सुनिश्चितम्।

वृषणाध: पादपार्ष्णी पार्ष्णिभ्यां परिबन्धयेत्॥ १२

Sīvanyāḥ Pārśvayōrnyasya Gulpayugmam Suniścitam |

Vruṣaṇādhaḥ Pādapārṣṇī Pārṣṇibhyām Paribandhayēt || 12

भद्रासनमिति प्रोक्तं योगिभि: परिपूजितम्।

ऊर्वो: पादौ क्रमान्यस्य जान्वो: प्रत्यङ्मुखाङ्गुली॥ १३

Bhadrāsaṇamiti Prōktam Yōgibhiḥ Paripūjitam |

Ūrvōḥ Pādou Kramānnyasya Jānvōḥ Pratyaṅ Mukāṅgulī || 13

करौ विदध्यादाख्यातं वज्रासनमनुत्तमम्।

एकं पादमध: कृत्वा विन्यस्योरुं तथोत्तरे॥ १४

Karou Vidadhyādākhyātam Vajrāsaṇamaṇuttamam |

Ēkam Pādamadhaḥ Krutvā Vinyasyōrum Tathōttarē || 14

ऋजुकायो विशेद्योगी वीरासनमितीरितम्।

इडयाकर्षयेद्वायुं बाह्यं षोडशमात्रया॥ १५

Rujukāyō Viśēdyōgī Vīrāsaṇamitīritam |

Iḍayākarṣayēdvāyum Bāhyam Ṣōḍaśamātrayā ǁ 15

धारयेत्पूरितं योगी चतुःषष्ट्या तु मात्रया।

सुषुम्णामध्यगं सम्यग्द्वात्रिंशन्मात्रया शनैः॥१६

Dhārayēpūritam Yōgī Catuḥ Ṣaṣṭyā Tu Mātrayā |

Suṣumṇāmadhyagam Samyagdvātrimśaṇmātrayā Śaṇaiḥ ǁ 16

नाड्या पिङ्गलया चैव रेचयेद्योगवित्तमः।

प्राणायाममिमं प्राहुर्योगशास्त्रविशारदाः॥१७

Nāḍyā Piṅgalayā Caiva Rēcayēdyōgavittamaḥ |

Prāṇāyāmamimam Prāhur Yōga Śāstra Viśāradāḥ ǁ 17

भूयो भूयः क्रमात्तस्य बाह्यमेवं समाचरेत्।

मात्रावृद्धिक्रमेणैव सम्यग्द्वादश षोडश॥१८

Bhūyō Bhūyaḥ Kramāttasya Bāhyamēvam Samācarēt |

Mātrāvruddhikramēṇaiva Samyagdvādaśa Ṣōḍaśa ǁ 18

जपध्यानादिभिः सार्धं सगर्भं तं विदुर्बुधाः।

तदपेतं विगर्भं च प्राणायामं परे विदुः॥१९

Japadhyāṇādibhiḥ Sārdham Sagarbham Tam Vidurbudhāḥ |

Tadapētam Vigarbham Ca Prāṇāyāmam Parē Viduḥ ǁ 19

क्रमादभ्यस्यतः पुंसो देहे स्वेदोद्गमोऽधमः।

मध्यमः कम्पसंयुक्तो भूमित्यागः परो मतः॥२०

Kramādabhyasyataḥ Pumsō Dēhē Svēdōdgamōdhamaḥ |

Madhyamaḥ Kampasamyuktō Bhūmityāgaḥ Parō Mataḥ ǁ 20

Place the soles of the feet completely under the thighs, keep the body straight and sit at ease. This is called the Svastikasan.

Bhadrasan consists in placing well the two heels on the two sides of the two nerves of the testicle, near the anus and catching by the two hands the two heels at the lower part of the testicles and then sitting at ease. This is very much liked by the Yogis. Vajrasan (diamond seat) consists in placing the feet on the two thighs respectively and placing the fingers below the thighs with the hands also there and then sitting at ease. Virasan consists in sitting cross on the knees in placing the right foot under the right thigh and the left foot under the left thigh and sitting at ease with body straight.

Taking in the breath by the Ida (the left nostril) so long as we count 'Om' sixteen, retaining it in the Sushumna so long as we count 'Om' sixty-four times and then exhaling it slowly by the Pingala nadi (the right nostril) as long as we count 'Om' thirty-two times. (The first process is called Pooraka, the second is called Kumbhaka and the third is called Rechaka). This is called *one* Pranayama by those versed in the Yogas. Thus, one should go on again and again with his Pranayama. At the very beginning, try with the number twelve, i.e., as we count 'Om' twelve times and then increase the number gradually. to sixteen and so on. Pranayama is of two kinds - Sagarbha and Vigarbha. It is called Sagarbha when Pranayama is performed with repeating the Ishta Mantra and Japam and meditation. It is called Vigarbha Pranayama when 'Om' is simply counted and no other Mantra. When this Pranayama is practiced repeatedly, perspiration comes first when it is called of the lowest order; when the body begins to tremble, it is called middling; and when one rises up in the air, leaving the ground, it is called the best Pranayama. (Therefore, one who practices Pranayama ought to continue it till he becomes able to rise in the air).

उत्तमस्य गुणावाप्तिर्यावच्छीलनमिष्यते ।
इन्द्रियाणां विचरतां विषयेषु निरर्गलम् ॥ २१

Uttamasya Guṇāvāptiryāvacchīlanamiṣyatē |

Indriyāṇām Vicaratām Viṣayēṣu Nirarkalam || 21

बलादाहरणं तेभ्यः प्रत्याहारोऽभिधीयते।
अङ्गुष्ठगुल्फजानूरुमूलाधोलिङ्गनाभिषु ॥२२

Balādāharaṇam Tēbhyaḥ Pratyāhārōbhidhīyatē |
Aṅguṣṭha Gulpa Jāṉūru Mūlādhōliṅga Nābhiṣu ॥ 22

हृद्ग्रीवाकण्ठदेशेषु लम्बिकायां ततो नसि।
भ्रूमध्ये मस्तके मूर्ध्नि द्वादशान्ते यथाविधि॥२३

Hrud Grīvā Kaṇṭha Dēśēṣu Lambikāyām Tatō Nasi |
Bhrūmadhyē Mastakē Mūrdhṉi Dvādaśāntē Yathāvidhi ॥ 23

धारणं प्राणमरुतो धारणेति निगद्यते।
समाहितेन मनसा चैतन्यान्तरवर्तिना॥२४

Dhāraṇam Prāṉamarutō Dhāraṇēti Nigadyatē |
Samāhitēṉa Maṉasā Caitaṉyāṉtaravartiṉā ॥ 24

आत्मन्यभीष्टदेवानां ध्यानं ध्यानमिहोच्यते।
समत्वभावना नित्यं जीवात्मपरमात्मनोः॥२५

Ātmaṉyabhīṣṭa Dēvāṉām Dhyāṉam Dhyāṉamihōcyatē |
Samatvabhāvaṉā Nityam Jīvātmaparamātmaṉōḥ ॥ 25

समाधिमाहुर्मुनयः प्रोक्तमष्टाङ्गलक्षणम्।
इदानीं कथये तेऽहं मन्त्रयोगमनुत्तमम्॥२६

Samādhimāhur Muṉayaḥ Prōktamaṣṭāṅka Lakṣaṇam |
Idāṉīm Kathayē Tēham Mantra Yōgamaṉuttamam ॥ 26

विश्वं शरीरमित्युक्तं पञ्चभूतात्मकं नग।
चन्द्रसूर्याग्नितेजोभिर्जीवब्रह्मैक्यरूपकम् ॥२७

Viśvam Śarīramityuktam Pañcabhūtātmakam Naga |
Candra Sūryāgṉi Tējōbhir Jīva Brahmaikya Rūpakam ॥ 27

तिस्त्रः कोट्यस्तदर्धेन शरीरे नाडयो मताः।

तासु मुख्या दश प्रोक्तास्ताभ्यस्तिस्त्रो व्यवस्थिताः॥ २८

Tisra: Kōṭyastadardhēṉa Śarīrē Nāḍyō Matāḥ |

Tāsu Mukhyā Daśa Prōktāstābhyas Tisrō Vyavasthitāḥ ‖ 28

प्रधाना मेरुदण्डेऽत्र चन्द्रसूर्याग्निरूपिणी।

इडा वामे स्थिता नाडी शुभ्रा तु चन्द्ररूपिणी॥ २९

Pradhāṉā Mērudaṇḍētra Candra Sūryāgṉi Rūpiṇī |

Iḍā Vāmē Sthitā Nāḍī Śubhrā Tu Candra Rūpiṇī ‖ 29

शक्तिरूपा तु सा नाडी साक्षादमृतविग्रहा।

दक्षिणे या पिङ्गलाख्या पुंरूपा सूर्यविग्रहा॥ ३०

Śaktirūpā Tu Sā Nāḍī Sākṣādamruta Vigrahā |

Dakṣiṉē Yā Piṅgalākhyā Pumrūpā Sūrya Vigrahā ‖ 30

Now comes Pratyahara. The senses travel spontaneously towards their objects, as if there are without anyone to check. To curb them perforce and to make them turn backwards from those objects is called 'Pratyahara'. To hold the Prana Vayu on toes, heels, knees, thighs, sacrum genital organs, navel, heart, neck, throat, the soft palate, nose, between the eyebrows and on the top of the head, at these twelve places respectively is called the 'Dharana'. Concentrate the mind on the consciousness inside and then meditate the Ishta Devata within the Jeevatma. This is the Dhyana. Samadhi is identifying always the Jeevatma and Paramatma. Thus, the sages say, (Samadhi is of two kinds (1) Samprajnata, or Savikalpa and (2) Nirvikalpa. When the ideas the Knower, Knowledge and the thing Known, remain separate in the consciousness and yet the mind feels the one Akhanda Sachchidananda Brahmam and his heart remains, there, that is called Samprajnata Samadhi; and when those three vanish away and the one Brahmam remains, it is called Asamprajnata Samadhi). Thus, I have described to you the Yoga with its eight limbs. Oh Mountain! This body composed of the five elements and with Jeeva endowed with the essence of the Sun the Moon and the Fire and Brahmam in it as one and the same, is denominated by the term 'Vishva'. There are the 350,000 nadis in this body of man; of these, the principal is ten. Out of the ten again, the three are most prominent. The foremost and first of these three is Sushumna, of the nature of the Moon, Sun and Fire, situated in the center of the spinal cord (it extends from the sacral plexus below to the Brahmarandhra in the head at the top where it looks like a blown Dhustura flower). On the left of this Sushumna is the Ida Nadi, white and looking like Moon; this Nadi is of the nature of Force, nectar-like. On the right side of the Sushumna is the Pingala Nadi of the nature of a male; it represents the Sun. The Sushumna comprises the nature of the all the Tejas (fires) and it represents Fire.

सर्वतेजोमयी सा तु सुषुम्णा वह्निरूपिणी।
तस्या मध्ये विचित्राख्ये इच्छाज्ञानक्रियात्मकम्॥ ३१

Sarvatējōmayi Sā Tu Suṣumṇā Vahṇi Rūpiṇī |

Tasyā Madhyē Vicitrākhyē Icchā Ñāṇa Kriyātmakam || 31

मध्ये स्वयम्भूलिङ्गं तु कोटिसूर्यसमप्रभम्।
तदूर्ध्वं मायाबीजं तु हरात्माबिन्दुनादकम्॥ ३२

Madhyē Svayambhūliṅgam Tu Kōṭi Sūrya Samaprabham |

Tadūrdhvam Māyābījam Tu Harātmā Bindu Nādakam || 32

तदूर्ध्वं तु शिखाकारा कुण्डली रक्तविग्रहा।
देव्यात्मिका तु सा प्रोक्ता मदभिन्ना नगाधिप॥ ३३

Tadūrdhvam Tu Śikhākārā Kuṇḍalī Rakta Vigrahā |

Dēvyātmikā Tu Sā Prōktā Madabhiṇṇā Nāgādhipa || 33

तद्बाहो हेमरूपाभं वादिसान्तचतुर्दलम्।
द्रुतहेमसमप्रख्यं पद्मं तत्र विचिन्तयेत्॥ ३४

Tadbāhyē Hēmarūpābham Vādhisānta Caturdalam |

Druta Hēma Samaprakhyam Padmam Tatra Vicintayēt || 34

तदूर्ध्वं त्वनलप्रख्यं षड्दलं हीरकप्रभम्।

बादिलान्तषड्वर्णेन स्वाधिष्ठानमनुत्तमम्॥ ३५

Tadūrdhvam Tva Nalaprakhyam Ṣaḍdalam Hīrakaprabham |

Bādilānta Ṣaḍvarṇēṇa Svādhiṣṭhāṇamaṇuttamam || 35

मूलमाधारषट्कोणं मूलाधारं ततो विदुः।

स्वशब्देन परं लिङ्गं स्वाधिष्ठानं ततो विदुः॥ ३६

Mūlamādhāra Ṣaṭkōṇam Mūlādhāram Tatō Viduḥ |

Svaśabdēṇa Param Liṅgam Svādhiṣṭhāṇam Tatō Viduḥ || 36

तदूर्ध्वं नाभिदेशे तु मणिपूरं महाप्रभम्।

मेघाभं विद्युदाभं च बहुतेजोमयं ततः॥ ३७

Tadūrdhvam Nābhidēśē Tu Maṇipūram Mahāprabham |

Mēghābham Vidyudābham Ca Bahutējōmayam Tataḥ || 37

मणिवद्भिन्नं तत्पद्मं मणिपद्मं तथोच्यते।

दशभिश्च दलैर्युक्तं डादिफान्ताक्षरान्वितम्॥ ३८

Maṇivadbhiṇṇam Tatpadmam Maṇipadmam Tatōcyatē |

Daśabhiśca Dalaiyuktam Ḍādiphāntākṣarāṇvitam || 38

विष्णुनाधिष्ठितं पद्मं विष्ण्वालोकनकारणम्।

तदूर्ध्वेनाहतं पद्ममुद्यदादित्यसन्निभम्॥ ३९

Viṣṇuṇādhiṣṭhitam Padmam Viṣṇvālōka Nakāraṇam |

Tadūrdhvēṇāhatam Padmamudyadādditya Saṇṇibham || 39

कादिठान्तदलैरर्कपत्रैश्च समधिष्ठितम्।

तन्मध्ये बाणलिङ्गं तु सूर्यायुतसमप्रभम्॥ ४०

Kādiṭhānta Dalairarka Patraiśca Samadhiṣṭhitam |

Taṇmadhyē Bāṇaliṅgam Tu Sūryāyuta Samaprabham || 40

शब्दब्रह्ममयं शब्दानाहतं तत्र दृश्यते।
अनाहताख्यं तत्पद्मं मुनिभिः परिकीर्तितम्॥ ४१

Śabta Brahmamayam Śabdānāhatam Tatra Druśyatē |

Anāhatākyam Tatpadmam Munibhiḥ Parikīrtitam || 41

The innermost of Sushumna is Vichitra or Chitrini Bhoolingam nadi (of the form of a cobweb) in the middle of which resides the Ichcha (will), Jnana (knowledge) and Kriya (action) Shaktis and resplendent like the Millions of Suns. Above Him is situated Hreem, the Maya Beeja *Haratma* with 'Ha' and Chandra bindu representing the Sound (Nada). Above this is the Flame, Kula Kundalini (the Serpent Fire) of a red colour and as it were, intoxicated. Outside Her is the Adhara Lotus of a yellow colour having a dimension of four digits and Comprising the four letters (व, च, श, स) 'va', 'sa', 'sha' and 'sa'. The Yogis meditate on this. In its center is the hexagonal space (Pittham). This is called the Mooladhara for it is the base and it supports all the six lotuses. Above it is the Svadhishthana Chakra, fiery and emitting luster like diamond and with six petals representing the six letters (ब, भ, म, य, र, ल) 'ba', 'bha', 'ma', 'ya', 'ra', 'la'. The word 'Sva' means "Param Lingam" (superior Male Symbol). Therefore, the sages call this "Svadhishthana Chakram". Above it is situated the "Manipoora Chakram" of the colour of lightning in clouds and very fiery; it comprises the ten Petals, comprising the 10 letters 'da', 'dha', 'na', 'ta', 'tha', 'da', 'dha', 'na', 'pa and 'pha' — (ड, ढ, ण, त, थ, द, ध, न, प, फ). The lotus resembles a full-blown pearl; hence it is 'Manipadma'. Vishnu dwells here. Meditation here leads to the sight of Vishnu, above it is 'Anahata' Padma with the twelve petals representing, the twelve letters (क, ख, ग, घ, ङ, च, च, ज, झ, ञ) Ka, Kha, Ga, Gha, Gna, Ca, Cha, Ja, Jha and Gja. In the middle is Banalingam, resplendent like the Sun. This lotus emits the sound Shabda Brahmam, without being struck; therefore, it is called the Anahata Lotus. This is the source of joy. Here dwells Rudra, the Highest Person.

आनन्दसदनं तत्तु पुरुषाधिष्ठितं परम्।
तदूर्ध्वं तु विशुद्धाख्यं दलं षोडशपङ्कजम्॥ ४२

Āṇandasadaṇam Tattu Puruṣādhiṣṭhitam Param |

Tadūrdhvam Tu Viśuddhākyam Dalam Ṣōḍapaṅkajam || 42

स्वैः षोडशभिर्युक्तं धूम्रवर्णं महाप्रभम्।
विशुद्धं तनुते यस्माजीवस्य हंसलोकनात्॥ ४३

Svaraiḥ Ṣōḍaśabhiryuktam Dhūmravarṇam Mahābhrapam |

Viśuddham Tanutē Yasmājjīvasya Hamsalōkaṇāt || 43

Above it is situated the Visuddhi Chakra of the sixteen petals, comprising the sixteen letters (अ - अः) a to ah — all vowels. This is of a smoky colour, highly lustrous and is situated in the throat. The Jeevatma sees the Paramatma (the Highest Self) here and it is purified; hence it is called Visuddha. This wonderful lotus is termed Akasha.

विशुद्धं पद्ममाख्यातमाकाशाख्यं महाद्भुतम्।
आज्ञाचक्रं तदूर्ध्वं तु आत्मनाधिष्ठितं परम्॥ ४४

Viśuddham Padmamākhyātamākāsākhyam Mahādbhutam |

Āgñā Cakram Tadūrdhvam Tu Ātmaṇādhiṣṭhitam Param || 44

आज्ञासंक्रमणं तत्र तेनाज्ञेति प्रकीर्तितम्।
द्विदलं हक्षसंयुक्तं पद्यं तत्सुमनोहरम्॥ ४५

Āgñā Saṅkramaṇam Tatra Tēṇāgñēti Prakīrtitam |

Dvidalam Hakṣasamyuktam Padmam Tatsu Maṇōharam || 45

Above that is situated betwixt the eyebrows the exceedingly beautiful Ajna Chakra with two petals comprising the two letters (ह, क्ष) 'Ha' and 'Ksha'. The Self-resides in this lotus. When persons are stationed here, they can see everything and know of the present, past and future. There one gets the commands from the Highest Deity (e.g. now this is for you to do and so on); therefore, it is called the Ajna Chakra.

कैलासाख्यं तदूर्ध्वं तु रोधिनी तु तदूर्ध्वतः।
एवं त्वाधारचक्राणि प्रोक्तानि तव सुव्रत॥ ४६

Kailāsākhyam Tadūrdhvam Tu Rōdhlṇī Tu Tadūrdhvataḥ |
Ēvam Tvādhāra Cakrāṇi Prōktāṇi Tava Suvrata ॥ 46

सहस्त्रारयुतं बिन्दुस्थानं तदूर्ध्वमीरितम्।
इत्येतत्कथितं सर्वं योगमार्गमनुत्तमम्॥ ४७

Sahasrārayutam Bindusthāṇam Tadūrdhvamīritam |
Ityētatkathitam Sarvam Yōgamārgamaṇuttamam ॥ 47

Above that is the Kailasa Chakra; over it is the Rodhini Chakra. Oh, One of good vows! Thus, I have described to you all about the Adhara Chakras. The prominent Yogis say that above that again, is the Bindu Sthan, the seat of the Supreme Deity with thousand petals.

Oh, Best of Mountains! Thus, I declare the best of the paths leading to Yoga.

आदौ पूरकयोगेनाप्याधारे योजयेन्मनः।
गुदमेढ्रान्तरे शक्तिस्तामाकुञ्च्य प्रबोधयेत्॥ ४८

Ādou Pūrakayōgēṇāpyādhārē Yōjayēṇmaṇah |
Gudamēḍhrāntarē Śaktistāmākuñcya Prabōdhayēt ॥ 48

Now bear what is the next thing to do. First by the 'Pooraka', Pranayama, fix the mind on the Mooladhara Lotus. Then contract and arouse the Kula Kundalini Shakti there, between the anus and the genital organs, by that Vayu.

लिङ्गभेदक्रमेणैव बिन्दुचक्रं च प्रापयेत्।
शम्भुना तां परां शक्तिमेकीभूतां विचिन्तयेत्॥ ४९

Liṅgabhēda Kramēṇaiva Bindu Cakram Ca Prāpayēt |

Śambhuṉā Tā Parām Śaktimēkībhūtām Vicintayēt || 49

Prime, then, the Lingams (the lustrous Svayambhu Adi Lingam) in the several Chakras above-mentioned and transfer along with it the heart united with the Shakti to the Sahasrara (the Thousand petalled Lotus). Then meditate the Shakti united with Shambhu there.

तत्रोत्थितामृतं यत्तु द्रुतलाक्षारसोपमम्।
पाययित्वा तु तां शक्तिं मायाख्यां योगसिद्धिदाम्॥ ५०

Tatrōtthitāmrutam Yattu Drutalākṣāra Sōpamam |

Pāyayitvā Tu Tām Śaktim Māyākhyām Yōgasiddhidām || 50

षट्चक्रदेवतास्तत्र सन्तप्र्यामृतधारया।
आनयेत्तेन मार्गेण मूलाधारं ततः सुधीः॥५१

Ṣaṭcakra Dēvatāstatra Santāpryāmruta Dhārayā |

Āṉayēttēṉa Mārgēṉa Mūlādhāram Tataḥ Sudhīḥ ||51

There is produced in the Bindu Chakra, out of the intercourse of Siva and Shakti, a kind of nectar-juice, resembling a sort of red-dye (lac). With that Nectar of Joy, the wise Yogis make the Maya Shakti, yielding successes in Yoga, drink; then pleasing all the Devas in the six Chakras with the offerings of that Nectar, the Yogi brings the Shakti down again on through Mooladhara Lotus.

एवमभ्यस्यमानस्याप्यहन्यहनि निश्चितम्।
पूर्वोक्तदूषिता मन्त्राः सर्वे सिद्ध्यन्ति नान्यथा॥ ५२

Ēvamabhyasyamāṉasyāpyahaṉyahaṉi Niścitam |

Pūrvōkta Dūṣitā Mantrāḥ Sarvē Siddhayanti Nāṉyathā || 52

Thus, by daily practising this, all the above mantras will no doubt, be made to come to complete success.

जरामरणदुःखाद्यैर्मुच्यते   भवबन्धनात् ।
ये गुणाः सन्ति देव्या मे जगन्मातुर्यथा तथा ॥ ५३

JarāmaranaduhKhādyairmucyatē Bhavabantanāt |

Yē Gunāḥ Santi Dēvyā Mē Jaganmāturyathā Tathā || 53

ते गुणाः साधकवरे भवन्त्येव न चान्यथा ।
इत्येवं   कथितं   तात   वायुधारणमुत्तमम् ॥ ५४

Tē Guṇāḥ Sādhakavarē Bhavantyēva Nā Cānyathā |

Ityēvam Kathitam Tāta Vāyudhāraṇamuttamam || 54

And one will be free from this Samsara, filled with old age and death, etc.

Oh Lord of Mountains! I am the World Mother; My devotee will get all My qualities; there is no doubt in this.

Oh Child! I have thus described to you the excellent Yoga, holding the Vayu (Pavana Dharana Yoga).

इदानीं धारणाख्यं तु शृणुष्वावहितो मम ।
दिक्कालाद्यनवच्छिन्नदेव्यां चेतो विधाय च ॥ ५५

Idānīm Dhāraṇākhyam Tu Śruṇuṣvāvahitō Mama |

Dikkālādyanavacchinna Dēvyām Cētō Vidhāya Ca || 55

Now hear from Me the Dharana Yoga. To fix thoroughly one's heart on the Supremely Lustrous Force of Mine, pervading all the quarters, countries and all time leads soon to the union of the Jeeva and the Brahmam.

तन्मयो भवति क्षिप्रं जीवब्रह्मैक्ययोजनात् ।
अथवा समलं चेतो यदि क्षिप्रं न सिद्ध्यति ॥ ५६

Taṇmayō Bhavati Kṣipram Jīvabrahmaikya Yōjaṇāt |
Athavā Samalam Cētō Yadi Kṣipram Na Siddhayati ‖ 56

तदावयवयोगेन योगी योगान्समभ्यसेत् ।
मदीयहस्तपादादावङ्गे तु मधुरे नग ॥ ५७

Tadāvayava Yōgēṇa Yōgī Yōgāṇ Samabhyasēt |
Madīyahasta Pādādāvaṅgē Tu Madhurē Naga ‖ 57

चित्तं संस्थापयेन्मन्त्री स्थानं स्थानजयात्पुनः ।
विशुद्धचित्तः सर्वस्मिन्रूपे संस्थापयेन्मनः ॥ ५८

Cittam Samsthāpayēṇ Mantrī Sthāṇam Sthāṇajayāt Puṇaḥ |
Viśuddhacittaḥ Sarvasmiṇ Rūpē Samsthāpayēṇ Maṇaḥ ‖ 58

If one does not quickly do this, owing to impurities of heart, then the Yogi ought to adopt what is called the "Avayava Yoga".

Oh, Chief of Mountains! The Sadhaka should fix his heart on my gentle hands, feet and other limbs one by one and try to conquer each of these places. Thereby his heart would be purified. Then he should fix that purified heart on My Whole Body.

यावन्मनो लयं याति देव्यां संविदि पर्वत ।
तावदिष्टमनुं मन्त्री जपहोमैः समभ्यसेत् ॥ ५९

Yāvaṇmaṇō Layam Yāti Dēvyām Samvidi Parvata |
Tāvadiṣṭamaṇum Mantrī Japahōmaiḥ Samabhyasēt ‖ 59

मन्त्राभ्यासेन योगेन ज्ञेयज्ञानाय कल्पते ।
न योगेन विना मन्त्रो न मन्त्रेण विना हि सः ॥ ६०

Mantrābhyāsēṇa Yōgēṇa Ñēyakñāṇāya Kalpatē |
Na Yōgēṇa Viṇā Mantrō Na Mantrēṇa Viṇā Hi Saḥ ‖ 60

द्वयोरभ्यासयोगो हि ब्रह्मसंसिद्धिकारणम् ।
तम: परिवृते गेहे घटो दीपेन दृश्यते ॥ ६१

Dvayōrabhyāsayōgō Hi Brahma Samsiddhi Kāraṇam |

Tamaḥ Parivrutē Gēhē Ghaṭō Dīpēṉa Druśyatē ||61

एवं मायावृतो ह्यात्मा मनुना गोचरीकृत: ।
इति योगविधि: कृत्स्न: साङ्ग: प्रोक्तो मयाधुना ।
गुरूपदेशतो ज्ञेयो नान्यथा शास्त्रकोटिभि: ॥ ६२

Ēvam Māyāvrutō Hyātmā Maṉuṉā Gōcarīkrutaḥ |

Iti Yōgavidhiḥ Krutsṉaḥ Sāṅgaḥ Prōktō Mayādhuṉā |

Gurupadēśatō Ñēyō Nāṉyathā Śāstra Kōṭibhiḥ || 62

The practicer must practice with Japam and Homam the Mantra till his mind be not dissolved in Me, My Consciousness. By the practice of meditating on the Mantra, the thing to be known (Brahma) is transformed into knowledge. Know this as certain, that the Mantra is futile without Yoga and the Yoga is futile without the Mantra. The Mantra and the Yoga are the two infallible means to realise Brahma. As the jar in a dark room is visible by a lamp, so this Jeevatma, surrounded by Maya is visible by means of Mantra to the Paramatma (the Highest Self).

Oh, Best of Mountains! Thus, I have described to you the Yogas with their Angas (limbs). You should receive instructions about them from the mouth of a Guru; else millions of Sastras will never be able to give you a true realisation of the meanings of the yogas.

ओं श्री जगदंबार्पणमस्तु । श्री चण्डिकापरमेश्वरी प्रीयताम् ।

Ōm Śrī Jagadambārpaṇamastu |

Śrī Caṇḍikā Paramēśvarī Prīyatām |

इति श्रीमद् देवी भागवते महापुराणेऽष्टादश साहस्रयां संहितायां श्री देवी गीतायांमन्त्र सिद्धि साधन वर्णनं नाम पञ्चमोऽध्याय: ॥

Iti Śrīmad Dēvī Bhāgavatē Mahāpurāṇēṣṣṭātaśa Sāhasrayām Samhitāyām Śrī Dēvī Gītāyām Mantra Siddhi Sādhana Varṇaṇam Nāma Pancamodyāyaḥ ॥

Here ends the fifth Chapter of Sri Devi Gita named as *Mantra Siddhi Sādhana Varṇaṇam* in the Mahapuranam *Shrimad Devi Bhagavatam* having 18,000 verses, by Maharshi Veda Vyasa.

Kundalini energy at Moolaadhaara chakra, getting up and going through the Sushumna Nadi and passing through the chakras to reach the Sahasrara Chakra – the dwelling place of unified Shiva-Shakti. This process has been described in almost all Sri Devi related texts like Soundaryalaharee, Sri Lalita Sahasranamam and so on.

In Bhagavad Gita as Krishna says that those who worship demigods go to their kingdom, so is it like attaining siddhis is kind of less achievement than attaining moksha/ nirvana/ enlightenment? Basically, we every time come to know that in order to make a mantra/ sadhana work for anyone, it should be siddha first. There are different types of sadhana/ siddhi for different purposes.

Krishna says in the Bhagavad Gita (2.59) – The embodied soul may be restricted from senses enjoyment, though the taste for sense objects remains. But, ceasing such engagements by experiencing a higher taste, he is fixed in consciousness.

Dhyana Yogaḥ
(*Devi Bhagavatam 7-36*)

This is the sixth chapter of *Sri Devi Gita*. The name of the chapter itself "Brahma Vidya Upadesha Varnanam". Here *Sri Devi* herself explains the *Brahma Vidya* to Himalaya King.

ओं नम: चण्डिकायै । *Ōm Namaḥ Caṇḍikāyai* |

देव्युवाच

इत्यादियोगयुक्तात्मा ध्यायेन्मां ब्रह्मरूपिणीम् ।
भक्त्या निर्व्याजया राजन्नासने समुपस्थित: ॥ १

Dēvyuvāca

Ityādi Yōgayuktātmā Dhyāyēṉ Mām Brahma Rūpiṇīm |

Bhaktyā Nirvyājayā Rājaṉṉāsaṉē Samupasthitaḥ | 1

आवि: सन्निहितं गुहाचरं नाम महत्पदम् ।
अत्रैतत्सर्वमर्पितमेजत्प्राणनिमिषच्च   यत् ॥ २

Āviḥ Saṉṉihitam Guhācaram Nāma Mahatpatam |

Atraitat Sarvamarpita Mējat Prāṇa Nimiṣacca Yat || 2

एतज्जानथ   सदसद्वरेण्यं   परं
         विज्ञानाद्यद्वरिष्ठं   प्रजानाम् ।
यदर्चिमद्यदणुभ्योऽणु   च
         यस्मिँल्लोका निहिता लोकिनश्च ॥ ३

Ētajjāṉatha Sadasadvarēṇyam Param Viñāṉātyatvariṣṭam
                                        Prajāṉām |

Yadarcimadyatanubhyōḍhu Ca Yasmilmlōkā Nihitā Lōkiṉaśca || 3

तदेतदक्षरं ब्रह्म स प्राणस्तदु वाङ्मन: ।
तदेतत्सत्यममृतं तद्वेद्धव्यं सौम्य विद्धि ॥ ४

Tadētadakṣaram Brahma Sa Prāṇastadu Vāṅmaṉaḥ |

Tadētatsatyamamrutam Tadvēddhavyam Saumya Viddhi ‖ 4

Sri Devi said - "Oh Himalayas! Thus, making one's own self attached to the Yoga by the above-mentioned process and sitting on a Yoga posture, one should mediate on My Brahmam Nature with an unfeigned devotion.

How the knowledge of that Formless Existence and Imperishable Brahmam arises, now hear. He is manifest, near, yea, even moving in the hearts of all beings. He is the well-known Highest Goal. Know that all this whatever, awaking, dreaming, or sleeping, which moves, breathes or blinks, is founded on Him. He is higher than Being and Non-being; higher than the Wisdom, He is the Best Object of adoration for all creatures. He is brilliant, smaller than the smallest and in Him the worlds are founded and the Rulers thereof. He is the Imperishable Brahmam. He is the Creator (Life), the Revealer of Sacred Knowledge (speech) and Omniscient (or the Cosmic Mind). This is the Truth. He is immortal, Oh Soumya! Know that He is the target to be hit.

Note – The words "higher than wisdom" mean higher than Brahmam. (Brahmam is the highest of all Jeevas, higher than Brahmam means higher than all creatures. The word Vijnana denotes Brahmam as we find in the following speech of Brahma in the Bhagavata Purana) "I, the Wisdom Energy (Vijnana-Shakti) was born from the navel of this Being resting on the Waters and possessed of the Infinite Powers".

Vishnu is called "Prana," because he is the leader of all (Prana-netri). He is called Vak, because He is the Teacher of all; Vishnu is called Manas because He is the adviser of all (Mantri). He is the Controller of all the Jeevas.

The third verse lays down that Brahmam is to be meditated upon or that the Manana should be performed; as the second verse teaches that Dhyana or concentration also is necessary.

धनुर्गृहीत्वौपनिषदं   महास्त्रं

शरं   ह्युपासानिशितं   सन्धयीत ।

आयम्य   तद्भावगतेन   चेतसा
लक्ष्यं तदेवाक्षरं सौम्य विद्धि॥ ५

Dhanur Gruhītvaupaniṣatam Mahāstram Śaram

Hyupāsāniśitam Sandhayīta |

Āyamya Tadbhāvagatēna Cētasā Lakṣyam

Tadēvākṣaram Soumya Viddhi ||

प्रणवो धनु: शरो ह्यात्मा ब्रह्म तल्लक्ष्यमुच्यते।
अप्रमत्तेन वेद्धव्यं शरवत्तन्मयो भवेत्॥ ६

Praṇavō Dhanuḥ Śarō Hyātmā Brahma Tallakṣya Mucyatē |

Apramattēna Vēddhavyam Śaravattanmayō Bhavēt || 6

Take hold of the Mystic name as the bow and know that the Brahmam is the aim to be hit. Put on this the great weapon (*Om*), the arrow (of the mind) sharpened by meditation. Withdraw yourself from all objects and with the mind absorbed in the idea of Brahmam, hit the aim; for now, Oh Soumya! That Imperishable alone to be the Mark. The Great name '*Om*' is the bow, the mind is the arrow and the Brahmam is said to be the mark. It is to be hit by a man whose thoughts are concentrated, for then he enters the target.

Thus Shravana, Manana and Dhyana of Brahmam have been taught. This is the method of Brahma-Upasana.

यस्मिन्द्यौश्च   पृथिवी   चान्तरिक्षमोतं
मन: सह   प्राणैश्च   सर्वै:।
तमेवैकं   जानथात्मानमन्या
वाचो विमुज्ञ्चथामृतस्यैष सेतु:॥ ७

Yasmindyouśca Pruthivī Cāntarikṣamōtam

$\qquad$ *Maṇaḥ Saha Prāṇaiśca Sarvaiḥ |*

Tamēvaikam Jānathātmānamanyā Vācō Vimuñcathāmrutas

$\qquad$ *Yaiṣa Sētuḥ || 7*

In Him are woven the heavens and the interspaces and mingle also with the senses. Know Him to be the one Support of all, the Atman. Leave off all other words (as well as the worship of other deities). This (Atman) is the refuge of the Immortals.

"He is the bridge of the Immortal" – the words Amruta or Immortal means Mukta Jeevas. In the Vedanta Sutra (I-32), it has been taught that the Lord is the refuge of the Muktas. So also, that "He is the Highest Goal of the Muktas".

अरा इव रथनाभौ संहता यत्र नाड्य: ।

स एषोऽन्तश्चरते बहुधा जायमान: ॥ ८

Arā Iva Rathaṉābhou Samhatā Yatra Nāḍyaḥ |

Sa Ēṣohtaścaratē Bahudhā Jāyamāṉaḥ ‖ 8

ओमित्येवं   ध्यायथात्मानं

स्वस्ति व: पाराय तमस: परस्तात् ।

दिव्ये ब्रह्मपुरे व्योम्नि आत्मा सम्प्रतिष्ठित: ॥ ९

Ōmityēvam Dhyāyathātmāṉam Svasti Vaḥ Pārāya

Tamasaḥ Parastāt |

Divyē Brahmapurē Vyōmṉi Ātmā Sam Pratiṣṭitaḥ ‖ 9

In Him the life-webs (nadis) are fastened, as the spokes to the nave of a chariot; He is this (Atman) that pervades the heart and by his own free will manifests Himself in diverse ways (as *Vishva*, *Taijasa*, etc., in waking, sleeping, etc., states); and also, as One as Prajna in the dreamless state. Meditate on the Atman as *Om* (full of all auspicious qualities and who is the chief aim of the Vedas), in order to acquire the knowledge of the *Paramatman*, who is beyond the Prakruti and the Sri Tattva. Your welfare consists in such knowledge.

This shows that Brahmam is the Antaryami Purusha. He resides in the heart where all the 72,000 Nadis meet, as the spokes meet in the navel of the wheel. He moves within the organs, not for His own pleasure, but to give life and energy to them all. The Om with all its attributes must be constantly meditated upon. He manifests Himself in manifold ways in the waking and dreaming stews as Vishva and Taijasa; while He manifests as One in the state of Sushupti or Dreamless sleep as Prajna. He is beyond darkness; He has no mortal body. Meditate on such Vishnu in the heart in order to get the Supreme Brahmam, with the help of the Mantra Om. The result of such meditation is that there is the welfare of yours – all evils will cease and you will get the bliss of the manifestation of the Divinity – your Real Self within your Heart.

मनोमयः   प्राणशरीरनेता

प्रतिष्ठितोऽन्ने   हृदयं   सन्निधाय।

तद्विज्ञानेन   परिपश्यन्ति   धीरा

आनन्दरूपममृतं   यद्विभाति ॥ १०

Maṉōmayaḥ Prāṇa Śarīraṉētā Pratiṣṭhitōḫṉē Hrudayam

Saṉṉidhāya |

Tadvikñāṉēṉa Paripaśyanti Dhīrā Āṉanda Rūpamrutam

Yadvibhāti ‖ 10

He who is all-wise and all-knowing, whose Greatness is thus manifested in the worlds, is to be meditated upon as the Atman residing in the Ether, in the Fourth Dimensional Space, in the shining city of Brahmam (the Heart). He is the Controller of the mind and the Guide of the senses and the body. He abides in the dense body, controlling the heart. He, the Atman, when manifesting Himself as the Blissful and Immortal, is seen by the wise through the purity of the heart.

भिद्यते   हृदयग्रन्थिश्छिद्यन्ते   सर्वसंशयाः।

क्षीयन्ते चास्य कर्माणि तस्मिन्दृष्टे परावरे॥ ११

Bhidyatē Hrudaya Granthiśchidyantē Sarva Samśayāḥ |

Kṣīyantē Cāsya Karmāṇi Tasmindruṣṭē Parāvarē ‖ 11

The fetters of the Jeevas are cut as under, the ties of Linga-dehas and Prakruti are removed (the effects of all) his works perish, when He is seen who is Supremely High (or when the Supremely High looks at the Jeeva.)

Note – Vishnu is Paravare, because Para or High Beings like Rama; Brahmas, etc., are Avatara or inferior in His comparison.

This shows the result of Divine Wisdom in the last verse. The Avidya covers both Ishvara and Jeeva. It prevents Ishvara being, seen by Jeeva and Jeeva, seeing Ishvara. It is a direct bondage of Jeeva and a metaphorical fetter of Ishvara. Avidya is the name given to Prakruti in Her active state. When Her three qualities Sattva, Rajas and Tamas, are actively manifest. Destruction of Avidya means putting these Gunas in their latent state. There is a great difference between the destruction of the Avidya fetters as taught in this verse and the unloosening of them as previously described in this verse! There Avidya still remained, for it was merely a Paroksha or intellectual apprehension of Truth. Here Avidya itself is destroyed by Aparoksha or Intuitive Knowledge of Brahmam.

The bonds are five –

1. The lowest is the Avidya bond,
2. Then the Lingadeha bond,
3. Then the Brahmacchadaka Prakruti bond,
4. The Kama bond and
5. The Karma bonds.

When all these bonds are destroyed, then the Jnani goes by the Path of Light to the Santamka Loka. Before proceeding further all have to salute the Sishumara – the Dweller on the threshold – the hub of the Universe.

Basically, Sishumara literally means the Infant Killer and also means the name of a constellation, in the north, near the Pole. It corresponds perhaps with the Draco or the Ursa Minor. For a fuller description of it, see Bhagavata Purana (5,23). Here it is a mystical reference to a Being of an exalted order, which every Jnani passes by, in his way beyond this Universe. It way corresponds with the ring-pass-not of the 'Secret Doctrine'! It is the name of Hari, also, as we find the following verse "The Supreme Hari, the Support of infinity of worlds and who is called Sishumara, is saluted by all knowers of Brahmam, on their way to the Supreme God".

हिरण्मये परे कोशे विराजं ब्रह्म निष्कलम् ।
तच्छुभ्रं ज्योतिषां ज्योतिस्तद्यदात्मविदो विदुः ॥ १२

Hiraṇmayē Parē Kōśē Virājam Brahma Niṣkalam |

Taccubhram Jyōtiṣām Jyōtistadyadātmavidō Vituḥ ॥ 12

The Brahmam (called Sishumaram) free from all passions and parts (manifesto in the external world) in the highest Golden Sheath (the Cosmic Egg). That is pure, that is the highest of Lights, it is that which the knowers of Atman know.

He is in the Centre of the Cosmic (as Sishumara, the Light of all Cosmic Suns. He is even in the center of our Sun and illumining all planets.

In the first respect He is meditated upon as Sishumara and in the second as Gayatri.

In man, the Brahmam manifests in the heart or the Auric Egg, called the city of Brahmam. In the Universe, He manifests Himself in the Cosmic Egg, called the "Golden Sheath". These are the two places where Brahmam may be meditated upon.

This verse has been explained in two different ways: First, as applying to Sishumara and secondly, as teaching how to meditate on Narayana in the Sun, the "Golden sheath" would then mean the Solar sphere. The Supremely High Brahmam resides in the excellent Golden Sheath. He is Pure and Without parts.

न तत्र सूर्यो भाति न चन्द्रतारकं
नेमा विद्युतो भान्ति कुतोऽयमग्निः ।

तमेव   भान्तमनुभाति   सर्वं
तस्य   भासा   सर्वमिदं   विभाति॥ १३

Na Tatra Sūryō Bhāti Na Candratārakam Nēmā

Vidyutō Bhānti Kutōyamagnih |

Tamēva Bhāntamanupāti Sarvam Tasya Bhāsā

Sarvamidam Vibhāti ǁ 13

The Sun does not shine there in His Presence nor the Moon and the Stars, for His Light is greater than theirs, they appear as if dark in that Effulgence, like the candle-light in the Sun. Nor do these lightnings and much less this fire shine there. When He shines, everything shines after Him; by His Light all this becomes manifest.

Him the Sun does not illumine nor the moon and the stars. Nor do these lightnings; much less this Fire illumines Him. When He illumines all (the Sun, etc.,) than they shine after (Him with His light). This whole Universe reveals His Light (is His Light and its Light is His).

Note – The Sun, etc., do not illumine Him, i.e., cannot make Him manifest.

This *shloka* is normally used as a mantra while showing camphor deepam to god/ goddess.

ब्रह्मैवेदममृतं   पुरस्ताद्ब्रह्म

पश्चाद्ब्रह्म   दक्षिणतश्चोत्तरेण।

अधश्चोर्ध्वं च प्रसृतं ब्रह्मैवेदं विश्वं वरिष्ठम्॥ १४

Brahmai Vēdamamrutam Purastād Brahma

Paścād Brahma Dakṣinataścōttarēṇa |

Adhaścōrdhvam Ca Prasrutam Brahmai

Vēdam Viśvam Variṣṭham ǁ 14

The Eternally Free is verily this Brahmam only. He is in the West, in the North and the South, in the Zenith and the Nadir. The

Brahmam alone is; it is He who pervades all directions. This Brahmam alone is it who pervades, This Brahmam alone is the Full (that exists in all time the Eternity). This Brahmam is the Best.

This *'idam'* Brahmam is alone the Vishvam or Infinity or full (*poornam*). This alone is the Best, the Highest of all. As the word *'idam'* is used several times in this verse, it qualifies the word Brahmam and not *'Vishvam'*.

Note – The Brahmam was taught to be meditated upon fully in the Heart and the Hiranmaya Kosha. But least one should mistake that He is thus limited in those two places, one is to infer that they are selected as the best.

एतादृगनुभवो यस्य स कृतार्थो नरोत्तमः।

ब्रह्मभूतः प्रसन्नात्मा न शोचति न काङ्क्षति॥ १५

Ētādrugaṇubhavō Yasya Sa Krutārthō Narōttamaḥ |

Brahmabhūtaḥ Prasaṇnātmā Na Śōcati Na Kāṅkṣati || 15

द्वितीयाद्वै भयं राजंस्तदभावाद् बिभेति न।

न तद्वियोगो मेऽप्यस्ति मद्वियोगोऽपि तस्य न॥ १६

Dvitīyādvai Bhayam Rājamstadabhāvād Bibhēti Na |

Na Tadviyōgō Mēpyasti Madviyōgōpi Tasya Na || 16

The man who realises thus is satisfied and has all that he wants to do and is considered as the best. He becomes Brahmam and his Self is pleased and he neither wants anything nor becomes sorry.

Oh King! Fear comes from the idea of a second; where there is no second, fear does not exist. No danger then arises for him to be separated from Me. Nor I also get separated from him.

अहमेव स सोऽहं वै निश्चितं विद्धि पर्वत।

मद्दर्शनं तु तत्र स्याद्यत्र ज्ञानी स्थितो मम॥ १७

Ahamēva Sa Sōham Vai Niścitam Viddhi Parvata |

Maddarśaṉam Tu Tatra Syādyatra Ñāṉi Sthitō Mama || 17

Oh Himavan! Know that I am he and he is I. Know that I am seen there where my Jnani resides.

नाहं तीर्थे न कैलासे वैकुण्ठे वा न कर्हिचित् ।
वसामि किं तु मज्ज्ञानिहृदयाम्भोजमध्यमे ॥ १८

Nāham Tīrthē Na Kailāsē Vaikuṇṭhē Vā Na Kar'hicit |

Vāsāmi Kim Tu Majñāṉi Hrudayām Bhōja Madhyamē || 18

Neither I dwell in any sacred place of pilgrimage, nor do I live in Kailasa nor in Vaikunda nor in any other place. I dwell in the heart lotus of My Jnani.

मत्पूजाकोटिफलदं सकृन्मज्ज्ञानिनोऽर्चनम् ।
कुलं पवित्रं तस्यास्ति जननी कृतकृत्यका ॥ १९

Matpūjākōṭiphaladam Sakruṉmajñāṉiṉōŕcaṉam |

Kulam Pavitram Tasyāsti Jaṉaṉī Krutakrutyakā || 19

The blessed man who worships once My Jnani, gets crores of times the fruit of worshipping Me. His family is rendered pure and his mother becomes blessed. He whose heart is diluted in the all-pervading Brahma-Consciousness, purifies this whole world. There is no doubt in this.

विश्वम्भरा पुण्यवती चिल्लयो यस्य चेतसः ।
ब्रह्मज्ञानं तु यत्पृष्टं त्वया पर्वतसत्तम ॥ २०

Viśvambharā Puṇyavatī Cillayō Yasya Cētasaḥ |

Brahmakñāṉam Tu Yatpruṣṭam Tvayā Paravata Sattama || 20

Oh Himavan! I have now told everything that you asked about Brahma-Jnana. Nothing now remains to be further described.

कथितं तन्मया सर्वं नातो वक्तव्यमस्ति हि।
इदं ज्येष्ठाय पुत्राय भक्तियुक्ताय शीलिने॥ २१

Kathitam Taṉmayā Sarvam Nātō Vaktavyamasti Hi |

Idam Jyēṣṭhāya Putrāya Bhaktiyuktāya Śīliṉē || 21

This Brahma-Vidya (science of the knowledge of Brahmam) is to be imparted to the eldest son, who is devoted and of good character and to him who is endowed with the good qualities as enumerated in the Shastras and not to be given to any other person.

शिष्याय च यथोक्ताय वक्तव्यं नान्यथा क्वचित्।
यस्य देवे परा भक्तिर्यथा देवे तथा गुरौ॥ २२

Śiṣyāya Ca Yathōktāya Vaktapyam Nāṉyathā Kvacit |

Yasya Dēvē Parā Bhaktiryathā Dēvē Tathā Gurou || 22

He who is fully devoted to his Ishta Devata and who is equally devoted to his Guru, to him the high-minded persons should declare the Brahma-Vidya.

तस्यैते कथिता ह्यर्थाः प्रकाशन्ते महात्मनः।
येनोपदिष्टा विद्येयं स एव परमेश्वरः॥ २३

Tasyaitē Kathitā Hyarthāḥ Prakāśantē Mahātmaṉaḥ |

Yēṉōpadiṣṭā Vidyēyam Sa Ēva Paramēśvaraḥ || 23

Verily, he is God himself, who advises this Brahma-Vidya; no one is able to repay the debts due to him.

यस्यायं सुकृतं कर्तुमसमर्थस्ततो ऋणी।
पित्रोरप्यधिकः प्रोक्तो ब्रह्मजन्मप्रदायकः॥ २४

Yasyāyam Sukrutam Kartumasamarthastatō Ruṇī |

Pitrōramyadhikaḥ Prōktō Brahma Jaṉma Pradāyakaḥ || 24

He who gives birth to a man in Brahmam, is, no doubt, superior to the ordinary father; for the birth that a father gives is destroyed; but the birth in Brahmam that is given by the Guru is never destroyed.

पितृजातं जन्म नष्टं नेत्थं जातं कदाचन।

तस्मै न द्रुह्येदित्यादि निगमोऽप्यवदन्नग॥ २५

Pitrujātam Janma Naṣṭam Nēttham Jātam Kadācaṇa |

Tasmai Na Druhyēdityādi Nigamōpyavadaṇṇaga ǁ 25

Hence, the *Shruti* says - Never do harm to the Guru who imparts the knowledge of *Brahmam.*

तस्माच्छास्त्रस्य सिद्धान्तो ब्रह्मदाता गुरुः परः।

शिवे रुष्टे गुरुस्त्राता गुरौ रुष्टे न शङ्करः॥ २६

Tasmācchāstrasya Siddhāntō Brahmadātā Guruḥ Paraḥ |

Śivē Ruṣṭē Gurustrātā Gurau Ruṣṭē Na Śaṅkaraḥ ǁ 26

In all the Siddhantas (decided conclusion) of the Shastras, it is stated that the Guru who imparts the knowledge of Brahmam is the best and the most honourable. If Shiva, becomes angry, the Guru can save; but when the Guru becomes angry, Shankara cannot save. Consequently, the Guru should be served with the utmost care.

तस्मात्सर्वप्रयत्नेन श्रीगुरुं तोषयेन्नग।

कायेन मनसा वाचा सर्वदा तत्परो भवेत्॥ २७

Tasmāt Sarva Prayatṇēṇa Śrīgurum Tōṣayēṇṇaga |

Kāyēṇa Maṇasā Vācā Sarvadā Tatparō Bhavēt ǁ 27

Hence, the Guru must be served with all the care that are possible by body, mind and word one should always please Him. Otherwise he becomes wild and he cannot be saved.

अन्यथा तु कृतघ्नः स्यात्कृतज्ञे नास्ति निष्कृतिः ।
इन्द्रेणाथर्वणायोक्ता   शिरश्छेदप्रतिज्ञया ॥ २८

Anyathā Tu Krutaghnah Syātkrutaghnē Nāsti Niṣkrutih |

Indrēnātharvaṇāyōktā Śiraśchēda Pratiknayā || 28

अश्विभ्यां कथने तस्य शिरश्छिन्नं च वज्रिणा ।

अश्वीयं तच्छिरो नष्टं दृष्ट्वा वैद्यौ सुरोत्तमौ ॥ २९

Aśvibhyām Kathanē Tasya Śiraśchinnam Ca Vajriṇā |

Aśvīyam Tacchirō Naṣṭam Druṣṭvā Vaidyou Surōttamou || 29

पुनः संयोजितं स्वीयं ताभ्यां मुनिशिरस्तदा ।

इति संकटसम्पाद्या ब्रह्मविद्या नगाधिप ।

लब्धा येन स धन्यः स्यात्कृतकृत्यश्च भूधर ॥ ३०

Punah Samyōjitam Svīyam Tābhyām Muni Śirastadā |

Iti Saṅkaṭa Sampādyā Brahma Vidyā Nagādhipa |

Labdhā Yēna Sa Dhanyah Syātkruta Krutyaśca Bhūdhara || 30

Oh, Best of Human! It is very difficult to acquire Brahma-Jnana. Hear goes a story. A Muni named Dadhyanga of Atharvana family went to Indra and prayed to him to give Brahma-Jnana. Indra said – "I would give you Brahma-Jnana, but if you impart it to anybody else, I would sever your head". Dadhyanga agreed to this and Indra gave him the Brahma-Jnana. After a few days, the twin Ashvins came to the Muni and prayed for Brahma-Vidya. The Muni said – "If I give you the Brahma-Vidya, Indra, will cut off my head". Hearing this the two Ashvins said – "We will cut your head and keep it elsewhere and we will attach the head of a horse to your body. Instruct us with the mouth of this horse and when Indra will cut off this mouth, we will replace your former head". When they said so, the Muni gave them the Brahma-Vidya. Indra cut off his head by his thunderbolt. When the horse-head of the Muni was cut off, the two physicians of the Devas replaced his original head. This is widely known in all the Vedas.

Oh, Head of Mountains! He becomes blessed who gets this the Brahma-Vidya.

ओं श्री जगदंबार्पणमस्तु । श्री चण्डिकापरमेश्वरी प्रीयताम् ।

Ōm Śrī Jagadambārpaṇamastu |

Śrī Caṇḍikā Paramēśvarī Prīyatām |

इति श्रीमद् देवी भागवते महापुराणेऽष्टादश साहस्रयां संहितायां श्री देवी गीतायां प्रह्मविद्योपदेश वर्णनं नाम षष्टोऽध्याय: ॥

Iti Śrīmad Dēvī Bhāgavatē Mahāpurāṇēṣṣṭātaśa Sāhasrayām Samhitāyām Śrī Dēvī Gītāyām Brahma Vidyopadeśa Varṇaṇam Nāma Ṣaṣṭōdyāyaḥ ॥

Here ends the sixth Chapter of Sri Devi Gita named as Highest Knowledge of Brahmam in the Mahapuranam Shrimad Devi Bhagavatam having 18,000 verses, by Maharshi Veda Vyasa.

In *Śrīmad Nārāyanīyam* also, the 95th *Daśakam* is called as *Dyāna Yoga*.

Chapter 6 of Shrimad Bhagawad Gita – Ashtanga-yoga, a mechanical meditative practice, controls the mind and the senses and focuses concentration on Paramatma (the Super soul, the

form of the Lord situated in the heart). This practice culminates in samadhi, full consciousness of the Supreme.

Mind is subdued by constant vigorous spiritual practice with perseverance and by detachment, Oh Arjuna! (6.35) A yogi is free from all Desires, has no Attachment to (fruits of work or) anything, has no personal Selfish motive and no Doership and Ownership.

Bhakti Yogaḥ
(Devi Bhagavatam 7-37)

This is the seventh chapter of *Sri Devi Gita*. The name of the chapter itself *"Bhakti Yogaḥ"*. This is very well comparable with the 12th chapter of Shrimad Bhagawad Gita, with the same name as "Bhakti Yogaḥ".

ओं नम: चण्डिकायै । *Ōm Namaḥ Caṇḍikāyai* ।

हिमालय उवाच

स्वीयां भक्तिं वदस्वाम्ब येन ज्ञानं सुखेन हि।

जायेत मनुजस्यास्य मध्यमस्याविरागिण:॥ १

Himālaya Uvāca

Svīyām Bhaktim Vadasvāmba Yēṉa Ñāṉam Sukhēṉa Hi |

Jāyēta Maṉujasyāsya Madhyamasyāvirāgiṇaḥ ‖ 1

The Himavan said - Oh Mother! Now describe the Bhakti Yoga, by which ordinary men who have no dispassion get the knowledge of Brahmam easily.

देव्युवाच

मार्गास्त्रयो मे विख्याता मोक्षप्राप्तौ नगाधिप।

कर्मयोगो ज्ञानयोगो भक्तियोगश्च सत्तम॥ २

Dēvyuvāca

Mārgāstrayō Mē Vikyātā Mōkṣaprāptau Nagādhipa |

Karmayōgō Ñāṉayōgō Bhaktiyōgaśca Sattama ‖ 2

Sri Devi said - "Oh Chief of Mountains! There are three paths, widely known, leading to the final liberation (Moksha). These are Karma Yoga, Jnana Yoga and Bhakti Yoga.

त्रयाणामप्ययं योग्य: कर्तुं शक्योऽस्ति सर्वथा।

सुलभत्वान्मानसत्वात्कायचित्ताद्यपीडनात् ॥ ३

Trayāṇāmapyayam Yōgyaḥ Kartum Śakyōsti Sarvathā |

Sulabhatvāṉ Māṉa Satvāt Kāya Cittādya Pīḍaṉāt ॥ 3

Of these three, Bhakti Yoga is the easiest in all respects; people can do it very well without incurring any suffering to the body and bringing the mind to a perfect concentration.

गुणभेदान्मनुष्याणां सा भक्तिस्त्रिविधा मता।

परपीडां समुद्दिश्य दम्भं कृत्वा पुर:सरम्॥ ४

Guṇabhēdāṉ Maṉuṣyāṇām Sā Bhaktistrividhā Matā |

Parapīḍām Samuddhisya Dambham Krutvā PuraḥSaram ॥ 4

मात्सर्यक्रोधयुक्तो यस्तस्य भक्तिस्तु तामसी।

परपीडादिरहित: स्वकल्याणार्थमेव च॥ ५

Mātsarya Krōdha Yuktō Yastasya Bhaktistu Tāmasī |

Parapīḍāti Rahitaḥ Svakalyāṇārtamēva Ca ॥ 5

नित्यं सकामो हृदयं यशोऽर्थी भोगलोलुप:।

तत्तत्फलसमावाप्त्यै मामुपास्तेऽतिभक्तित:॥ ६

Nityam Sakāmō Hrudayam Yaśōŕthī Bhōgalōlupaḥ |

Tattatphala Samāvāptyai Māmupāstēti Bhaktitaḥ ॥ 6

भेदबुद्ध्या तु मां स्वस्मादन्यां जानाति पामर:।

तस्य भक्ति: समाख्याता नगाधिप तु राजसी ॥ ७

Bhēdabuddhyā Tu Mām Svasmādaṉyām Jāṉāti Pāmaraḥ |

Tasya Bhaktiḥ Samākhyātā Nagādhipa Tu Rājasī ॥ 7

परमेशार्पणं कर्म पापसंक्षालनाय च।

वेदोक्तत्वादवश्यं तत्कर्तव्यं तु मयानिशम्॥ ८

Paramēśārpaṇam Karma Pāpasamkṣālaṇāya Ca |

Vēgōk Tatvādavaśyam Tatkartavya Tu Mayāṇiśam || 8

इति निश्चितबुद्धिस्तु भेदबुद्धिमुपाश्रितः ।
करोति प्रीतये कर्म भक्ति: सा नग सात्त्विकी ॥ ९

Iti Niścita Buddhistu Bhēdabuddhimupāśritaḥ |

Karōti Prītayē Karma Bhaktiḥ Sā Naka Sātvikī || 9

परभक्ते: प्रापिकेयं भेदबुद्ध्यवलम्बनात् ।
पूर्वप्रोक्ते ह्युभे भक्ती न परप्रापिके मते ॥१०

Parabhaktēḥ Prāpikēyam Bhēdabuddhyavalambaṇāt |

Pūrva Prōktē Hyubhē Bhaktī Na Paraprāpikē Matē ||10

This Bhakti (devotion) again is of three kinds as the Gunas are three. His Bhakti is Tamasa who worships Me, to pain others, being filled with vanity and jealousy and anger.

That Bhakti is Rajasic, when one worships Me for one's own welfare and does not intend to do harm to others. He has got some desire or end in view, some fame or to attain some objects of enjoyments and ignorantly and thinking himself different from Me, worships Me with greatest devotion.

Again, that Bhakti is Sattvic when anybody worships Me to purify his sins and offers to Me the result of all his Karmas, thinking that Jeeva and Ishvara are separate and knowing that this action of his is authorized in the Vedas and therefore must be observed.

This Sattvic Bhakti is different from the Supreme Bhakti as the worshippers think Me separate; but it leads to the Supreme Bhakti. The other two Bhaktis do not lead to Para Bhakti (the Supreme Bhakti or the Highest unselfish Love).

अधुना परभक्तिं तु प्रोच्यमानां निबोध मे ।
मद्गुणश्रवणं नित्यं मम नामानुकीर्तनम् ॥ ११

Adhuṇā Parabhaktim Tu Prōcyamāṇām Nibōdha Mē |

Madguṇa Śravaṇam Nityam Mama Nāmāṇukīrtaṇam ‖ 11

कल्याणगुणरत्नानामाकरायां मयि स्थिरम्।

चेतसो वर्तनं चैव तैलधारासमं सदा॥१२

Kalyāṇa Guṇa Ratṇāṇāmākarāyām Mayi Sthiram |

Cētasō Vartaṇam Caiva Tailadhārāsamam Sadā ‖ 12

हेतुस्तु तत्र को वापि न कदाचिद्द्रवेदपि।

सामीप्यसार्ष्टिसायुज्यसालोक्यानां न चैषणा॥१३

Hētustu Tatra Kō Vāpi Na Kadācidbhavēdapi |

Sāmīpya Sārṣṭi Sāyujya Sālōkyāṇām Na Caiṣaṇā ‖ 13

मत्सेवातोऽधिकं किञ्चिन्नैव जानाति कर्हिचित्।

सेव्यसेवकताभावात्तत्र मोक्षं न वाञ्छति॥१४

Matsēvātōdhikam Kiñciṇṇaiva Jāṇāti Kar’hicit |

Sēvya Sēvakatā Bhāvāt Tatra Mōkṣam Nā Vāñcati ‖14

परानुरक्त्या मामेव चिन्तयेद्यो ह्यतन्द्रितः।

स्वाभेदेनैव मां नित्यं जानाति न विभेदतः॥१५

Parāṇuraktyā Māmēva Cintayēdyō Hyatandritaḥ |

Svābhēdēṇaiva Mām Nityam Jāṇāti Na Vibhēdataḥ ‖ 15

Now hear attentively about the Para-Bhakti that I am now describing to you. He who hears always My Glories and recites My Name and whose mind dwells always, like the incessant flow of oil, in Me Who is the receptacle of all auspicious qualities and Gunas. But he has not the least trace of any desire to get the fruits of his Karma; yet he does not want Saameepya, Sarshti, Saayujya and Saalokya and other forms of liberations! He becomes filled with devotion for Me alone, worships Me only; knows nothing higher than to serve Me and he does not want final liberation even. He does not like to forsake this idea of Sevya (to he served) and Sevaka (servant who serves).

He always meditates on Me with constant vigilance and actuated by a feeling of Supreme Devotion; he does not think himself separate from Me but rather thinks himself "that I am the Bhagavati". He considers all the Jeevas as Myself and loves Me as he loves himself. He does not make any difference between the Jeevas and myself as he finds the same Chaitanya everywhere and manifested in all.

मद्रूपत्वेन जीवानां चिन्तनं कुरुते तु यः।
यथा स्वस्यात्मनि प्रीतिस्तथैव च परात्मनि॥१६

Madrūpatvēṉa Jīvāṉām Cintaṉam Kurutē Tu Yaḥ |

Yathā Svasyātmaṉi Prītistathaiva Ca Parātmaṉi ‖16

चैतन्यस्य समानत्वान्न भेदं कुरुते तु यः।
सर्वत्र वर्तमानानां सर्वरूपां च सर्वदा॥१७

Caitaṉyasya Samāṉatvāṉṉa Bhēdam Kurutē Tu Yaḥ |

Sarvatra Vartamāṉām Sarvarūpām Ca Sarvadā ‖ 17

नमते यजते चैवाप्याचाण्डालान्तमीश्वर।
न कुत्रापि द्रोहबुद्धिं कुरुते भेदवर्जनात्॥१८

Namatē Yajatē Caivāpyācāṇḍālantamīśvara |

Na Kutrāpi Drōhabuddhim Kurutē Bhēdavarjaṉāt ‖18

मत्स्थानदर्शने श्रद्धा मद्भक्तदर्शने तथा।
मच्छास्त्रश्रवणे श्रद्धा मन्त्रतन्त्रादिषु प्रभो॥१९

Mat Sthāṉa Darśaṉē Śraddhā Madbhakta darśaṉē Tathā |

Macchāstra Śravaṉē Śraddhā Mantra Tantrā Diṣu Prabhō ‖ 19

मयि प्रेमाकुलमती रोमाञ्चिततनुः सदा।
प्रेमाश्रुजलपूर्णाक्षः कण्ठगद्गदनिःस्वनः॥२०

Mayi Prēmā Kulamatī Rōmāñcita Taṉuḥ Sadā |

Prēmā Śru Jala Pūrṇākṣaḥ Kaṇṭhagad Gada NiḥSvaṉaḥ ‖ 20

He does not quarrel with anybody as he has abandoned all ideas about separateness; he bows down and worships the Chandalas and all the Jeevas. He who becomes filled with devotion to Me whenever he sees My place, My devotees and hears the Shastras, describing My deeds and whenever he meditates on My Mantras, he becomes filled with the highest love and his hairs stand on their ends out of love to Me and tears of love flow incessantly from both his eyes; he recites My name and My deeds in a voice, choked with feelings of love for Me.

N.B. - The Para-Prema-Bhakti is like the maddening rush of a river to the Ocean; thence in the shape of vapour to the highest; Himalayan Mountain peaks to be congealed into snow where various plays of bright colours take place.

अनन्येनैव भावेन पूजयेद्यो नगाधिप।

मामीश्वरीं जगद्योनिं सर्वकारणकारणम्॥ २१

Ananyēṉaiva Bhāvēṉa Pūjayēdyō Nagādhipa |

Māmīśvarīm Jakadyōṉim Sarvakāraṇakāraṇam || 21

व्रतानि मम दिव्यानि नित्यनैमित्तिकान्यपि।

नित्यं यः कुरुते भक्त्या वित्तशाठ्यविवर्जितः॥ २२

Vratāṉi Mama Divyāṉi Nitya Naimittikāṉyapi |

Nityam Yaḥ Kurutē Bhaktyā Vittaśāṭhyavivarjitaḥ ||22

मदुत्सवदिद्दृक्षा च मदुत्सवकृतिस्तथा।

जायते यस्य नियतं स्वभावादेव भूधर॥ २३

Madutsavadidrukṣā Ca Madutsavakrutistathā |

Jāyatē Yasya Niyatam Svabhāvādēva Bhūdhara || 23

उच्चैर्गायंश्च नामानि ममैव खलु नृत्यति।

अहङ्कारादिरहितो देहतादात्म्यवर्जितः॥ २४

Uccairhāyamśca Nāmāṉi Mamaiva Khalu Nrutyati |

Ahaṅkārādirahitō Dēhatādātmya Varjitaḥ || 24

प्रारब्धेन यथा यच्च क्रियते तत्तथा भवेत् ।

न मे चिन्तास्ति तत्रापि देहसंरक्षणादिषु ॥ २५

Prārabdhēna Yathā Yacca Kriyatē Tattathā Bhavēt |

Na Mē Cintāsti Tatrāpi Dēha Samrakṣaṇādiṣu ॥ 25

इति भक्तिस्तु या प्रोक्ता परभक्तिस्तु सा स्मृता ।

यस्यां देव्यतिरिक्तं तु न किञ्चिदपि भाव्यते ॥ २६

Iti Bhaktistu Yā Prōktā Parabhaktistu Sā Smrutā |

Yasyām Dēvyatiriktam Tu Na Kiñcidapi Bhāvyatē ॥ 26

इत्थं जाता परा भक्तिर्यस्य भूधर तत्त्वतः ।

तदैव तस्य चिन्मात्रे मद्रूपे विलयो भवेत् ॥ २७

Ittham Jātā Parā Bhaktiryasya Bhūdhara Tatvataḥ |

Tadaiva Tasya Ciṉmāṉtra Madrūpē Vilayō Bhavēt ॥ 27

भक्तेस्तु या पराकाष्ठा सैव ज्ञानं प्रकीर्तितम् ।

वैराग्यस्य च सीमा सा ज्ञाने तदुभयं यतः ॥ २८

Bhaktēstu Yā Parākāṣṭhā Saiva Ñāṉam Prakīrtitam |

Vairāgyasya Ca Sīmā Sā Ñāṉē Tadubhayam Yataḥ ॥ 28

भक्तौ कृतायां यस्यापि प्रारब्धवशतो नग ।

न जायते मम ज्ञानं मणिद्वीपं स गच्छति ॥ २९

Bhaktou Krutāyām Yasyāpi Prārabdhavaśatō Naga |

Na Jāyatē Mama Ñāṉam Maṇidvīpam Sa Gacchati ॥ 29

तत्र गत्वाखिलान्भोगानिच्छन्नपि चच्छति ।

तदन्ते मम चिद्रूपज्ञानं सम्यग्भवेन्नग ॥ ३०

Tatra Gatvākhilāṉ bhōgāṉaṉicchaṉṉapi Carchati |

Tadantē Mama Cidrūpañāṉam Samyagbhavēṉṉaga ॥ 30

Oh Lord of the mountains! He worships Me with intense feeling as the Mother of this Universe and the Cause of all causes. He performs the daily and occasional duties and all My vows and sacrifices without showing any miserly feeling in his expenditure of money. He naturally longs to perform My festivities and to visit places where My Utsavs are held. He sings My name loudly and dances, being intoxicated with My love and has no idea of egoism and is devoid of his body-idea, thinking that the body is not his.

He thinks that whatever is Praarabdha (sins done in his previous births) must come to pass and therefore does not become agitated as to the preservation of his body and soul. This sort of Bhakti is called the Para-Bhakti or the Highest Devotion. Here the predominant idea is the idea of Sri Devi and no other idea takes its place.

Oh Mountain! He gets immediately dissolved in My Nature of Consciousness whose heart is really filled with such Para Bhakti or All Love. The sages call the limiting stage of this devotion and dispassion as Jnana (knowledge). When this Jnana arises, Bhakti and dispassion get their ends satisfied. Yea! He goes then to the Mani Dveepa, when his Ahamkara does not crop up by his Praarabdba Karma, though he did not fail to give up his life in devotion.

Oh Mountain! That man enjoys there all the objects of enjoy merits, though unwilling and at the end of the period, gets the knowledge of My Consciousness. By that he attains the Final Liberation forever. Without this Jnana, the Final Liberation is impossible.

तेन मुक्तः सदैव स्याज्ज्ञानान्मुक्तिर्न चान्यथा।

इहैव यस्य ज्ञानं स्याद्धृद्गतप्रत्यगात्मनः ॥ ३१

Tēna Muktaḥ Sadaiva Syāj Ñānān Muktirṇa Cāṇyathā |

Ihaiva Yasya Ñāṇam Syād Dhrudgata Pratyagātmaṇah ॥ 31

मम संवित्परतनोस्तस्य प्राणा व्रजन्ति न।

ब्रह्मैव संस्तदाप्नोति ब्रह्मैव ब्रह्म वेद य:॥ ३२

Mama Samvit Paratanēs Tasya Prāṇā Vrajanti Na |

Brahmaiva Sams Tadāpṇōti brahmaiva Brahma Vēda Yaḥ || 32

कण्ठचामीकरसममज्ञानात्तु   तिरोहितम्।

ज्ञानादज्ञाननाशेन लब्धमेव हि लभ्यते॥ ३३

Kaṇṭhacāmīkara Samamakñāṇāttu Tirōhitam |

Ñāṇādakñāṇa Nāśēṇa Labdhamēva Hi Labhyatē ||33

He realises Parabrahmam who gets in this body of the above Jnana of the Pratyak Atma in his heart; when his Prana leaves his body, he does not get re-birth. The Shruti says - "He, who knows Brahmam, becomes Brahmam". In the logic of Kantha Chameekara, (gold on the neck) the ignorance vanishes. When this ignorance is destroyed by knowledge, he attains all his knowledge the object to be attained, when he recognises the gold on his neck.

विदिताविदितादन्यन्नगोत्तम   वपुर्मम।

यथादर्शे तथात्मनि यथा जले तथा पितृलोके॥ ३४

Viditāviditādaṇyaṇ Nagōttama Vapurmama |

Yathādarśē Tathātmaṇi Yathā Jalē Tathā Pitrulōkē || 34

छायातपौ यथा स्वच्छौ विविक्तौ तद्वदेव हि।

मम लोके भवेज्ज्ञानं द्वैतभावविवर्जितम्॥ ३५

Chāyātapau Tathā Svacchou Viviktou Tadvadēva Hi |

Mama Lōkē Bhavējñāṇam Dvaita Bhāva Vivarjitam || 35

यस्तु वैराग्यवानेव ज्ञानहीनो म्रियेत चेत्।

ब्रह्मलोके वसेन्नित्यं यावत्कल्पं तत: परम्॥ ३६

Yastu Vairāgya Vāṉēva Ñāṉahīṉō Mriyēta Cēt |

Brahmalōkē Vasēṉnityam Yāvatkalpam Tataḥ Param ||36

शुचीनां श्रीमतां गेहे भवेत्तस्य जनिः पुनः।

करोति साधनं पश्चात्ततो ज्ञानं हि जायते॥ ३७

Śucīṉām Śrīmatām Gēhē bhavēttasya Jaṉiḥ Puṉaḥ |

Karōti Sādhaṉam Paccāttatō Ñāṉam Hi Jāyatē || 37

Oh, Best of Mountains! This My consciousness is different from the perceived pots, etc. and unperceived Maya. The image of this Paramatma is seen in bodies other than the Atma as the image falls in a mirror; as the image falls in water, so also this Paramatma is seen in the Pitrulokas. As the shadow and light are quite distinct, so in My Manidveepa, the knowledge of oneness without a second arises. That man resides in the Brahma Loka for the period of a Kalpa who leaves his body without attaining Jnana, though he had his Vairagyam. Then he takes his birth in the family of a pure prosperous family and practising again his Yoga habits, gets My Consciousness.

अनेकजन्मभी राजन् ज्ञानं स्यान्नैकजन्मना।

ततः सर्वप्रयत्नेन ज्ञानार्थं यत्नमाश्रयेत्॥ ३८

Aṉēka Jaṉmabhī Rājaṉ Ñāṉam Syāṉnaika Jaṉmaṉā |

Tataḥ Sarva Prayatṉēṉa Ñāṉārtham Yatṉamāśrayēt || 38

नोचेन्महान् विनाशः स्याजन्मैतदुर्लभं पुनः।

तत्रापि प्रथमे वर्णे वेदप्राप्तिश्च दुर्लभा॥ ३९

Nōcēṉ Mahāṉ Viṉāśaḥ Syāj Jaṉmai Tad Dhurlabham Puṉaḥ |

Tatrāpi Prathamē Varṇē Vēda Prāptiśca Durlabhā || 39

शमादिषट्कसम्पत्तिर्योगसिद्धिस्तथैव च।

तथोत्तमगुरुप्राप्तिः सर्वमेवात्र दुर्लभम्॥ ४०

Śamādi Ṣaṭka Sampattir Yōga Siddhis Tathaiva Ca |

Tathōttama Guru Prāptiḥ Sarva Mēvātra Durlabham || 40

तथेन्द्रियाणां पटुता संस्कृतत्वं तनोस्तथा।

अनेकजन्मपुण्यैस्तु मोक्षेच्छा जायते ततः॥ ४१

Tathēndriyāṇām Paṭutā Samskrutatvam Taṇōstathā |

Aṇēka Jaṇma Puṇyaistu Mōkṣēcchā Jāyatē Tataḥ ||41

साधने सफलेऽप्येवं जायमानेऽपि यो नरः।

ज्ञानार्थं नैव यतते तस्य जन्म निरर्थकम्॥ ४२

Sādhaṇē Saphalēpyēvam Jāyamāṇēpi Yō Naraḥ |

Ñāṇārtham Naiva Yatatē Tasya Jaṇma Nirarthakam || 42

तस्माद्राजन् यथाशक्त्या ज्ञानार्थं यत्नमाश्रयेत्।

पदे पदेऽश्वमेधस्य फलमाप्नोति निश्चितम्॥ ४३

Tasmād Rājaṇ Yathāśaktyā Ñāṇārtham Yatṇamāśrayēt |

Padē Padēćvamēdhasya Phalamāpṇōti Niścitam || 43

घृतमिव पयसि निगूढं भूते भूते च वसति विज्ञानम्।

सततं मन्थयितव्यं मनसा मन्थानभूतेन॥ ४४

Ghrutamiva Payasi Nigūḍam Bhūtē Bhūtē Ca Vasati Vigñāṇam |

Satatam Manthayitavyam Maṇasā Manthāṇa Bhūtēṇa || 44

ज्ञानं लब्ध्वा कृतार्थः स्यादिति वेदान्तडिण्डिमः।

सर्वमुक्तं समासेन किं भूयः श्रोतुमिच्छसि॥ ४५

Ñāṇam Labdhvā Krutārthaḥ Syāditi Vēdāntaḍiṇḍimaḥ |

Sarvamuktam Samāsēṇa Kim Bhūyaḥ Śrōtu Micchasi || 45

Oh, King of Mountains! This Jnana arises after many births it does not come in one birth; so, one should try one's best to get this Jnana. If, attaining this rare human birth, one does not attain this Jnana, know that a great calamity has befallen to him. For this human birth is very hard to attain; and then the birth in a Brahmin family is rarer; moreover, amongst the Brahmins, the knowledge of the Veda (the Consciousness is exceedingly rare). The attaining of the six qualities (which are considered as six wealth), restraint of passions, etc.; the success in Yoga and the acquisition of a pure real Guru, all these are very hard to be attained in this life.

Oh Mountain! The maturity and the activities of the organs of the senses and the purification of the body according to the Vedic rites are all very difficult to attain. Know this again that to get a desire for final liberation is acquired by the merits acquired in many births. That man's birth is entirely futile, who attaining all the above qualifications does not try his best to attain this Jnana, Hence, one should try one's best to acquire the Jnana. Then, at every moment, he gets the fruits of the Ashvamedha sacrifice. There is no doubt in this. As *ghee* resides potentially in milk, so also the Vigjnana Brahmam resides in every body. Hence make the mind the churning rod and always churn with it. Then, by slow degrees, the knowledge of Brahmam will be attained.

Man attains blessedness when he gets this Jnana; so, the Vedanta says – thus, I have described to you in brief, Oh King of Mountains! all that you wanted to hear. Now what more do you want?

ओं श्री जगदंबार्पणमस्तु । श्री चण्डिकापरमेश्वरी प्रीयताम् ।

Ōm Śrī Jagadambārpaṇamastu |

Śrī Caṇḍikā Paramēśvarī Prīyatām |

इति श्रीमद् देवी भागवते महापुराणेऽष्टादश साहस्रयां संहितायां श्री देवी गीतायां भक्तिमहिमवर्णनं नाम सप्तमोऽध्याय: ॥

Iti Śrīmad Dēvī Bhāgavatē Mahāpurāṇēṣṣṭātaśa Sāhasrayām Samhitāyām Śrī Dēvī Gītāyām Bhakti Mahima Varṇaṇam Nāma Samptamōdyāyaḥ ॥

Here ends the seventh Chapter of Sri Devi Gita named as *Bhakti Mahima Varṇaṇam Nāma* in the Mahapuranam *Shrimad Devi Bhagavatam* having 18,000 verses, by Maharshi Veda Vyasa.

In *Śrīmad Nārāyanīyam* also, the 96th *Daśakam* is called as *Bhakti Yoga.*

Shrimad Bhagavad Gita chapter 12 - Bhakti-yoga, says – pure devotional service to Lord Krishna, is the highest and most expedient means for attaining pure love for Krishna, which is the highest end of spiritual existence. Those who follow this supreme path develop divine qualities.

For the wise who seeks to attain yoga (of meditation, or the equanimity of mind), Karma Yoga is said to be the means. For the one who has attained yoga, the calmness becomes the means of Self-realization (6.03).

Those who perceive Me in everything and behold everything in Me, are not separated from Me and I am not separated from them (6.30).

Worship of a personal form of God with loving devotion is easier and faster for most people.

The five easy paths to reach God are;

1.   Focus your mind on Me,
2.   Let your intellect dwell upon Me alone through meditation and contemplation.
3.   Perform any ritual or Sadhana of your choice.
4.   Perform your duty just to serve and please Him. Work for God without any selfish motive just as an instrument.
5.   Just surrender unto My will and renounce the attachment to and the anxiety for the fruits of all work with subdued mind - by learning to accept all results, as God's grace with calmness.

One should sincerely try to develop divine qualities discussed in lot many other verses especially 2.55-59, 5.18-26, 6.27-32, 12.13-20, 13.07-11, 14.22-25 and 16.01-03.

Shrimad Vishnu Bhagavatam (7.5.23), through the voice of Prahalada describes 9 types of devotion (bhakti).

Shravaranam	Hearing
Keertanam	Reading
Smraranam	Thinking
Paada Sevanam	Worshipping Lotus feet

Archanam	Namavali
Vandanam	Praying
Daasyam	Submitting
Shakyam	Friendship
Atma Nivedhanam	Surrendering

∾∾○∾∾

Virata Festivals of *Sri Devi*
(Devi Bhagavatam 7-38)

This is the eighth chapter of *Sri Devi Gita*. The name of the chapter is *"Sri Devi Virata Mahotsava"*. This explains different festivals and *vratams* of *Sri Devi*. Details about the different dwelling places of Sri Devi, mostly within India, are also given.

ॐ नम: चण्डिकायै । *Ōm Namaḥ Caṇḍikāyai* ।

हिमालय उवाच

कति स्थानानि देवेशि द्रष्टव्यानि महीतले।

मुख्यानि च पवित्राणि देवीप्रियतमानि च॥१

Himālaya Uvāca

Kati Sthāṉāṉi Dēvēśi Draṣṭavyāṉi Mahītalē |

Mukhyāṉi Ca Pavitrāṇi Dēvī Priyatamāṉi Ca ॥ 1

व्रतान्यपि तथा यानि तुष्टिदान्युत्सवा अपि।

तत्सर्वं वद मे मातः कृतकृत्यो यतो नरः॥२

Vratāṉyapi Tathā Yāṉi Tuṣṭidāṉyusavā Api |

Tatsarvam Vada Mē Mātaḥ Krutakrutyō Yatō Naraḥ ॥ 2

The Himavan said - "On this earth that are prominent, sacred and worth visiting and which you are the best. Oh Mother! Also sanctify us by describing the vows (vratams) and utsavs that are pleasing to Thee and by performing which, men become blessed and get themselves satisfied.

देव्युवाच

सर्वं दृश्यं मम स्थानं सर्वे काला व्रतात्मका:।

उत्सवा: सर्वकालेषु यतोऽहं सर्वरूपिणी॥३

Dēvyuvāca

Sarvam Druśyam Mama Sthāṉam Sarvē Kālā Vrātmakāḥ |

Utsavāḥ Sarvakālēṣu Yatōham Sarva Rūpiṇī ॥ 3

तथापि भक्तवात्सल्यात्किञ्चित्किञ्चिदथोच्यते ।

शृणुष्वावहितो भूत्वा नगराज वचो मम ॥ ४

Tathāpi Bhakta Vātsalyāt Kiñcit Kiñcidathōcyatē |

Śruṇuṣvāvahitō Bhūtvā Nagarāja Vacō Mama || 4

कोलापुरं महास्थानं यत्र लक्ष्मीः सदा स्थिता ।

मातुःपुरं द्वितीयं च रेणुकाधिष्ठितं परम् ॥ ५

Kōlāpuram Mahāsthānam Yatra Lakṣmīḥ Sadā Stitā |

Mātuḥ Puram Dvītīyam Ca Rēṇukādhiṣṭhitam Param || 5

तुलजापुरं तृतीयं स्यात्सप्तशृङ्गं तथैव च ।

हिङ्गुलाया महास्थानं ज्वालामुख्यास्तथैव च ॥ ६

Tulajāpuram Trutīyam Syāt Sapta Śruṅgam Tathaiva Ca |

Hiṅgulāyā Mahāsthānam Jvālā Mukhyāstathaiva Ca || 6

शाकम्भर्याः परं स्थानं भ्रामर्याः स्थानमुत्तमम् ।

श्रीरक्तदन्तिकास्थानं दुर्गास्थानं तथैव च ॥ ७

Śākambharyāḥ Param Sthāṇam Bhrāmaryāḥ Sthāṇa Muttamam |

Śrīrakta Dantikāsthāṇam Durgāsthāṇam Tathaiva Ca || 7

विन्ध्याचलनिवासिन्याः स्थानं सर्वोत्तमोत्तमम् ।

अन्नपूर्णामहास्थानं काञ्चीपुरमनुत्तमम् ॥ ८

Vindhyācala Nivāsinyāḥ Sthāṇam Sarvōttamōttamam |

Aṇṇapūrṇā Mahāsthāṇam Kāñcīpuramaṇuttamam || 8

भीमादेव्या परं स्थानं विमलास्थानमेव च ।

श्रीचन्द्रलामहास्थानं कौशिकीस्थानमेव च ॥ ९

Śrīmādēvyā Param Sthāṇam Vimalāsthāṇamēva Ca |

Śrīcandralā Mahā Sthāṇam Kauśikī Sthāṇamēva Ca || 9

नीलाम्बायाः परं स्थानं नीलपर्वतमस्तके ।

जाम्बूनदेश्वरीस्थानं तथा श्रीनगरं शुभम् ॥ १०

Nīlāmbāyāḥ Param Sthāṉam Nīla Parvatamastakē |

Jāmbūṉa Dēśvarī Sthāṉam Tathā Śrīnagaram Śubham ǁ 10

Sri Devi spoke - "Oh Himavan! All the places that are on this earth are all Mine and all should be visited. And every moment is fit for taking vratas and utsavas. For I am of the nature pervading every moment; so whatever actions are performed at any moment are all equal to taking My vratas and utsavas.

Oh, King of Mountains! Still I am now telling something out of My affection to My Bhaktas. Hear.

- There is a great place of pilgrimage named Kolhapur in the southern country. Here Sri Devi Lakshmi always dwells.
- The second place is Matripura in the Sahyadri mountain; here Sri Devi Renuka dwells.
- The third place is Tulajapur;
- Next is the place Saptashringa, the great places of Hingula and Jvala Mukhee.
- Then the great places of Shakambhari, Bhraamari, Sri Raktadantika and Durga.
- The best of all places is that of Vindhyachala Vasini, the great places of Annapurna and the excellent Kanchipuram.
- Next come the places of Bhima Devi, Vimala Devi, Shri Chandrakala Devi of Karnataka and the place of Kaushiki.
- Then the great place of Nilamba on the top of the Nilaparvata, the place of Jambunadeshvari and the beautiful Srinagar.

गुह्यकाल्या महास्थानं नेपाले यत्रप्रतिष्ठितम् ।

मीनाक्ष्याः परमं स्थानं यच्च प्रोक्तं चिदम्बरे ॥ ११

Guhyakālyā Mahāsthāṉam Nēpālē Yat Pratiṣṭhitam |

Mīṉākṣyāḥ Paramam Stāṉam Yacca Prōktam Cidambarē ǁ 11

वेदारण्यं महास्थानं सुन्दर्याः समधिष्ठितम् ।

एकाम्बरं महास्थानं परशक्त्या प्रतिष्ठितम् ॥ १२

Vēdāraṇyam Mahāsthāṉam Sundaryāḥ Samadhiṣṭhitam |
Ēkāmbaram Mahāsthāṉam Paraśaktyā Pratiṣṭhitam || 12

महालसा परं स्थानं योगेश्वर्यास्तथैव च।
तथा नीलसरस्वत्याः स्थानं चीनेषु विश्रुतम्॥ १३

Mahālasā Param Sthāṉam Yōgēśvaryās Tathaiva Ca |
Tathā Nīla Sarasvatyāḥ Sthāṉam Cīṉēṣu Viśrutam || 13

वैद्यनाथे तु बगलास्थानं सर्वोत्तमं मतम्।
श्रीमच्छ्रीभुवनेश्वर्या मणिद्वीपं मम स्मृतम्॥ १४

Vaidyanāthē Tu Bagalā Sthāṉam Sarvōttamam Matam |
Śrīmacchrī Bhuvaṉēśvaryā Maṇidvīpam Mama Smrutam || 14

श्रीमत्रिपुरभैरव्याः कामाख्यायोनिमण्डलम्।
भूमण्डले क्षेत्ररत्नं महामायाधिवासितम्॥ १५

Śrīmat Tripura Bhairavyāḥ Kāmākhyā Yōṉi Maṇḍalam |
Bhūmaṇḍalē Kṣētraraṉam Mahāmāyādhivāsitam || 15

नातः परतरं स्थानं क्वचिदस्ति धरातले।
प्रतिमासं भवेद्देवी यत्र साक्षाद्रजस्वला॥ १६

Nātaḥ Parataram Sthāṉam Kvacidasti Dharātalē |
Pratimāsam Bhavēddhēvī Yatra Sākṣād Rajasvalā || 16

तत्रत्या देवताः सर्वाः पर्वतात्मकतां गताः।
पर्वतेषु वसन्त्येव महत्यो देवता अपि॥ १७

Tatratyā Dēvatāḥ Sarvāḥ Parvatātmakatām Gatāḥ |
Parvatēṣu Vasantyēva Mahatyō Dēvatā Api || 17

तत्रत्या पृथिवी सर्वा देवीरूपा स्मृता बुधैः।
नातः परतरं स्थानं कामाख्यायोनिमण्डलात्॥ १८

Tatratyā Pruthivī Sarvā Dēvī Rūpā Smrutā Bhutaiḥ |
Nātaḥ Parataram Sthāṉam Kāmākyāyōṉi Maṇḍalāt || 18

गायत्र्याश्च परं स्थानं श्रीमत्पुष्करमीरितम् ।
अमरेशे चण्डिका स्यात्प्रभासे पुष्करेक्षिणी ॥ १९

Gāyatrayāśca Param Sthānam Śrīmatpuṣkaramīritam |

Amarēśē Caṇḍikā Syāt Prabhāsē Puṣkarēkṣiṇī ॥ 19

नैमिषे तु महास्थाने देवी सा लिङ्गधारिणी ।
पुरुहूता पुष्कराक्षे आषाढौ च रतिस्तथा ॥ २०

Naimiṣē Tu Mahāsthānē Dēvī Sā Liṅga Dhāriṇī |

Purūhūtā Puṣkarākṣē Āṣāḍou Ca Ratistathā ॥ 20

- The great place of Shri Guhya Kali, well established in Nepal and that of Shri Meenakshi Devi established in Chidambaram[3].
- The great place named Vedaranya where the Sundari Devi is residing;
- Then the place named Ekambaram and
- The place Bhuvaneshvara near Purushottama where I always dwell as Para Shakti Bhuvaneshvari*.
- The famous place of Mahalasa, known in the south by the name Mallari;
- The place of Yogeshvari Varat and the widely known place of Neela Sarasvati[4] in China.
- The excellent place of Bagalamukhee* in Baidyanath
- The supreme place Manidveepa of Shri Bhuvaneshvari where I always reside.
- The Yonimandala Kamakhya, the place of Shri Tripura Bhariavi*,
- The excellent of all the places in this earth, where Sri Devi Maha-Maya always dwells.

The sages say - That all these places are of the nature of Sri Devi;

---

[3] Madurai Meenakshi is only referred here. Probably at that time, when this text was written, Madurai should have been within the area of Chidambaram.

[4] * Neela Saraswati, Bagalamuki, Bhuvaneshwari, Tripura Bhairavi, are all Goddesses within Dasha Maha Vidya.

- There is no better place than this Kamakhya Yonimaindala.
- Pushkara, the sacred place, is the seat of Gayatri;
- The place of Chandika in Amaresha: and
- The excellent place of Pushkarekshini in Frabhasa.
- The place of Linga-Dhaarini Devi in Naimisaranya and
- The place of Purubuta in Puskaraksha;
- Rati Devi dwells in Asadhi.

There is no other place better than this on the earth. Here Sri Devi becomes every month in Her course of menstruation and where the virtuous men are seen. Here all the Devas remain in the form of mountains and where on the mountains the excellent Devas inhabit.

चण्डमुण्डी महास्थाने दण्डिनी परमेश्वरी।
भारभूतौ भवेद्भूतिर्नाकुले नकुलेश्वरी॥ २१

Caṇḍamuṇḍī Mahāsthāṉē Daṇḍiṉī Paramēśvarī |

Bhārabhūtou Bhavētbhūtirnākulē Nakulēśvarī || 21

चन्द्रिका तु हरिश्चन्द्रे श्रीगिरौ शाङ्करी स्मृता।
जप्येश्वरे त्रिशूला स्यात्सूक्ष्मा चाम्रातकेश्वरे॥ २२

Candrikā Tu Hariścandrē Śrīgirou Śaṅkarī Smrutā |

Japyēśvarē Triśūlā Syātsūkṣmā Cāmrātakēśvarē || 22

शाङ्करी तु महाकाले शर्वाणी मध्यमाभिधे।
केदाराख्ये महाक्षेत्रे देवी सा मार्गदायिनी॥ २३

Śaṅkarī Tu Mahākālē Śarvāṇī Madhyamābhidhē |

Kēdārākyē Mahākṣētrē Dēvī Sā Mārgadāyiṉī || 23

भैरवाख्ये भैरवी सा गयायां मङ्गला स्मृता।
स्थाणुप्रिया कुरुक्षेत्रे स्वायम्भुव्यपि नाकुले॥ २४

Bhairavākhyē Bhairavī Sā Gayāyām Maṅgalā Smrutā |

Sthāṇupriyā Kurukṣētē Svāyambhuvyapi Nākulē || 24

कनखले भवेदुग्रा विश्वेशा विमलेश्वरे।
अट्टहासे महानन्दा महेन्द्रे तु महान्तका॥ २५

Kaṇakhalē Bhavēdugrā Viśvēśā Vimalēśvarē |
Aṭṭahāsē Mahāṇandā Mahēndrē Tu Mahāntakā || 25

भीमे भीमेश्वरी प्रोक्ता स्थाने वस्त्रापथे पुनः।
भवानी शाङ्करी प्रोक्ता रुद्राणी त्वर्धकोटिके॥ २६

Bhīmē Bhīmēśvarī Prōktā Sthāṇē Vastrāpathē Puṇaḥ |
Bhavāṇī Śāṅkarī Prōktā Rudrāṇī Tvardhakōṭikē || 26

अविमुक्ते विशालाक्षी महाभागा महालये।
गोकर्णे भद्रकर्णी स्याद्भद्रा स्याद्भद्रकर्णके॥ २७

Avimuktē Viśālākṣī Mahābhāgā Mahālayē |
Gōkarṇē Bhatrakarṇī Syādbhadrā Syād Bhadrakarṇakē || 27

उत्पलाक्षी सुवर्णाक्षे स्थाण्वीशा स्थाणुसंज्ञके।
कमलालये तु कमला प्रचण्डा छगलण्डके॥ २८

Utpalākṣī Suvarṇākṣē Sthāṇvīśā Sthāṇu Saṅkñakē |
Kamalālayē Tu Kamalā Pracaṇḍā Chagalaṇḍakē || 28

कुरण्डले त्रिसन्ध्या स्यान्माकोटे मुकुटेश्वरी।
मण्डलेशे शाण्डकी स्यात्काली कालञ्जरे पुनः॥ २९

Kuraṇḍalē Trisandhyā Syāṇmākōṭē Mukuṭēśvarī |
Maṇḍalēśē Śāṇḍakī Syātkālī Kālañjarē Puṇaḥ || 29

शङ्कुकर्णे ध्वनिः प्रोक्ता स्थूला स्यात्स्थूलकेश्वरे।
ज्ञानिनां हृदयाम्भोजे ह्ल्लेखा परमेश्वरी॥ ३०

Śaṅkukarṇē Dhvaṇiḥ Prōktā Sthūlā Syāt Sthūla Kēśvarē |
Ñāṇiṇām Hrudayāmbhōjē Hrullēkhā Paramēśvarī || 30

- Dandini Parameshvari dwells in Chandamundi.

- Bhuti dwells in Bharabhuti; and
- Nakuleshvari dwells in Nakula.
- Chandrika dwells in Harishchandra;
- Shankari in Sringeri;
- Trishula in Japeshvara; and
- Sukshma in Amrata Keshvara.
- Shankari dwells in Ujjain,
- Sharvani in the place Madhyama and
- Marga Dayini dwells in the holy Kshetra Kedara.
- The celebrated Bhairavi dwells in the place named Bhairava;
- Mangala in Gaya Kshettra;
- Sthanupriya in Kurukshetra; and
- Svayambhuvi Devi dwells in Nakula;
- Ugra dwells in Kankhal;
- Vishvesa dwells in Vimaleshvara,
- Mahananda in Attahasa and
- Mahantaka in Mahendra.
- Bhimeshvari dwells in Bhima;
- The Bhavani Shankari dwells in Vastrapadma; and
- Rudrani in Ardha Koti.
- Visalakshi dwells in Avimukta (Banaras);
- Mahabhaga dwells in Mahalaya;
- Bhadrakarni in Gokarna; and
- Bhadra resides in Bhadrakarnak;
- Utpalakshi dwells in Suvarnaksha;
- Sthanavisha in Sthanu;
- Kamala in Kamalalaya;
- Chanda in Chhagalandaka, situated in the south near the sea coast.
- Trisandhya dwells in Kurundala;
- Mukuteshvari in Makota;
- Shandaki in Mandalesha;
- Kali in Kalanjara;
- Dhvani in Shankukarna;
- Sthula in Sthulakeshvara; and
- Parameshvari Hrullekha dwells in the heart lotuses of the Jnanins.

प्रोक्तानीमानि स्थानानि देव्याः प्रियतमानि च।

तत्तत्क्षेत्रस्य माहात्म्यं श्रुत्वा पूर्वं नगोत्तम॥ ३१

Prōktāṉīmāṉi Sthāṉāṉi Dēvyāḥ Priyatamāṉi Ca |

Tattatkṣētrasya Māhātmyam Śrutvā Pūrvam Nagōttama ‖ 31

तदुक्तेन विधानेन पश्चाद्देवीं प्रपूजयेत्।

अथवा सर्वक्षेत्राणि काश्यां सन्ति नगोत्तम॥ ३२

Taduktēṉa Vidhāṉēṉa Paścād Dēvīm Prapūjayēt |

Athavā Sarvakṣētrāṇi Kācyām Santi Nagōttama ‖ 32

अतस्तत्र वसेन्नित्यं देवीभक्तिपरायणः।

तानि स्थानानि सम्पश्यञ्जपन्देवीं निरन्तरम्॥ ३३

Atas Tatra Vasēṉ Nityam Dēvī Bhakti Parāyaṇaḥ |

Tāṉi Sthāṉāṉi Sampaśyañ Japaṉ Dēvīm Nirantaram ‖ 33

ध्यायंस्तच्चरणाम्भोजं मुक्तो भवति बन्धनात्।

इमानि देवीनामानि प्रातरुत्थाय यः पठेत्॥ ३४

Dhyāyams Taccaraṇām Bhōjam Muktō Bhavati Bandhaṉāt |

Imāṉi Dēvīṉāmāṉi Prātarutthāya Yaḥ Paṭhēt ‖ 34

The places mentioned above are all dearest to Sri Devi. First the merits of these places are to be heard; next Sri Devi is to be worshipped by the rites and ceremonies according to the prescribed rules.

Or - Oh Mountain! All the holy places of pilgrimages exist in Kashi. Sri Devi always dwells there. Persons, devoted to Sri Devi, see these places and if they make Japam and meditate on the lotus-feet of Sri Devi, they will certainly be freed from the bonds of Samsara; there is no doubt in this. If anybody, getting up in the morning, recite the names of these places, all his sins would instantly be burnt away.

भस्मीभवन्ति पापानि तत्क्षणान्नग सत्वरम्।
श्राद्धकाले पठेदेतान्यमलानि द्विजाग्रतः ॥ ३५

Bhasmī Bhavanti Pāpāni Tatkṣaṇānnaga Satvaram |
Śrāddhakālē Paṭhēdētānyamalāni Dvijāgrataḥ || 35

And if one reads, in the time of Shraddha, before the Brahmins, these holy names of Sri Devi, his Pitrus will be purified of their sins in the Mahakasha by the Maha Prana and will get their highest goal.

मुक्तास्तत्पितरः सर्वे प्रयान्ति परमां गतिम्।
अधुना कथयिष्यामि व्रतानि तव सुव्रत ॥ ३६

Muktāstatpitaraḥ Sarvē Prayānti Paramām Gatim |
Adhunā Kathayiṣyāmi Vratāni Tava Suvrata || 36

नारीभिश्च नरैश्चैव कर्तव्यानि प्रयत्नतः।
व्रतमनन्ततृतीयाख्यं रसकल्याणिनीव्रतम् ॥ ३७

Nārībhiśca Naraiścaiva Kartavyāni Prayatnataḥ |
Vratamananta Trutīyākhyam Rasakalyāṇi Nīvratam || 37

आर्द्रानन्दकरं नाम्ना तृतीयाया व्रतं च यत्।
शुक्रवारव्रतं चैव तथा कृष्णाचतुर्दशी ॥ ३८

Ārdrā Nandakaram Nāmnā Trutīyāyā Vratam Ca Yat |
Śukravāra Vratam Caiva Tathā Kruṣṇa Caturdaśī || 38

भौमवारव्रतं चैव प्रदोषव्रतमेव च।
यत्र देवो महादेवो देवीं संस्थाप्य विष्टरे ॥ ३९

Bhoumavāra Vratam Caiva Pradōṣa Vratamēva Ca |
Yatra Dēvō Mahādēvō Dēvīm Samsthāpya Viṣṭarē || 39

नृत्यं करोति पुरतः सार्धं देवैर्निशामुखे।
तत्रोपोष्य रजन्यादौ प्रदोषे पूजयेच्छिवाम् ॥ ४०

Nrutyam Karōti Puratah Sārdham Dēvair Niśāmukhē |

Tatrō Pōṣya Rajanyādou Pradōṣē Pūjayēcchivām ॥ 40

Oh, king of Mountains! I will now describe to you the vratas that are to be carefully observed by men and women; hear.

Ananta Tritiya Vrata (vow), Rasakalyani Vrata and Arudra Vrata, these three Vratas are to be observed in the Tritiya (third) tithi. The next come the Friday vrata, the Krishna Chaturdashi vratas, the Tuesday vrata and the evening twilight (pradosha) vrata. In this twilight vow, Maha Deva placed Sri Devi in the evening on a high Asana; and He, along with the other Devas, began to dance before Her. Fasting is enjoined in this vrata; and then in the evening one must worship Sri Devi, the Giver of all auspicious things. Especially in every fortnight, if Sri Devi be worshipped, she gets extremely pleased.

प्रतिपक्षं विशेषेण तद्देवीप्रीतिकारकम्।

सोमवारव्रतं चैव ममातिप्रियकृन्नग ॥ ४१

Pratipakṣam Viśēṣēṇa Taddēvī Prītikārakam |

Sōmavāravratam Caiva Mamāti Priyakruṇṇaga ॥ 41

Oh, Best of Mountains! The Monday vrata is very much agreeable to Me; the worship of Sri Devi should be done and then only in the night one must take one's food.

तत्रापि देवीं सम्पूज्य रात्रौ भोजनमाचरेत्।

नवरात्रद्वयं चैव व्रतं प्रीतिकरं मम ॥ ४२

Tatrāpi Dēvīm Sampūjya Rātrau Bhōjanamācarēt |

Navarātra dvayam Caiva Vratam Prītikaram Mama ॥ 42

एवमन्यान्यपि विभो नित्यनैमित्तिकानि च।

व्रतानि कुरुते यो वै मत्प्रीत्यर्थं विमत्सरः ॥ ४३

Ēvamanyānyapi Vibhō Nityanaimittikāni Ca |

Vratāṇi Kurutē Yō Vai Matprītyartham Vimatsarah ॥ 43

The two nine nights vratas called Navaratri are to be observed, one in the autumn and the other in the spring season. These are very dear to Me. He is certainly My devotee and very dear who for My satisfaction performs these and the other Nitya Naimittika vratas, free from any pride and jealousy. He certainly gets the Sayujya Mukti with Me.

प्राप्नोति मम सायुज्यं स मे भक्तः स मे प्रियः।

उत्सवानपि कुर्वीत दोलोत्सवमुखान्विभो ॥ ४४

Prāpṇōti Mama Sāyujyam Sa Mē Baktaḥ Sa Mē Priyaḥ |

Utsavāṇapi Kurvīta Dōlōtsava Mukhāṇivibhō ॥ 44

शयनोत्सवं तथा कुर्यात्तथा जागरणोत्सवम्।

रथोत्सवं च मे कुर्याद्दमनोत्सवमेव च ॥ ४५

Śayaṇōtsavam Tathā Kuryāttathā Jāgaraṇōtsavam |

Rathōtsavam Ca Mē Kuryāddamaṇōtsavamēva Ca ॥ 45

पवित्रोत्सवमेवापि श्रावणे प्रीतिकारकम्।

मम भक्तः सदा कुर्यादेवमन्यान्महोत्सवान् ॥ ४६

Pavitrōtsavamēvāpi Śrāvaṇē Prītikārakam |

Mama Bhaktaḥ Sadā Kuryā Dēva Maṇyāṇ Mahōtsavāṇ ॥ 46

Oh Raja! The Holy (Dol) festival in the month of Chaitra on the third day of the white fortnight is very pleasing to Me and should be observed by all. My devotees perform

- The Shayanotsava[5] in the full Moon day in the month of Ashadha;
- The Jagaranotsava* in the full Moon day in the month of Kartikai,
- The Ratha Jatra in the 3rd of the bright fortnight in Ashadha;
- The Damanotsava in month of Chaitra.

---

[5] * Shayanam is to lie down. Jagrath is to wake up.

- And my dear festivals in the month of Shravana and various other festivals.

मद्भक्तान्भोजयेत्प्रीत्या तथा चैव सुवासिनीः ।

कुमारीर्वटुकांश्चापि मद्बुद्ध्या तद्गतान्तरः ॥ ४७

Madbhaktān Bhōjayēt Prītyā Tathā Caiva Suvāsiṇīḥ |

Kumārīr Vaṭukāmccāpi Madbuddhyā Tadgatāntaraḥ || 47

वित्तशाठ्येन रहितो यजेदेतान्सुमादिभिः ।

य एवं कुरुते भक्त्या प्रतिवर्षमतन्द्रितः ॥ ४८

Vittaśāṭhyēṇa Rahitō Yajēdētāṇ Sumādibhiḥ |

Ya Ēvam Kurutē Bhaktyā Prati Varṣamatantritaḥ || 48

स धन्यः कृतकृत्योऽसौ मत्प्रीतेः पात्रमञ्जसा ।

सर्वमुक्तं समासेन मम प्रीतिप्रदायकम् ।

नाशिष्याय प्रदातव्यं नाभक्ताय कदाचन॥ ४९

Sa Dhaṇyaḥ Kruta Krutyōṣau Matprītēḥ Pātra Mañjasā |

Sarvamuktam Samāsēṇa Mama Prīti Pradāyakam |

Nāśiṣyāya Pradātavyam Nābhaktāya Kadācaṇa || 49

In all these festivals one should feast well with gladness all My devotees and the Kumaris (virgins), well clothed and dressed and the boys, thinking them all to be of My very nature. No miserliness is to be entertained and I should be worshipped with flowers, etc. He is blessed and attains his goal and is dear to Me who carefully and devotedly observes every year all these festivals.

Oh Nagendra! Thus, I have described to you in brief all the vows that are pleasing to Me. These instructions Share not to be given who is not a disciple nor to one who is not My devotee.

ॐ श्री जगदंबार्पणमस्तु । श्री चण्डिकापरमेश्वरी प्रीयताम् ।

Ōm Śrī Jagadambārpaṇamastu I

Śrī Caṇḍikā Paramēśvarī Prīyatām I

इति श्रीमद् देवी भागवते महापुराणेऽष्टादश साहस्रयां संहितायां श्री देवी गीतायांश्री देव्या महोत्सव व्रत स्तानवर्णनं नाम अष्टमोऽध्याय: ॥

Iti Śrīmad Dēvī Bhāgavatē Mahāpurāṇēऽṣṭātaśa Sāhasrayām Samhitāyām Śrī Dēvī Gītāyām Sri Devyā Mahotsava Vrata Stāna Varṇaṉam Nāma Aṣṭamōऽdyāyaḥ II

Here ends the eighth Chapter of Sri Devi Gita named as *Śrī Dēvī Mahotsava Vrata* in the Mahapuranam *Shrimad Devi Bhagavatam* having 18,000 verses, by Maharshi Veda Vyasa.

Devi Pooja Vidhi
(Devi Bhagavatam 7-39)

This is the nineth chapter of *Sri Devi Gita*. The name of the chapter itself *"Sri Devi Devyā Pūja Vidhi Varṇaṇam"*. This explains the processes of performing pujas to *Sri Devi*.

ओं नम: चण्डिकायै । *Ōm Namaḥ Caṇḍikāyai* ।

हिमालय उवाच

देवदेवि महेशानि करुणासागरेऽम्बिके।
ब्रूहि पूजाविधिं सम्यग्यथावदधुना निजम्॥ १

Himālaya Uvāca

Dēvadēvi Mahēśāṇi Karuṇāsāgarēmbikē ।

Brūhi Pūjāvidhim Samyagyathāvadadhuṇā Nijam ॥ 1

The Himalayas said - Oh Devi! Oh Maheshwari! Oh Thou, the Ocean of Mercy! Oh World-Mother! Now describe in detail how Thy worship is conducted, the rules and ceremonials thereof.

श्रीदेव्युवाच

वक्ष्ये पूजाविधिं राजन्नम्बिकाया यथाप्रियम्।
अत्यन्तश्रद्धया सार्धं शृणु पर्वतपुङ्गव॥ २

Śrī Dēvyuvāca

Vakṣyē Pūjāvidhim Rājaṇṇambikāyā Yathāpriyam ।

Atyanta Śraddhayā Sārdham Śruṇu Parvata Puṅgava ॥ 2

द्विविधा मम पूजा स्याद् बाह्या चाभ्यन्तरापि च।
बाह्यापि द्विविधा प्रोक्ता वैदिकी तान्त्रिकी तथा॥ ३

Dvividhā Mama Pūjā Syād Bāhyā Cābhyantarāpi Ca ।

Bāhyāpi Dvividhā Prōktā Vaidikī Tāntrikī Tathā ॥ 3

वैदिक्यर्चापि द्विविधा मूर्तिभेदेन भूधर।

वैदिकी वैदिकैः कार्या वेददीक्षासमन्वितैः ॥ ४

Vaidikyarcāpi Dvividhā Mūrtibhēdēṉa Bhūdhara |

Vaidikī Vaidikaiḥ Kāryā Vēdadīkṣā Samaṉvitaiḥ ॥ 4

तन्त्रोक्तदीक्षावद्भिस्तु तान्त्रिकी संश्रिता भवेत्।

इत्थं पूजारहस्यं च न ज्ञात्वा विपरीतकम् ॥ ५

Tantrōkta Dīkṣā Vadbhistu Tāntrikī Samśritā Bhavēt |

Ittham Pūjā Rahasyam Ca Na Ñātvā Viparītakam ॥ 5

Sri Devi said – Oh King of Mountains! I will now describe to you the rites and ceremonies and the methods of My worship that are pleasing to Me. Hear it attentively and with faith.

- My worship is of two kinds – External and internal.
- The external worship is again twofold – one is Vaidik and the other is Tantric.
- The Vaidik worship is also of two kinds according to the differences in My forms.

Those who are initiated in the Vedic Mantrams worship according to the Vedic rites and ceremonies and those who are initiated in the Tantric-Mantra worship; according to the Tantric rites.

That stupid man, who knowing the secrets of worship, act contrary to them, is entirely ruined and goes to Hell.

First, I will describe to you the Vaidik worship; hear.

The below 2 names of Sri Lalita Sahasranama is worth comparable here;

- 870th name – Antarmukhasamārādhyā – अन्तर्मुख समाराध्या – One who is well adored by those who are inward looking.

- 871st name -- Bahirmukhasudurlabhā – बहिर्मुख सुदुर्लभा – One who is rare for those whose mental gaze goes on outward things.

करोति यो नरो मूढः स पतत्येव सर्वथा।
तत्र या वैदिकी प्रोक्ता प्रथमा तां वदाम्यहम्॥ ६

Karōti Yo Narō Mūḍaḥ Sa Patatyēva Sarvathā |
Tatra Yā Vaidikī Prōktā Prathamā Tām Vadāmyaham || 6

यन्मे साक्षात्परं रूपं दृष्टवानसि भूधर।
अनन्तशीर्षनयनमनन्तचरणं महत्॥ ७

Yaṉmē Sākṣātparam Rūpam Drustavāṉasi Bhūdhara |
Aṉanta Śīrṣa Nayaṉamaṉanta Caraṇam Mahat || 7

सर्वशक्तिसमायुक्तं प्रेरकं यत्परात्परम्।
तदेव पूजयेन्नित्यं नमेद् ध्यायेत्स्मरेदपि॥ ८

Sarvaśakti Samāyuktam Prēkam Yatparātparam |
Tadēva Pūjayēṉnityam Namēd Dhyāyēt Smarēdapi || 8

इत्येतत्प्रथमाचार्याः स्वरूपं कथितं नग।
शान्तः समाहितमना दम्भाहङ्कारवर्जितः॥ ९

Ityētat Prathamārcāyāḥ Svarūpam Kathitam Naga |
Śāntaḥ Samāhitamaṉā Dambhāhaṅkāra Varjitaḥ || 9

तत्परो भव तद्याजी तदेव शरणं व्रज।
तदेव चेतसा पश्य जप ध्यायस्व सर्वदा॥ १०

Tatparō Bhava Tadyājī Tadēva Śaraṇam Vraja |
Tadēva Cētasā Paśya Japa Dhyāyasva Sarvadā || 10

अनन्यया प्रेमयुक्तभक्त्या मद्भावमाश्रितः।
यज्ञैर्यज तपोदानैर्मामेव परितोषय॥ ११

Ananyayā Prēmayukta Bhaktyā Madbhāvamāśritaḥ |

Yañairyaja Tapōdānair Māmēva Paritōṣaya ‖ 11

Shrimad Bhagawad Gita (9.22) also says, those who worship Me with devotion, without any other thinking (*ananya chinta*) meditating on My transcendental form, I carry what they lack and preserve what they have.

इत्थं ममानुग्रहतो मोक्ष्यसे भवबन्धनात् ।

मत्परा ये मदासक्तचित्ता भक्तवरा मताः ॥ १२

Ittham Mamānugrahatō Mōkṣyasē Bhava Bandhanāt |

Matparā Yē Madā Sakta Cittā Bhaktavarā Matāḥ ‖ 12

प्रतिजाने भवादस्मादुद्धराम्यचिरेण तु ।

ध्यानेन कर्मयुक्तेन भक्तिज्ञानेन वा पुनः ॥ १३

Pratijānē Bhavādasmāduddharāmyacirēṇa Tu |

Dhyānēna Karmayuktēna Bhakti Ñānēna Vā Puṇaḥ ‖ 13

प्राप्याहं सर्वथा राजन्न तु केवलकर्मभिः ।

धर्मात्सञ्जायते भक्तिर्भक्त्या सञ्जायते परम् ॥ १४

Prāpyāham Sarvathā Rājanna Tu Kēvala Karmabhiḥ |

Dharmāt Sañjāyatē Bhaktir Bhaktyā Sañjāyatē Param ‖ 14

श्रुतिस्मृतिभ्यामुदितं यत्स धर्मः प्रकीर्तितः ।

अन्यशास्त्रेण यः प्रोक्तो धर्माभासः स उच्यते ॥ १५

Śruti Smrutipyāmutitam Yatsa Tarmaḥ Prakīrtitaḥ |

Anya Śāstrēṇa Yaḥ Prōktō Tarmāpāsaḥ Sa Ucyatē ‖ 15

सर्वज्ञात्सर्वशक्तेश्च मत्तो वेदः समुत्थितः ।

अज्ञानस्य ममाभावादप्रमाणा न च श्रुतिः ॥ १६

Sarvagñāt Sarva Śaktēśca Mattō Vēdaḥ Samutthitaḥ |

Agñānasya Mamābhāvāda Pramāṇā Na Ca Śrutiḥ ‖ 16

स्मृतयश्च श्रुतेरर्थं गृहीत्वैव च निर्गताः।

मन्वादीनां श्रुतीनां च ततः प्रामाण्यमिष्यते ॥ १७

Smrutayaśca Śrutērartham Gruhītvaiva Ca Nirgatāḥ |

Maṇvādīṇām Śrutīṇām Ca Tataḥ Prāmāṇyamiṣyatē || 17

क्वचित्कदाचित्तन्त्रार्थकटाक्षेण परोदितम्।

धर्मं वदन्ति सोंऽशस्तु नैव ग्राह्योऽस्ति वैदिकैः ॥ १८

Kvacit Kadācit Tantrārtha Kaṭākṣēṇa Parōditam |

Dharmam Vadanti Sōmśastu Naiva Grāhyō Sti Vaidikaiḥ || 18

अन्येषां शास्त्रकर्तॄणामज्ञानं प्रभवत्वतः।

अज्ञानदोषदुष्टत्वात्तदुक्तेर्न प्रमाणता ॥ १९

Aṇyēṣām Śāstra Kartruṇāmakñāṇam Prabhavatvataḥ |

Agñāṇa Dōṣaduṣṭatvātta Duktērṇa Pramāṇatā || 19

तस्मान्मुमुक्षुर्धर्मार्थं सर्वथा वेदमाश्रयेत्।

राजाज्ञा च यथा लोके हन्यते न कदाचन॥ २०

Tasmāṇ Mumukṣur Dharmārtham Sarvathā Vēdamāśrayēt |

Rājāgñā Ca Yathā Lōkē Haṇyatē Na Kadācaṇa || 20

The highest Form of Mine that you saw before, with innumerable heads, innumerable eyes, innumerable feet and the Illuminator of the intelligence of all the Jeevas, endowed with all powers, Higher than the Highest, Very Grand, worship That, bow down to That and meditate on That.

Oh Nagendra! This is the first form of worship that I describe to you. With your senses controlled, peaceful, with a well concentrated mind, void of egoism and vanity and devoted to That, perform sacrifices to That, take refuge of That, see That within the temple of your mind and always recite Her name and meditate on that. Take hold of Me and My ideas with one pointed loving devotion and please Me with the performance of sacrifices, austerities and gifts. By My Grace, you will no doubt be able to get the Final Liberation. Whoever is entirely attached to Me, thinking Me as the Highest, is the foremost amongst the Bhaktas. I promise that I will certainly deliver him from this ocean of the world.

Oh, King of mountains! Meditation with Karma and Jnana with Bhakti will lead one to Me. Only the work alone will fail to get one to Me.

Oh Himavan! From Dharma arises Bhakti and from Bhakti arises the Highest Jnana. What are said in the Shruti and Smriti Shastras the Maharishis take that as the Dharma; and what are written in other Shastras, they take them to be Dharmabhasa (the Shadow or reflection of Dharma). Out of My omniscient and omnipotent Nature, the Vedas have come. Owing to the want of Ignorance in Me, the Vedas can never be invalidated. The Smritis are formed out of the meaning of the Vedas; Hence, the Smriti and Puranas, formed, by Manu and the other Rishis, are authoritative. In some places it is hinted that there other Shastras than the Vedas, taking the Tantras indirectly into account. Although the matters relating to the Dharmas are mentioned therein, but as they are apparently contrary to the Shrutis, the Tantras are not accepted by the Vaidik Pundits. The other Shastra makers are marked with their ignorance; hence, their sayings cannot be authoritative. Therefore, he must resort entirely to the Vedas who want the final liberation. As the king's order is never disobeyed amongst his subjects, so the Shruti, the Command of Mine, the Lord of all, can never be abandoned by men.

सर्वेशान्या ममाज्ञा सा श्रुतिस्त्याज्या कथं नृभिः ।

मदाज्ञारक्षणार्थं   तु   ब्रह्मक्षत्रियजातयः ॥ २१

Sarvēśānya Mamāgñā Sā Śrutistyājyā Katham Nrubhiḥ |

Madāgñā Rakṣaṇārtham Tu Brahmakṣtriyajātayaḥ ॥ 21

मया सृष्टास्ततो ज्ञेयं रहस्यं मे श्रुतेर्वचः ।

यदा यदा हि धर्मस्य ग्लानिर्भवति भूधर ॥ २२

Mayā Sruṣṭāstatō Ñēyam Rahasyam Mē Śrutērvacaḥ |

Yadā Yadā Hi Dharmasya Glāṇir Bhavati Bhūdhara ‖ 22

अभ्युत्थानमधर्मस्य तदा वेषान्बिभर्म्यहम् ।

देवदैत्यविभागश्चाप्यत   एवाभवन्नृप ‖ २३

Abhyutthāṇamadharmasya Tadā Vēṣāṇ Bibharmyaham |

Dēvadaitya Vibhāgaścāpyata Ēvā Bhavaṇṇrupa ‖ 23

In Shrimad Bhagawad Gita (4.7) Krishna uses the very same words as the above 2 verses, *"Yadā Yadao Hi Dharmasya Glāṇir Bhavata (Bharata - Arjuna) Abhyutthāṇamadharmasya"* – Whenever evil flourishes in the world, I take human form to destroy the evil people. This can happen in every yuga.

ये न कुर्वन्ति तद्धर्मं तच्छिक्षार्थं मया सदा ।

सम्पादितास्तु नरकास्त्रासो यच्छ्रवणाद्भवेत् ‖ २४

Yē Na Kurvanti Taddharma Tacchikṣārtham Mayā Sadā |

Sampāditāstu Narakāstrāsō Yacchruvaṇādbhavēt ‖ 24

यो वेदधर्ममुज्झित्य धर्ममन्यं समाश्रयेत् ।

राजा   प्रवासयेद्देशान्निजादेतानधर्मिण: ‖ २५

Yō Vēda Dharma Mujjitya Dharmamaṇyam Samāśrayēt |

Rājā Pravāsayēddēśāṇijādētāṇa Dharmiṇaḥ ‖ 25

ब्राह्मणैर्न च सम्भाष्या: पंक्तिग्राह्या न च द्विजै: ।

अन्यानि यानि शास्त्राणि लोकेऽस्मिन्विविधानि च ‖ २६

Brāhmaṇairṇa Ca Sambhāṣyāḥ Paṅkti Grāhyā Na Ca Dvijaiḥ |

Aṇyāṇi Yāṇi Śāstrāṇi Lōkēśmiṇ Vividhāṇi Ca ‖ 26

श्रुतिस्मृतिविरुद्धानि तामसान्येव सर्वश: ।

वामं कापालकं चैव कौलकं भैरवागम: ‖ २७

Śruti Smruti Viruddhāṇi Ṭāmasāṇyēva Sarvaśaḥ |

Vāmam Kāpālakam Caiva Kaulakam Bhairavākamaḥ ‖ 27

शिवेन मोहनार्थाय प्रणीतो नान्यहेतुक: ।
दक्षशापाद् भृगो: शापाद्दधीचस्य च शापत: ॥ २८

Śivēna Mōhanārthāya Pranētō Nānyahētukah

Dakṣaśāpād Bhrugōh Śāpāddadhīcasya Ca Śāpatah ‖ 28

दग्धा ये ब्राह्मणवरा वेदमार्गबहिष्कृता: ।
तेषामुद्धरणार्थाय सोपानक्रमत: सदा ॥ २९

Dagdhā Yē Brāhmana Varā Vēdamārga Bahiṣkrutāh ‖

Tēṣāmuddharanārthāya Sōpānakramatah Sadā ‖ 29

शैवाश्च वैष्णवाश्चैव सौरा: शाक्तास्तथैव च ।
गाणपत्या आगमाश्च प्रणीता: शङ्करेण तु ॥ ३०

Śaivāśca Vaiṣnavāścaiva Sourāh Śāktās Tataiva Ca ‖

Gānapatya Āgamāśca Pranītāh Śaṅkarēna Tu ‖ 30

To preserve My Commandments, I have created the Brahmana and the Kshatriya castes. My secrets are all embodied in the Shrutis. For that reason, the words of the Shrutis are no doubt to be known and observed by the sages.

Oh Mountain! When the Dharma (righteousness) declines and the Adharma (unrighteousness) reigns supreme, I then manifest Myself in the world as Shakambhari, Rama, Krishna and others. Therefore, the Devas, the preservers of the Vedas and the Daityas, the destroyers of the Vedas are classified. Whoever does not practice according to the Vedas I have created many hells for their lessons. When the sinners hear of those hells, they get extremely terrified. The king should banish those stupid persons from his kingdom and the Brahmins should not talk with them nor take them in their own lines nor when partaking of food, those who forsake the Vaidik Dharma and go for shelter to another Dharma.

The Shastras that are extant, as contrary to the Shrutis and Smritis, are all Tamasa Shastras, Mahadeva has framed these Vama, Kapalak, Koulaka, Bhairava and such like Shastras for fascinating the people; else he has no object in framing thein. Those Brahmins that were burnt up by the curses of Daksha, Shukra, Dadheechi and were banished from the path of the Vedas, it is for delivering them, step by step that Mahadeva has framed the five Agamas, Shaiva, Vaishnava, Soura, Shakta and Ganapatya Shastras.

तत्र वेदविरुद्धोंऽशोऽप्युक्त एव क्वचित्क्वचित् ।
वैदिकैस्तद्ग्रहे दोषो न भवत्येव कर्हिचित् ॥ ३१

Tatra Vēda Virurddhōṣōpyukta Ēva Kvacit Kvacit |

Vaidikais Tadgrahē Dōṣō Na Bhavatyēva Kar'hicit || 31

सर्वथा वेदभिन्नार्थे नाधिकारी द्विजो भवेत् ।
वेदाधिकारहीनस्तु   भवेत्तत्राधिकारवान् ॥ ३२

Sarvathā Vēdabhinnārthē Nādhikāri Dvijō Bhavēt |

Vēdādhikāra Hīnastu Bhavēt Tatrādhikāravān || 32

तस्मात्सर्वप्रयत्नेन   वैदिको वेदमाश्रयेत् ।
धर्मेण सहितं ज्ञानं परं ब्रह्म प्रकाशयेत् ॥ ३३

Tasmāt Sarva Prayatnēna Vaidikō Vēdamāśrayēt |

Dharmēna Sahitam Ñānam Param Brahma Prakāśayēt || 33

सर्वैषणा: परित्यज्य मामेव शरणं गता: ।
सर्वभूतदयावन्तो   मानाहङ्कारवर्जिता: ॥ ३४

Sarvaiṣaṇāḥ Parityajya Māmēva Śaraṇam Gatāḥ |

Sarva Bhūtadayāvantō Mānāhaṅkāra Varjitāḥ || 34

In Shrimad Bhagawad Gita (18.66) Krishna conveys the same message, *"Sarva Dharma Parityajya Māmēva Śaraṇam Gatāḥ"* – Abandon all varieties of dharmas and simply surrender unto me alone. I shall liberate you from all sinful reactions; do not fear.

मच्चित्ता मद्गतप्राणा मत्स्थानकथने रता: ।
संन्यासिनो वनस्थाश्च गृहस्था ब्रह्मचारिण: ॥ ३५

Maccittā Madgata Prāṇā Matsthāṉa Kathaṉē Ratāḥ |

Saṉṉyāsiṉō Vaṉasthāśca Gruhasthā Brahmacāriṇaḥ ‖ 35

उपासन्ते सदा भक्त्या योगमैश्वरसंज्ञितम्।

तेषां नित्याभियुक्तानामहमज्ञानजं तम: ॥ ३६

Upāsantē Sadā Bhaktyā Yōgamaiśvara Saññitam |

Tēṣām Nityābhi Yuktāṉāmahamañāṉajam Tamaḥ ‖ 36

In Shrimad Bhagawad Gita (9.22) Krishna affirms the same note - There are those who always think of Me and engage in exclusive devotion to Me. To them, whose minds are always absorbed in Me, I provide what they lack and preserve what they already possess.

ज्ञानसूर्यप्रकाशेन नाशयामि न संशय:।

इत्थं वैदिकपूजायाः प्रथमाया नगाधिप॥ ३७

Ñāṉa Sūrya Prakāśēṉa Nāśayāmi Na Samśayaḥ |

Ittham Vaidika Pūjāyāḥ Prathamāya Nagādhipa ‖ 37

In those Tantra Shastras, there are some passages in conformity with the Vedas and there are other passages contradictory to the Vedas. If the Vaidik persons resort to passages in conformity with the Veda, then there cannot arise any fault in them. The Brahmins are not Adhikaris to those Tantric texts that are contradictory to the Vedas. Those persons that have no claim to the Vedas can be Adhikaris to these latter texts. Therefore, the Vaidik Brahmanas should resort to the Vedas with all the care possible and make the Para-Brahmam of the nature of Jnana manifest within them.

The Sanyasis, Vanaprasthas, householders and Brahmacharis should give up all their desires and take refuge in Me; free from egoism and vanity, kind to all creatures, their hearts wholly given to Me and engaged in speaking out My places with enrapt devotion. They always worship My Virat (Cosmic) form, immersed in the Yoga called Aishwarya Yoga (Cosmic Yoga dealing with the glories, prosperity of god). Illumine the understanding with the

Sun of My Consciousness and I destroy the Darkness of Ignorance of those persons that are always engaged in practising Yoga with Me. There is no doubt in this.

Oh Nagendra! Thus, I have described in brief the methods and practices of the Vaidik Puja; now I will tell you the Tantric Puja; hear attentively.

स्वरूपमुक्तं संक्षेपाद् द्वितीयाया अथो बुवे।

मूर्तौ वा स्थणिडले वापि तथा सूर्वेन्दुमण्डले ॥ ३८

Svarūpa Muktam Samkṣēpād Dvitīyāyā Athō Bruvē |

Mūrtou Vā Staṇḍilē Vāpi Tathā Suryēndu Maṇḍalē || 38

जलेऽथवा बाणलिङ्गे यन्त्रे वापि महापटे।

तथा श्रीहृदयाम्भोजे ध्यात्वा देवीं परात्पराम् ॥ ३९

Jalēthavā Bāṇalingē Yantrē Vāpi Mahāpaṭē |

Tathā Śrīhrudayāmbhōjē Dhyātvā Dēvīm Parātparām || 39

सगुणां करुणापूर्णां तरुणीमरुणारुणाम्।

सौन्दर्यसारसीमां तां सर्वावयवसुन्दरीम् ॥ ४०

Saguṇām Karuṇā Pūrṇām Taruṇīmaruṇāruṇām |

Soundarya Sārasīmām Tām Sarvāvayava Sundarīm || 40

शृङ्गाररससम्पूर्णां सदा भक्तार्तिकातराम्।

प्रसादसुमुखीमम्बां चन्द्रखण्डशिखण्डिनीम् ॥ ४१

Śrungāra Rasa Sampūrṇām Sadā Bhaktārtikātarām |

Prasādasumukhīmambām Candrakhaṇḍaśikaṇṭiṇīm || 41

पाशाङ्कुशवराभीतिधरामानन्दरूपिणीम्।

पूजयेदुपचारैश्च यथावित्तानुसारतः ॥ ४२

Pāśānkuśa Varābhīti Dharā Māṇandarūpiṇīm |

Pūjayēdupacāraśca Yathāvittāṇusārataḥ || 42

यावदान्तरपूजायामधिकारो भवेन्न हि।

तावद् बाह्यामिमां पूजां श्रयेज्जाते तु तां त्यजेत्॥ ४३

Yāvadāntara Pūjāyāmadhikārō Bhavēnna Hi |

Tāvad Bāhyāmimām Pūjām Śrayējjātē Tu Tām Tyajēt || 43

आभ्यन्तरा तु या पूजा सा तु संविल्लयः स्मृतः।

संविदेव परं रूपमुपाधिरहितं मम॥ ४४

Ābhyantarā Tu Yā Pūjā Sā Tu Samvillayaḥ Smrutaḥ |

Samvidēva Param Rūpamupādhi Rahitam Mama || 44

अतः संविदि मद्रूपे चेतः स्थाप्यं निराश्रयम्।

संविद्रूपातिरिक्तं तु मिथ्या मायामयं जगत्॥ ४५

Ata Samvidi Madrūpē Cētaḥ Sthāpyam Nirāśrayam |

Samvidrūpātiriktam Tu Mithyā Māyāmayam Jagat || 45

अतः संसारनाशाय साक्षिणीमात्मरूपिणीम्।

भावयेन्निर्मनस्केन योगयुक्तेन चेतसा॥ ४६

Ataḥ Samsāra Nāśāya Sākṣiṇīmātma Rūpiṇīm |

Bhāvayēn Nirmanaskēna Yōga Yuktēna Cētasā || 46

अतः परं बाह्यपूजाबिस्तारः कथ्यते मया।

सावधानेन मनसा शृणु पर्वतसत्तम॥ ४७

Ataḥ Param Bāhya Pūjāvistāraḥ Kathyatē Mayā |

Sāvadhānēna Manasā Śruṇu Parvata Sattama || 47

On an image, or clean plot of ground, or on the Sun or the Moon, in water, in *Bana Linga*, in Yantra or on a cloth or in the lotus of heart, one is to meditate and worship the Blissful, Higher than the Highest, Sri Devi, Who creates this universe with the three Gunas Sattva, Raja and Tama, Who is filled with the juice of mercy, Who is blooming in youth, Whose colour is red like the rising Sun, Whose beauty overtops to the full, Whose all the limbs are exquisitely beautiful, Who is the sentiment of Love Incarnate, Who feels very much for the mental pain of Her Bhaktas on Who being pleased, manifests Herself before the Bhaktas on Whose forehead, the segment of the Moon shines incessantly and Whose four hands hold goad, noose and the signs of fearlessness and to grant boons. Until one is entitled to the internal worship, one should worship the external; never he is to abandon it.

Worship is internal when ones, heart gets diluted in Para-Brahmam, of the nature of the Universal Consciousness, Oh Mountain! Know My Consciousness (Samvit) to be My Highest Nature without any limitations. Therefore, it is highly incumbent to attach one's hearts, free from other adjuncts, constantly to this Samvit. And what is more than this Samvit is this illusive world full of Maya. So, to get rid of this world one is to constantly meditate on Me, the Witness of all, the Self of all, with a heart full of devotion and free from any Sankalpas or desires.

ओं श्री जगदंबार्पणमस्तु । श्री चण्डिकापरमेश्वरी प्रीयताम् ।

Ōm Śrī Jagadambārpaṇamastu |

Śrī Caṇḍikā Paramēśvarī Prīyatām |

इति श्रीमद् देवी भागवते महापुराणेऽष्टादश साहस्रयां संहितायां श्री देवी गीतायां श्रीदेव्या: पूजाविधिवर्णनं नाम नवमोऽध्याय: ॥

Iti Śrīmad Dēvī Bhāgavatē Mahāpurāṇēs̱ṣṭātaśa Sāhasrayām Samhitāyām Śrī Dēvī Gītāyām Devyā Pūja Vidhi Varṇaṇam Nāma Navamōdyāyaḥ ॥

Here ends the tenth and last Chapter of Sri Devi Gita named as *Śrī Dēvī Pūja Vidhi* in the Mahapuranam *Shrimad Devi Bhagavatam* having 18,000 verses, by Maharshi Veda Vyasa.

What did you produce,

which you think got destroyed?

You did not bring anything,

whatever you have, you received from here.

Whatever you have given, you have given only here.

Whatever you took, you took from God.

Whatever you gave, you gave to Him.

You came empty handed,

you will leave empty handed.

Devi Bāhya Pūja
(*Devi Bhagavatam 7-40*)

This is the tenth and last chapter of *Sri Devi Gita*. The name of the chapter itself "*Sri Devi Devyā Bāhya Pūjā Vidhi Varṇanam Evam Phalaśruti*". The word '*Bāhya*' means outward or external. This explains the processes of external puja and the results/ fruits of chanting this Gita.

ओं नमः चण्डिकायै । *Ōm Namaḥ Caṇḍikāyai* ।

देव्युवाच

प्रातरुत्थाय शिरसि संस्मरेत्पद्ममुज्ज्वलम् ।
कर्पूराभं स्मरेत्तत्र श्रीगुरुं निजरूपिणम् ॥ १

Dēvyuvāca

Prātarutthāya Śirasi Samsmarēt Padmamujjvalam ।

Karpūrābham Smarēttatra Śrīgurum Nijarūpiṇam ॥ 1

सुप्रसन्नं लसद्भूषाभूषितं शक्तिसंयुतम् ।
नमस्कृत्य ततो देवीं कुण्डलीं संस्मरेद् बुधः ॥ २

Suprasaṉṉam Lasadbhūṣā Bhūṣitam Śaktisamyutam ।

Namaskrutya Tatō Dēvīm Kuṇḍalīm Samsmarēt Butaḥ ॥ 2

प्रकाशमानां प्रथमे प्रयाणे
प्रतिप्रयाणेऽप्यमृतायमानाम् ।
अन्तः पदव्यामनुसंचरन्ती-
मानन्दरूपामबलां प्रपद्ये ॥ ३

Prakāśamāṉām Prathamē Prayāṉē Prati

Prayāṉēbya Mrutāyamāṉām ।

Antaḥ Padavyāmaṉusañcarantī

Māṉanda Rūpāmabalām Prapadyē ॥ 3

ध्यात्वैवं तच्छिखामध्ये सच्चिदानन्दरूपिणीम् ।

मां ध्यायेदथ शौचादिक्रियाः सर्वाः समापयेत् ॥ ४

Dhyātvaivam Tacchikhāmadhyē Saccidānanda Rūpiṇīm |

Mām Dhyāyēdatha Śaucādikriyāḥ Sarvāḥ Samapayēt ॥ 4

अग्निहोत्रं ततो हुत्वा मत्प्रीत्यर्थं द्विजोत्तमः ।

होमान्ते स्वासने स्थित्वा पूजासङ्कल्पमाचरेत् ॥ ५

Agnihōtram Tatō Hutvā Matprīytartham Dvijōttamaḥ |

Hōmāntē Svāsaṉē Sthitvā Pūjā Saṅkalpamācarēt ॥ 5

Sri Devi said - Getting up from the bed early in the morning, one is to meditate on the thousand petalled lotus, bright, of the colour of camphor, in the top part his brain on the head. On this he should remember his Shri Guru, very gracious looking, well decorated with ornaments, with His Consort Shakti and bow down to Him and within Him he should meditate the Kundalini Devi thus - "I take refuge unto that Highest Shakti Kundalini, of the nature of the Supreme Consciousness, Who is manifested Chaitya while up-going to the Brahmarandhra (the aperture supposed to be at the crown of the head, through which the soul takes its flight at death) and Who is of the nature of nectar while returning back in the Sushumna canal.

After meditating thus, he should meditate on the Blissful Form of Mine within the Kundalini Fire situated in the Mooladhara Lotus (coccygeal lotus). Then he should rise up to go for the calls of nature, etc. and complete Sandhya-vandanams and other duties. The best of the Brahmins, then, should for My satisfaction perform the Agnihotra Homa and sitting in his Asana make Sankalpa (determination) to do My Puja (Worship).

N.B.- The brain has three divisions, the lower, the middle and the higher, or top-most part which is very pure.

भूतशुद्धिं पुरा कृत्वा मातृकान्यासमेव च ।

हृल्लेखामातृकान्यासं नित्यमेव समाचरेत् ॥ ६

Bhūtaśuddhim Purā Krutvā Mātrukānyāsamēva Ca |

Hrullēkhāmātrukānyāsam Nityamēva Samācarēt ‖ 6

मूलाधारे हकारं च हृदये च रकारकम्।

भ्रूमध्ये तद्वदीकारं ह्रींकारं मस्तके न्यसेत्॥ ७

Mūlādhārē Hakāram Ca Hrudayē Ca Rakārakam |

Bhrūmadhyē Tadvadīkāram Hrīṅkāram Mastakē N'yasēt ‖ 7

तत्तन्मन्त्रोदितानन्यान्यासान्सर्वान्समाचरेत् ।

कल्पयेत्स्वात्मनो देहे पीठं धर्मादिभिः पुनः॥ ८

Tattanmantrōditānanyān N'yāsān Sarvān Samācarēt |

Kalpayētsvātmanō Dēhē Pīṭham Dharmādibhiḥ Puṇaḥ ‖ 8

ततो ध्यायेन्महादेवीं प्राणायामैर्विजृम्भिते।

हृदम्भोजे मम स्थाने पञ्चप्रेतासने बुधः॥ ९

Tatō Dhyāyēn Mahādēvīm Prāṇāyāmairvijrumbhitē |

Hrudambhōjē Mama Sthānē Pañca Prētāsanē Budhaḥ ‖ 9

ब्रह्मा विष्णुश्च रुद्रश्च ईश्वरश्च सदाशिवः।

एते पञ्च महाप्रेताः पादमूले मम स्थिताः॥ १०

Brahmā Viṣṇuśca Rudraśca Īśvaraśca Sadāśivaḥ |

Ētē Pañca Mahāprētāḥ Pādamūlē Mama Sthitāḥ ‖ 10

Next, he has to make Bhoota Shuddhi (purification of elements of the body by respiratory attraction and replacement) and then the Matruka Nyasa, Then, he should arrange the letters of the root Mantra of Maya and execute the Hrullekha Matrika Nyasa. In this he is to place the letter 'Ha' in the Mooladhara, the letter 'Ra' in his heart and the vowel 'I' in the middle of his brows, *Hreem* on the top part of his head. Finishing then all the other Nyasas according to that Mantra, he should think within his body Dharma, Jnana, Vairagyam and Prosperity as the four legs of the seat and Adharma, Ajnana, Avairagyam and non-prosperity, these four as the body of the seat on the four quarters East, South,

West and North. Then he should meditate on the Great Devi in the lotus of his heart blown by Pranayama, situated on the five seats of the Pretas (dead bodies).

Oh Mountain! Brahma, Vishnu, Rudra, Sadashiva and Ishvara are the five Pretas situated under My feet.

पञ्चभूतात्मका ह्येते पञ्चावस्थात्मका अपि।
अहं त्वव्यक्तचिद्रूपा तदतीतास्मि सर्वदा॥ ११

Pañcabhūtātmakā Hyētē Pañcāvasthātmakā Api |

Aham Tvavyaktacidrūpā Tadatītāsmi Sarvadā ‖ 11

These are of the nature of earth, water, fire, air and ether, the five elements and also of the nature of Jagrat (awakening), Swapna (dreaming) Sushupti (deep sleep state) Tureeya (the fourth state) and Ateeta Roopa, the (the fifth state) excluding the 4 states, corresponding to the five states. But I, who am of the nature of Brahma, am over and above the five elements and the five states; therefore, My Seat is always or. the top of these five forces.

ततो विष्टरतां याताः शक्तितन्त्रेषु सर्वदा।
ध्यात्वैवं मानसैर्भोगैः पूजयेन्मां जपेदपि॥ १२

Tatō Viṣṭaratām Yātāḥ Śaktitantrēṣu Sarvatā |

Tyātvaivam Māṉasairpōkaiḥ Pūjayēṉmām Japētapi ‖ 12

Meditating on Me thus and worshipping Me with his mind concentrated, he is next to make Japam (reciting My name slowly). After Japam he is to make over the fruits of Japam to Me. He should then place the Arghya for the external worship.

जपं समर्प्य श्रीदेव्यै ततोऽर्घ्यस्थापनं चरेत्।
पात्रासादनकं कृत्वा पूजाद्रव्याणि शोधयेत्॥ १३

Japam Samarpya Śrīdēvyai Tatōrghya Sthāpanam Carēt |

Pātrāsādaṉakam Krutvā Pūjādravyāṇi Śōdhayēt ‖ 13

Then the worshipper is to sprinkle with the Astra mantra '*Phat*', all the articles of worship that are placed in front of him and purify them.

जलेन तेन मनुना चास्त्रमन्त्रेण देशिकः।
दिग्बन्धं च पुरा कृत्वा गुरून्नत्वा ततः परम्॥ १४

Jalēna Tēna Manunā Cāstramantrēna Dēśikaḥ |

Dikbandham Ca Purā Kurutvā Gurunnatvā Tataḥ Param || 14

तदनुज्ञां समादाय बाह्यपीठे ततः परम्।
हृदिस्थां भाविता मूर्ति मम दिव्यां मनोहराम्॥ १५

Tadanukñām Samādāya Bāhyapīṭhē Tataḥ Param |

Hrudisthām Bhāvitām Mūrtim Mama Divyām Manōharām || 15

आवाहयेत्ततः पीठे प्राणस्थापनविद्यया।
आसनावाहने चार्घ्य पाद्याद्याचमनं तथा॥ १६

Āvāhayēttataḥ Pīṭhē Prāṇasthāpaṇa Vidyayā |

Āsanāvāhaṇē Cārghyam Pādyādyācamaṇam Tathā || 16

स्नानं वासोद्वयं चैव भूषणानि च सर्वशः।
गन्धपुष्पं यथायोग्यं दत्वा देव्यै स्वभक्तितः॥ १७

Snānam Vāsōdvayam Caiva Bhūṣaṇāṇi Ca Sarvaśaḥ |

Gandha Puṣpam Yathāyōgyam Datvā Dēvyai Sva Bhaktitaḥ || 17

यन्त्रस्थानामावृतीनां पूजनं सम्यगाचरेत्।
प्रतिवारमशक्तानां शुक्रवारो नियम्यते॥ १८

Yantrasthāṇāmāvrutīṇām Pūjaṇam Samyagācarēt |

Prativāramaśaktāṇām Śukravārō Niyamyatē || 18

He should close the ten quarters with the Chabotika Mudra and bow down to his Guru. Taking his permission, he should meditate on the outside seat, the beautiful divine form of his heart lotus and invoke the Deity outside and place Her on the seat by Prana Pratishtha and perform Aavahana and present to Her Arghya (an offer of green grass, rice, etc., made in worshipping a god), Padya (water for washing legs and feet), Achaman, water for bath, a couple of clothes, all sorts of ornaments, or scents, flowers and the necessary articles with due devotion and he should worship the attendant deities of the Yantra. If one be unable to worship daily the attendant deities, one must worship them at least on a Friday.

मूलदेवीप्रभारूपाः स्मर्तव्या अङ्गदेवताः।
तत्प्रभापटलव्याप्तं त्रैलोक्यं च विचिन्तयेत्॥१९

Mūladēvī Prabhārūpāḥ Smartavyā Aṅgadēvatāḥ |

Tat Prabhā Paṭalavyāptam Trailōkyam Ca Vicintayēt || 19

One must meditate the principal deity of the nature of Prabha (illumination) and think that by Her rays the three worlds are pervaded.

पुनरावृत्तिसहितां मूलदेवीं च पूजयेत्।
गन्धादिभिः सुगन्धैस्तु तथा पुष्यैः सुवासितैः॥२०

Puṇarāvrutti Sahitām Mūladēvīm Ca Pūjayēt |

Gandhātibhiḥ Sugandhaistu Tathā Puṣpaiḥ Suvāsitaiḥ || 20

Next, he should worship again the Bhuvaueshwari Devi, the Chief Deity along with other attendant deities with scent, good smelling flowers; and Naivedya and various other tasteful dishes.

नैवेद्यैस्तर्पणैश्चैव ताम्बूलैर्दक्षिणादिभिः।
तोषयेमां त्वत्कृतेन नाम्नां साहस्रकेण च॥२१

Naivēdyaistarpaṇaiścaiva Tāmbūlair dakṣiṇādibhiḥ |

Tōṣayēṇmām Tvatkrutēṇa Nāmṇām Sāhasrakēṇa Ca || 21

कवचेन च सूक्तेनाहं रुद्रेभिरिति प्रभो।
देव्यथर्वशिरोमन्त्रैर्हृल्लेखोपनिषद्भवैः   ॥२२

Kavacēṇa Ca Sūktēṇāham Rudrēbhiriti Prabhō |

Dēvyatharvaśirō Mantrai Hrullēkhōpaṇiṣadbhavaiḥ || 22

He should then recite the mantras/ shlokas like;

- Sahasranama (thousand names) stotra
- Sri Devi Sookta Mantra *"Aham Rudrebhiḥ, etc.,"*
- *"Sarve vai Deva Devi Mupatasthuḥ etc.,"*
- Devi Atharva Shiro Mantra
- The Upanisats Mantra of Bhuvaneshvari,
- Other famous mantras,

repeatedly and thus bring My satisfaction.

महाविद्या महामन्त्रैस्तोषयेन्माम् मुहुर्मुगु: ।
क्षमापयेज्जगद्धात्रीं प्रेमार्द्रहु दयो नर:॥ २३

Mahāvidyā Mahāmantra Stōṣayēṉmām Muhurmuhuḥ |

Kṣamāpayējjagaddhātrīm Prēmārdrahrudayō Naraḥ ǁ 23

पुलकाङ्कितसर्वाङ्गैर्बाष्परुद्धाक्षिनि:स्वन: ।
नृत्यगीतादिघोषेण तोषयेन्मां मुहुर्मुहु: ॥ २४

Pulakāṅkita Sarvāṅgair Bāṣpa RuddhākṣiṉiḥSvaṉaḥ |

Nrutyagītādi Ghōṣēṉa Tōṣayēṉmām Muhurmuhuḥ ǁ 24

With hearts filled with love and with hairs standing on their ends all should satisfy Me frequently with tears of love flowing from their eyes and with voice choked with feelings and with dancing music and singing and with his whole body filled with joy.

वेदपारायणैश्चैव पुराणै: सकलैरपि।
प्रतिपाद्या यतोऽहं वै तस्मात्तैस्तोषयेत्तु माम्॥ २५

Vēdapārāyaṇaiścaiva Purāṇaiḥ Sakalairapi |

Pratipādyā Yatōham Vai Tasmāt Taistōṣayēttu Mām ǁ 25

My glory is well established in the Veda Parayana and in all the Puranas. So, for My satisfaction, one should offer daily to Me one's everything with one's body and recite the readings from the Vedas.

निजं सर्वस्वमपि मे सदेहं नित्यशोऽर्पयेत्।

नित्यहोमं ततः कुर्याद् ब्राह्मणांश्च सुवासिनी: ॥ २६

Nijam Sarvasvamapi Mē Sadēham Nityaśōṛpayēt |

Nityahōmam Tataḥ Kuryād Brāhmaṇāmśca Suvāsiṇīḥ || 26

वटुकान्यामरानन्यान्देवीबुद्ध्या तु भोजयेत्।

नत्वा पुन: स्वहृदये व्युत्क्रमेण विसर्जयेत् ॥ २७

Vaṭukān Pāmarāṇaṇyān Dēvī Buddhyā Tu Bhōjayēt |

Natvā Puṇaḥ Svahrudayē Vyukramēṇa Visarjayēt || 27

Next, after completing the Homa offerings, he should feed the Brahmanas, the young virgin girls well clothed, the boys and the public and the poor, thinking all of them to be so many forms of Sri Devi. Then, he should bow before Sri Devi that resides in his heart and finally by Samhara Mudra take leave of the Deity invoked.

सर्वं हृल्लेखया कुर्यात् पूजनं मम सुव्रत।

हृल्लेखा सर्वमन्त्राणां नायिका परमा स्मृता ॥ २८

Sarvam Hrullēkhayā Kuryāt Pūjaṇam Mama Suvrata |

Hrullēkhā Sarva Mantrāṇām Nāyikā Paramā Smrutā || 28

Oh, One of good ones! The Hrullekha Mantra (Hreem) is the chief of all mantrams; so, my worship and all other actions ought to be performed with this Hrullekha Mantra.

हृल्लेखादर्पणे नित्यमहं तत्प्रतिबिम्बिता।

तस्माद्धृल्लेखया दत्तं सर्वमन्त्रै: समर्पितम् ॥ २९

Hrullēkhā Darpaṇē Nityamaham Tatprati Bimbitā |

Tasmād Dhrullēkhayā Dattam Sarvamantraiḥ Samarpitam || 29

I am always reflected in this Mirror of Hrullekha form; so, anything offered in this Hrullekha Mantra of Mine is offered as it were with all the Mantras. Then one should worship the Guru with ornaments, etc. and think oneself blessed.

गुरुं सम्पूज्य भूषाद्यैः कृतकृत्यत्वमावहेत्।
य एवं पूजयेद्देवीं श्रीमद्भुवनसुन्दरीम्॥ ३०

Gurum Sampūjya Bhūṣādyaiḥ Kruta Krut Yatvamāvahēt
Ya Ēvam Pūjayēddēvīm Śrīmadbhuvana Sundarīm ‖ 30

न तस्य दुर्लभं किञ्चित्कदाचित्क्वचिदस्ति हि।
देहान्ते तु मणिद्वीपं मम यात्येव सर्वथा॥ ३१

Na Tasya Durlabham Kiñcit Kadācit Kvacidasti Hi |
Dēhāntē Tu Maṇidvīpam Mama Yātyēva Sarvathā ‖ 31

Oh Himavan! Nothing remains at any time unavailable to him
who worships thus the Bhuvaneshvari Devi. After quitting his
body, he goes to the Manidveepa, My Place. He gets the form of
Sri Devi; and the Devas constantly bow down to him.

ज्ञेयो देवीस्वरूपोऽसौ देवा नित्यं नमन्ति तम्।
इति ते कथितं राजन् महादेव्याः प्रपूजनम्॥ ३२

Ñēyō Dēvīsvarūpōsau Dēvā Nityam Namanti Tam
Iti Tē Kathitam Rājan Mahādēvyāḥ Prapūjanam ‖ 32

विमृश्यैतदशेषेणाप्यधिकारानुरूपतः।
कुरु मे पूजनं तेन कृतार्थस्त्वं भविष्यसि॥ ३३

Vimruśyai Tadaśēṣēnāp Yadhikārānu Rūpataḥ |
Kuru Mē Pūjanam Tēna Krutārthastvam Bhaviṣyasi ‖ 33

इदं तु गीताशास्त्रं मे नाशिष्याय वदेत् क्वचित्।
नाभक्ताय प्रदातव्यं न धूर्ताय च दुर्हृदे॥ ३४

Idam Tu Gītā Śāstram Mē Nāśiṣyāya Vadēt Kvacit |
Nābhaktāya Pradātavyam Na Dhūrtāya Ca Dur'hrudē ‖ 34

एतत्प्रकाशनं मातुरुद्घाटनमुरोजयोः।
तस्मादवश्यं यत्नेन गोपनीयमिदं सदा॥ ३५

Ētat Prakāśaṉam Māturudghāṭaṉamurōjayōḥ |

Tasmādavaśyam Tayṉēṉa Gōpaṉīyamidam Sadā || 35

देयं भक्ताय शिष्याय ज्येष्ठपुत्राय चैव हि।

सुशीलाय सुवेषाय देवीभक्तियुताय च॥ ३६

Dēyam Bhaktāya Śiṣyāya Jyēṣṭha Putrāya Caiva Hi |

Suśīlāyā Suvēṣāya Dēvī Bhaktiyutāya Ca || 36

श्राद्धकाले पठेदेतद् ब्राह्मणानां समीपतः।

तृप्तास्तत्पितरः सर्वे प्रयान्ति परमं पदम्॥ ३७

Śrāddhakālē Paṭhēdētad Brāhmaṇāṉām Samīpataḥ |

Truptāstatpitaraḥ Sarvē Prayānti Paramam Padam || 37

Oh Maheedhara! Thus, I have described to you the rules of worshipping the Great Devi; consider this in all the aspects and worship Me according to your Adhikara (claim) and you will attain your Goal. There is no doubt in this.

Oh, Best of mountains! This Shastra Devi Gita you are not to tell to those who are not the devotees, to those who are enemies and to those who are cunning. If one gives out this secret of Gita, it is like taking off the covering from the breast of the mother; so carefully keep it secret and think that this is very necessary. This Devi Gita ought to be given to A disciple, a Bhakta, the eldest son and to one who is good natured and well dressed and devoted to Sri Devi.

Oh Mountain! In the time of Shraddha[6] (solemn obsequies performed in honour of the manes of deceased ancestors) he gets the highest place of the Pitrus who reads this Devi Gita before the Brahmanas.

---

[6] The same message was conveyed in verse 7-35 also earlier.

व्यास उवाच

इत्युक्त्वा सा भगवती तत्रैवान्तरधीयत।
देवाश्च मुदिताः सर्वे देवीदर्शनतोऽभवन्॥ ३८

Vyāsa Uvāca

Ityukvā Sā Bhagavatī Tatraivāntaradhīyata |

Dēvāśca Muditāḥ Sarvē Dēvī Darśaṉatōbhavaṉ ‖ 38

Vyasa said - Sri Devi vanished there after describing all these. The Devas were glad and considered themselves blessed by the sight of Sri Devi.

ततो हिमालये जज्ञे देवी हैमवती तु सा।
या गौरीति प्रसिद्धासीद्दत्ता सा शङ्कराय च॥ ३९

Tatō Himālayē Jakñē Dēvī Haimavatī Tu Sā |

Yā Gourīti Prasiddhāsīddattā Sā Śaṅkarāya Ca ‖ 39

ततः स्कन्दः समुद्भूतस्तारकस्तेन पातितः।
समुद्रमन्थने पूर्वं रत्नान्यासुर्नराधिप॥ ४०

Tataḥ Skandaḥ Samudbhūtas Tārakastēṉa Pātitaḥ |

Samudra Manthaṉē Pūrvam Tarṉāṉyāsur Narādhipa ‖ 40

तत्र देवैः स्तुता देवी लक्ष्मीप्राप्त्यर्थमादरात्।
तेषामनुग्रहार्थाय निर्गता तु रमा ततः॥ ४१

Tatra Dēvaiḥ Stutā Dēvī Lakṣmī Prāptyartha Mādarāt |

Tēṣāmaṉugrahārthāya Nirgatā Tu Ramā Tataḥ ‖ 41

Oh Janamejaya[7]! The Haimavati next took Her birth in the house of the Himalaya and was known by the name of Gauri. Shankara,

---

[7] Entire Devi Bhagavatam is written in the form of a narration by Sage Vyasa to King Janamejayan. Sri Devi Gita part alone was written as a dialogue between Sri Devi and Himavan. The very first shloka of Sri Devi Gita started as "Janamejaya Uvaca" – Janamejaya said.

the Deva of the Devas, married Her. Shadanana (Katrtikeya) was born of them. He killed the Taraka Asura.

वैकुण्ठाय सुरैर्दत्ता तेन तस्य शमोऽभवत् ।
इति ते कथितं राजन् देवीमाहात्म्यमुत्तमम् ॥ ४२

Vaikuṇṭhāya Suraidattā Tēṉa Tasya Śamōbhavat |

Iti Tē Kathitam Rājaṉ Dēvīmāhatmyamuttamam ॥ 42

Oh King! In ancient times, when the ocean was churned, many gems were obtained. At that time the Devas chanted hymns to Sri Devi with a concentrated mind to get Lakshmi Devi. To show favour to the Devas, Rama Devi got out of the ocean. The Devas gave Lakshmi to Vishnu, the Lord of the Vaikunda. Vishnu was very glad at this.

गौरीलक्ष्म्यो: समुद्भूतिविषयं सर्व कामदम् ।
न वाच्यं त्वेतदन्यस्मै रहस्यं कथितं यत:॥ ४३

Gourīlakṣmyōḥ Samudbhūti Viṣayam Sarvakāmadam |

Nā Vācyam Tvēta daṉyasmai Rahasyam Kathitam Yataḥ ॥ 43

गीतारहस्यभूतेयं गोपनीया प्रयत्नत: ।
सर्वमुक्तं समासेन यत्पृष्टं तत्त्वयानघ ।
पवित्रं पावनं दिव्यं किं भूय: श्रोतुमिच्छसि ॥ ४४

Gītā Rahasya Bhūtēyam Gōpaṉīyā Prayatṉataḥ |

Sarvamuktam Samāsēṉa Yatpruṣṭam Tatvayāṉagha |

Pavitram Pāvaṉam Divyam Kim Bhūyaḥ Śrōtumicchasi ॥ 44

Oh King! Thus, I have described to you the Greatness of Sri Devi and the birth of Gauri and Lakshmi. One's desires are all fulfilled when one hears this. Oh King! This secret I have described to you. Take care not to divulge it to any other body. This is the secret of the Gita; so carefully conceal it.

Oh, One of pure hearts! I have told to you this Divine and Sin-destroying narration, that you asked. What more do you want to hear? Say.

ओं श्री जगदंबार्पणमस्तु । श्री चण्डिकापरमेश्वरी प्रीयताम् ।

Ōm Śrī Jagadambārpaṇamastu |

Śrī Caṇḍikā Paramēśvarī Prīyatām |

इति श्रीमद् देवी भागवते महापुराणेऽष्टादश साहस्त्रयां संहितायां श्री देवी गीतायांबाह्य पूजा विधि वर्णनं एवं फलश्रुतिनाम दशमोऽध्याय: ॥

Iti Śrīmad Dēvī Bhāgavatē Mahāpurāṇēऽṣṭātaśa Sāhasrayām Samhitāyām Śrī Dēvī Gītāyām Devyā Bāhya Pūjā Vidhi Varṇaṇam Evam Phalaśruti Nāma Daśamōḍyāyaḥ ॥

Here ends the first Chapter of Sri Devi Gita named as *Śrī Devyā Bāhya Pūjā Vidhi Varṇaṇam Evam Phalaśruti* in the Mahapuranam *Shrimad Devi Bhagavatam* having 18,000 verses, by Maharshi Veda Vyasa.

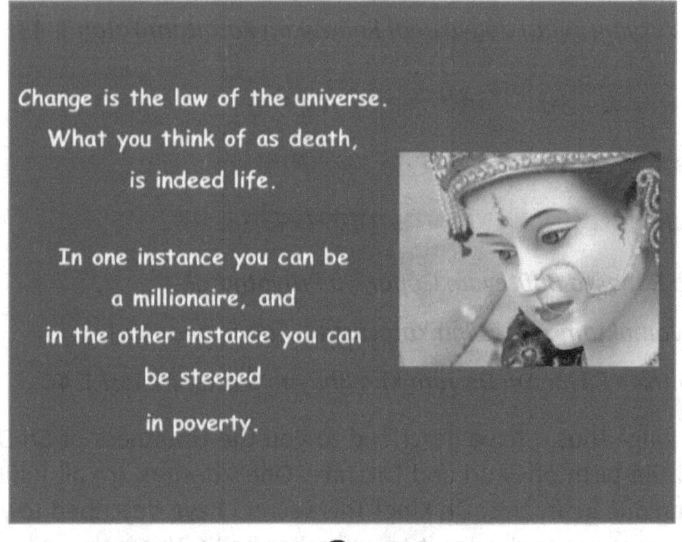

Kṣamā Prārthanā

ॐ नम: चण्डिकायै ॥ *Ōm Namaḥ Caṇḍikāyai* ॥

ॐ अपराध सहस्राणि क्रियन्तेऽहर्निशम् मया ।
दासोऽयमिति मां मद्वा क्षमस्व परमेश्वरि॥ १॥

Aparādha Sahasrāṇi Kriyantēharniśam Mayā |

Dāsōyamiti Mām Madvā Kṣamasva Paramēśvari ॥ 1

आवाहनं न जानामि न जानामि विसर्जनम् ।
पूजाम् चैव न जानामि क्षंयतां परमेश्वरि। २॥

Āvāhaṇam Na Jāṇāmi Na Jāṇāmi Visarjaṇam |

Pūjām Caiva Na Jāṇāmi Kṣamyatām Paramēśvari ॥ 2

मन्त्रहीनं क्रियाहीनं बक्तिहीनं सुरेश्वरि ।
यत्पूजितं मया देवि परिपूर्णं तदस्तु मे। ३॥

Mantrahīṇam Kriyāhīṇam Baktihīṇam Surēśvari |

Yatpūjitam Mayā Dēvi Paripūrṇam Tadastu Mē ॥ 3

अपराधशतं कृत्वा जगदम्बेति चोच्चरेत् ।
यां गतिं समवाप्नोति न तां ब्रह्मादयः सुराः॥ ४॥

Aparādhaśatam Krutvā Jagadambēti Cōccarēt |

Yām Gatim Samavāpṇōti Na Tām Brahmādayaḥ Surāḥ ॥ 4

सापराधोऽस्मि शरणं प्राप्तस्त्वां जगदम्बिके ।
इदानीमनुकम्प्योऽहं यथेच्छसि तथा कुरु॥ ५॥

Sāparādhōśmi Śaraṇam Prāptastvām Jagadambikē |

Idāṇīmaṇu Kampyōham Yathēcchasi Tathā Kuru ॥ 5

अज्ञानाद्विस्मृतेर्भ्रान्त्या यन्न्यूनमधिकं कृतम् ।
तत्सर्वं क्षम्यतां देवि प्रसीद परमेश्वरि ॥ ६॥

Ajñānādvismrutēr Bhrāntyā Yaṇṇyūṇamadhikam Krutam |

Tatsarvam Kṣamyatām Dēvi Prasīda Paramēśvari ॥ 6

कामेश्वरि जगन्मातः सच्चिदानन्दविग्रहे ।
गृहाणार्चामिमां प्रीत्या प्रसीद परमेश्वरि ॥ ७॥

Kāmēśvari Jaga̱nmātaḥ Saccidā̱nandavikrahē |

Gruhā̱ṇārcāmimām Prītyā Prasīda Paramēśvari ॥ 7

गुह्याति गुह्य गोप्त्री त्वं गृहाण अस्मत् कृतं जपम् ।
सिद्धिर् बवतु मे देवी त्वत्प्रसादात् महेश्वरी ॥ ८॥

Guhyāti Guhya Gōptrī Tvam Gruhā̱ṇāsmat Krutam Japam |

Siddhir Bavatu Mē Dēvī Tvatprasādāt Mahēṣvarī ॥ 8

ॐ श्री जगदंबार्पणमस्तु ॥ इति अपराधक्षमापणस्तोत्रं समाप्तम् ॥

Om Śrī Jagatambārpaṇamastu |

Iti Aparādhakṣamāpaṇastōtram Samāptam ॥

*****

Dēvyaparāta Kṣamāpaṇa Stōtra

ॐ नम: चण्डिकायै ॥ *Ōm Namaḥ Caṇḍikāyai* ॥

न मन्त्रं नो यन्त्रं तदपि च न जाने स्तुतिमहो
न चाह्वानं ध्यानं तदपि च न जाने स्तुतिकथाः ।
न जाने मुद्रास्ते तदपि च न जाने विलपनं
परं जाने मातस्त्वदनुसरणं क्लेशहरणम् ॥ १॥

Na Mantram Nō Yantram Tadapi Ca Na Jāṉē Stutimahō
Na Cāhvāṉam Dhyāṉam Tadapi Ca Na Jāṉē Stutikathāḥ |
Na Jāṉē Mudrāstē Tadapi Ca Na Jāṉē Vilapaṇam
Param Jāṉē Mātastvadaṉusaraṇam Klēśaharaṇam || 1

विधेरज्ञानेन द्रविणविरहेणालसतया
विधेयाशक्यत्वात्तव चरणयोर्या च्युतिरभूत् ।
तदेतत् क्षन्तव्यं जननि सकलोद्धारिणि शिवे
कुपुत्रो जायेत क्वचिदपि कुमाता न भवति ॥ २॥

Vidhērajñāṉēṉa Draviṇa Virahēṉālasatayā
Vidhēyāśakyatvāttava Caraṇayōryā Cyuti Rabhūt |
Tadētat Kṣantavyam Jaṉaṉi Sakalōddhāriṇi Śivē
Kuputrō Jāyēta Kvacidapi Kumātā Na Bhavati || 2

पृथिव्यां पुत्रास्ते जननि बहवः सन्ति सरलाः
परं तेषां मध्ये विरलतरलोऽहं तव सुतः ।
मदीयोऽयं त्यागः समुचितमिदं नो तव शिवे
कुपुत्रो जायेत क्वचिदपि कुमाता न भवति ॥ ३॥

Pruthivyām Putrāstē Jaṉaṉi Bahava: Santi Saralāḥ
Param Tēṣām Madhyē Viralataralōham Tava Sutaḥ |
Madīyōýam Tyāgaḥ Samucita Midam Nō Tava Śivē
Kuputrō Jāyēta Kvacidapi Kumātā Na Pavati || 3

जगन्मातर्मातिस्तव चरणसेवा न रचिता
न वा दत्तं देवि द्रविणमपि भूयस्तव मया ।

तथापि त्वं स्नेहं मयि निरुपमं यत्प्रकुरुषे
कुपुत्रो जायेत क्वचिदपि कुमाता न भवति॥ ४॥

Jaganmātar Mātastava Caraṇasēvā Na Racitā
Na Vā Dattam Dēvi Draviṇa Mapi Bhūyastava Mayā |
Tathāpi Tvam Snēham Mayi Nirūpamam Yatprakuruṣē
Kuputrō Jāyēta Kvacidapi Kumātā Na Bhavati ‖ 4

परित्यक्ता देवा विविधविधसेवाकुलतया
मया पञ्चा शीतेरधिकमपनीते तु वयसि।
इदानीं चेन्मातस्तव यदि कृपा नापि भविता
निरालम्बो लम्बोदरजननि कं यामि शरणम्॥ ५॥

Parityaktā Dēvā Vividha Vidha Sēvākulatayā
Mayā Pañcā Śītē Radhika Mapanītē Tu Vayasi |
Idānīm Cēnmātastava Yadi Krupā Nāpi Bhavitā
Nirālambō Lambōdara Janani Kamyāmi Śaraṇam ‖ 5

श्वपाको जल्पाको भवति मधुपाकोपमगिरा
निरातङ्को रङ्को विहरति चिरं कोटिकनकैः।
तवापर्णे कर्णे विशति मनु वर्णे फलमिदं
जनः को जानीते जननि जननीयं जपविधौ॥ ६॥

Śvapākō Jalpākō Bhavati Madhupākōpamagirā
Nirātaṅkō Raṅkō Viharati Ciram Kōṭi Kaṇakaiḥ |
Tavāparṇē Karṇē Viśati Maṇuvarṇē Phalamitam
Janaḥ Kō Jāṇītē Janani Japaṇīyam Japavidhou ‖ 6

चिताभस्मालेपो गरलमशनं दिक्पटधरो
जटाधारी कण्ठे भुजगपतिहारी पशुपतिः।
कपाली भूतेशो भजति जगदीशैकपदवीं
भवानि त्वत्पाणिग्रहणपरिपाटीफलमिदम्॥ ७॥

Citābhasmālēpō Garala Maśaṇam Dikpaṭadharō
Jaṭādhārī Kaṇṭhē Bhujaga Patihārī Paśupatiḥ |

Kapālī Bhūtēśō Bhajati Jakadīśaika Padavīm

Bhavāni Tvatpāṇigrahaṇa Pariphāṭīpalamidam ‖ 7

न मोक्षस्याकाङ्क्षा भवविभववाञ्छापि च न मे
न विज्ञानापेक्षा शशिमुखि सुखेच्छापि न पुनः ।
अतस्त्वां संयाचे जननि जननं यातु मम वै
मृडानी रुद्राणी शिव शिव भवानीति जपतः ॥ ८॥

Na Mōkṣasyā Kāṅkṣā Bhava Vibhava Vāñchāpi Ca Na Mē

Na Vijñānāpēkṣā Śaśimuki Sukēcchāpi Na Puṇaḥ ।

Atastvām Samyācē Janani Jananam Yātu Mama Vai

Mruḍāṇī Rudrāṇī Śiva Śiva Bhavāṇīti Japataḥ ‖ 8

नाराधितासि विधिना विविधोपचारैः किं रुक्षचिन्तनपरैर्न कृतं वचोभिः ।
श्यामे त्वमेव यदि किञ्चन मय्यनाथे धत्से कृपामुचितमम्ब परं तवैव।

Nārādhitāsi Vidhiṇā Vividhōpacāraiḥ Kim Rūkṣacintaṇaparair Na

         Krutam Vacōpiḥ ।

Śyāmē Tvamēva Yadi Kiñcaṇa Mayyaṇāthē

Dhatsē Krupā Mucita Mamba Param Tavaiva ‖ 9

आपत्सु मग्नः स्मरणं त्वदीयंकरोमि दुर्गे करुणार्णवेशि ।
नैतच्छठत्वं मम भावयेथाः क्षुधातृषार्ता जननीं स्मरन्ति॥ १०॥

Āpatsu Magṇaḥ Smaraṇam Tvadīyam Karōmi Durkē

         Karuṇārṇavēśi ।

Naitacchaṭhatvam Mama Bhāvayēthāḥ Kṣudhātruṣārtā Jaṇaṇīm

         Smaranti ‖ 10

जगदम्ब विचित्र मत्र किं परिपूर्णा करुणास्ति चेन्मयि ।
अपराधपरम्परापरं न हि माता समुपेक्षते सुतम्॥ ११॥

Jagadamba Vicitra Mantra Kim Paripūrṇā Karuṇāsti Cēṇmayi ।

Aparādha Paramparāparam Na Hi Mātā Samupēkṣatē Sutam ‖ 11

मत्समः पातकी नास्ति पापघ्नी त्वत्समा न हि ।
एवं ज्ञात्वा महादेवि यथायोग्यं तथा कुरु॥ १२॥ ॐ ॥

Matsamaḥ Pātakī Nāsti Pāpaghnī Tvatsamā Na Hi |
Ēvam Jñātvā Mahādēvi Yathāyōgyam Tathā Kuru || 12

ॐ श्री जगदंबार्पणमस्तु || *Om Śrī Jagadambārpaṇamastu ||*

इति श्रीशङ्कराचार्य विरचितं देव्यपरादक्षमापन स्तोत्रम् सम्पूर्णम् ।
Iti Śrīśaṅkarācārya Viracitam Dēvyaparādakṣamāpaṇa Stōtram Sampūrṇam |

*****

Other Books of the Author

http://ramamurthy.jaagruti.co.in/

#	Title	Remarks	Pages
	Indology Related		
1.	*Shrī Lalitā Sahasranāmam*	English translation of Shrī *Bhāskararāya's Bhāṣyam*	750
2.	Power of *Shrī Vidyā*	The secrets demystified – with lucid English rendering and commentaries	80
3.	*Samatā*	An exposition of Similarities in *Lalitā Sahasranāma* with *Soundaryalaharī*, *Saptaśatī*, *Viṣṇu Sahasranāma* and *Shrīmad Bhagavad Gīta*	172
4.	*Advaita* in *Shākta*	Advaita Philosophy discussed in Shakta related Books	80
5.	*Shrī Lalitā Triśatī*	300 divine names of the celestial Mother – **English** translation of *Shrī Ādhi Śaṅkara's Bhāṣyam*	193
6.	Secrets of *Mahāśakti*	Chandi demystified	78
7.	*Daśa Mahā Vidyā*	Ten cosmic forms of the Divine mother	60
8.	ஸ்ரீவித்யா பேதங்கள்	ஸ்ரீவித்யா உபாசனையின் படிகள் - கோவை ஸுதச் சண்டி மலர்	51
9.	ஸ்ரீ தேவீ ஸ்துதிகள்	பல முக்கிய அம்பாள் ஸ்தோத்ரங்கள்	133
10.	Śrī Devī Stutis – श्री देवी स्तुति:	Various important stotras of Sri Devi	223
11.	ஷண்மத மந்த்ரங்கள் - षण्मत मन्त्रा:	பொள்ளாச்சி ஸ்ரீ ஸஹஸ்ரசண்டி மஹாயாக நினைவு மலர்	145
12.	*Ṣanmata Mantras* - षण्मत मन्त्रा:	Important Mantras relating to Gods of six religions	87
13.	தேவதா மந்த்ரங்கள்	அக்கரைப்பட்டி ஸஹஸ்ரசண்டி மஹாயாக நினைவு மலர்	32
14.	ஆதி ஸங்கரரும் ஷண்மதமும்	ஷண்மதங்களைப் பற்றிய ஒரு அறிமுகம்	32
15.	ஸ்ரீ ஷண்மத தேவதா அர்ச்சனை	ஸ்ரீ மஹா கும்பாபிஷேக மலர்	64
16.	*Vaidhīka* Wedding	Typical Wedding process in English	56
17.	வைதீகத் திருமணம்	Typical Wedding process in Tamil	57
18.	ஸ்ரீ லலிதா திரிஸதி	300 divine names of the celestial Mother – Tamil translation of *Shrī Ādi Śaṅkara's Bhāṣyam*	234

#	Title	Remarks	Pages
19.	ஸ்ரீகுரு பாத பூஜா விதானம்	சித்தகிரி ஸஹஸ்ரசண்டி மலர்	44
20.	ஸ்ரீவித்யா ஸடாம்னாய மந்த்ரங்கள்	சித்தகிரி ஸஹஸ்ரசண்டி மலர்	60
21.	*Ekatā*	Oneness among Shiva, Vishnu and Shakti	277
22.	*Vedas* – An Analytical Perspective	A description of Veda, Vedanta, Vedanga, Jyotisha, Shastra, etc.	240
23.	*Shrīvidya* Variances	Variances in Srividya Upasana	50
24.	வேதங்கள் – ஒரு பகுப்பாய்வு	A description of Veda, Vedanta, Vedanga, Jyotisha, Shastra, etc.	280
25.	பரமாச்சார்யாள் நோக்கில் ஸ்ரீலலிதாம்பிகா	The explanation given by Paramacharya on some of the names in Lalita Sahasranama	175
26.	*Ṣaṇṇavati Tarpaṇa*	Repaying Debts to Ancestors	42
27.	ஷண்ணவதி தர்பணம்	முன்னோர் கடன் தீர்த்தல்	48
28.	*Shrī Mahā Pratyangirā Devī*	Holy Divine mother in ferocious form	41
29.	ஸ்ரீ மஹா ப்ரத்யங்கிரா தேவீ	தெய்வீக அன்னையின் பயங்கர வடிவம்	51
30.	*Śrī Chakra Navāvarṇam*	Marvels of *Śrī Chakra*	115
31.	ஸ்ரீ சக்ர நவாவர்ணம்	ஸ்ரீ சக்ரத்தின் அதிசயங்கள்	130
32.	அம்பிகையின் (திரு) அவதாரங்கள்	ஸ்ரீ தேவியின் பல்வேறு அவதாரங்கள்	142
33.	Incarnations of Holy Mother	Different Incarnations of *Śrī Devī*	140
34.	ஸ்ரீ பிரணவானந்தர் - ஒரு சரிதம்	ஒரு அரிய ஸ்வாமிகளின் திவ்ய சரிதம்	91
35.	ஸன்யாஸம் - ஓர் அலசல்	ஹிந்து மத ஸன்யாஸ பேதங்கள் - ஒரு பகுப்பாய்வு	140
36.	Asceticism – an Analysis	A Study of Hindu *Sanyasam*	140
37.	ஶாந்தமும் ப்ரணவமும்	(ஸ்ரீ ஶாந்தானந்தரும் ஸ்ரீ ப்ரணவானந்தரும்) குரு சிஷ்யருக்கு உபதேசங்கள்	120
38.	ஸ்ரீ ஸஹஸ்ராக்ஷரீ வித்யா	2020 சாதுர்மாஸ்ய மலர்	84
39.	ஶாக்த	ஸ்ரீ தேவியைப் பற்றிய	400

#	Title	Remarks	Pages
	உபநிஷதங்கள்	உபநிஷதங்கள்	
40.	*Shakta Upanishats*	*Upanishats* about *Sri Devi*	385
41.	ஸ்ரீ தேவீ கீதை	Sri Devi Geeta	193
42.	*Śrī Devī Gīta*	Sri Devi Geeta	180
Applied Samskrutam Based			
43.	*Paribhāshā Stora*-s	An exploration of *Lalitā Sahasranāmam*	96
44.	*Shrī Cakra*, An Esoteric Approach	Mathematical Construction to draw *Shrī Cakra*	64
45.	Number System in Samskrutam	An overview of Mathematics based on Samskrutam	123
46.	*Vedic* Mathematics	30 formulae elucidated	146
47.	Vedic IT	Information Technology and Samskrutam	162
IT Based			
48.	Orthogonal Array	A Statistical Tool for Software Testing	180
Banking Based			
49.	Retail Banking	A guide book for Novice	213
50.	Corporate Banking	A guide book for Novice	232
51.	Dictionary of Financial Terms	A Guide Book for all – Demystifying Myriad Global Financial Terms	215
52.	GRC in BFS Industry	(**G**overnance, **R**isk Management and **C**ompliance by Banking & Finance Industry)	200

Let him be blessed to share his knowledge and experience with others through more books. Let us wish him all the best.

*****

Bibliography

The following books were referred to write this book. Lot many thanks to the authors and the publishers. They were very useful.

#	Title of the book	Author/ Publishers
1.	श्रीमद्देवीभागवतमहापुराणम्	Gita Press, Gorakpur
2.	ஸ்ரீமத் தேவி பாகவதம்	ஸ்ரீ ராம நாம வங்கியின் பகவன் நாமா பப்ளிகேஷன்ஸ்
3.	ஸ்ரீ தேவீ பாகவதம்	ஸ்ரீ டி. எஸ். கிருஷ்ண ஐயர்
4.	Other books of the same author.	

Om Tat Sat ॐ तत् सत्